D0214410

Snow Job?

RAND Studies Published with Transaction

The Gradual Revolution:
China's Economic Reform Movement
Hui Wang

The Icarus Syndrome:
The Role of Air Power Theory in the Evolution
and Fate of the U.S. Air Force
Carl H. Builder

Linking Economic Policy and Foreign Policy
Charles Wolf, Jr.

Snow Job?
The War Against International Cocaine Trafficking
Kevin Jack Riley

Troubled Partnership:
A History of U.S.-Japan Collaboration on the FS-X Fighter
Mark Lorell

NATIONAL UNIVERSITY
LIBRARY   SAN DIEGO

Snow Job?

The War Against International Cocaine Trafficking

Kevin Jack Riley

Transaction Publishers

New Brunswick (U.S.A.) and London (U.K.)

Copyright © 1996 by RAND.

All rights reserved under International and Pan-American Copyright Conventions. No part of this book may be reproduced or transmitted in any form or by any means, electronic or mechanical, including photocopy, recording, or any information storage and retrieval system, without prior permission in writing from the publisher. All inquiries should be addressed to Transaction Publishers, Rutgers—The State University, New Brunswick, New Jersey 08903.

This book is printed on acid-free paper that meets the American National Standard for Permanence of Paper for Printed Library Materials.

Library of Congress Catalog Number: 95-44247
ISBN: 1-56000-242-5
Printed in the United States of America

Library of Congress Cataloging-in-Publication Data

Riley, Kevin Jack, 1964–
    Snow job? : the war against international cocaine trafficking / Kevin Jack Riley.
        p. cm.
    Based on author's Rand Graduate School dissertation.
    Includes bibliographical references and index.
    ISBN 1-56000-242-5 (alk. paper)
    1. Narcotics, Control of—Andes Region.   2. Narcotics, Control of—United States.   3. Drug traffic—Andes Region.   4. Drug traffic—United States.   5. Cocaine industry—Andes Region.   6. Cocaine habit—United States.   I. Title.
HV5840.A5R56   1995
363.4′5′098—dc20   95-44247
                                                                              CIP

This is a RAND study.

RAND books are available on a wide variety of topics. To obtain information on other publications, write or call Distribution Services, RAND, 1700 Main Street, P.O. Box 2138, Santa Monica, CA 90407-2138, (310) 393-0411, ext 6686.

Contents

List of Figures and Tables

Figures

Tables

Preface

Like most authors, I hope this book sells well. More importantly, I hope that it elevates the debate about drug policy, not only among the people that make and implement the laws, but among the public at large. That having been said, however, I feel a disclaimer is in order. There are a number of people whom I think should be spared the expense and aggravation of buying and reading this book. If your mind is closed about drug policy, if you believe that international drug traffickers are solely responsible for this nation's drug problems, and if you believe that any change in international drug control policies is tantamount to a retreat from international terrorists, you should not bother with this book. If you are curious about the costs and consequences of our existing drug policy, if you think that there might be a better way, or if you simply want to learn more about international cocaine trafficking, this might be the book for you.

Readers should be aware that this book is based on a quantitative study presented in *Snow Job? The Efficacy of Source Country Cocaine Control Policies,* which was published by the RAND Graduate School in 1993. In that document, an economic model of the cocaine trade and the Bolivian, Peruvian, and Colombian economies is used to explore the effects of various source-country control policies. Those interested in an empirical examination of source-country policies are encouraged to review the 1993 report.

I am often asked why, given the unambiguous conclusion that source-country policies do not, and cannot, *control* the export of cocaine from Latin America, that I do not remove the "?" from the title. One reason is that source-country policies can *affect* drug production and exports, just not very effectively over the long run. This leads to another reason why it remains: I do not advocate abandoning source-country control policies. Rather, I support a policy that considers source-country programs' strengths and weaknesses, and adjusts policy implementation accordingly. Finally, I leave it in because I do not wish to imply that the public has been deceived by policymakers. To a large extent, the public is getting what it asks for.

Reasonable people disagree, often passionately, about international cocaine control policy and its contribution to drug control objectives, and the continuation of present policies results largely from these disagreements. The presence of the question mark, however, should not be taken to indicate uncertainty or ambiguity about the book's main themes and conclusions. Quite simply, we need to recognize the very real limits to what source-country policies can accomplish. We need to formulate more realistic goals. We need to educate the public and policymakers. In short, we need to do better.

Acknowledgments

A great many people contributed to making this book possible and most, in one way or another, are connected to the RAND Graduate School and RAND. I cannot imagine a more stimulating and vibrant environment in which to write a book than the one these organizations provided. Charles Wolf, Jr., Steve Drezner, and Rob MacCoun got the process started by supporting my proposal for post-doctoral work at the RAND Graduate School. The book itself is based upon research and ideas contained in my dissertation, *Snow Job? The Efficacy of Source Country Cocaine Control Policies* (RAND, 1993). RAND's Drug Policy Research Center, headed at that time by Peter Reuter and Audrey Burnham, and RAND's International Policy Department, then led by Jonathan Pollack, provided generous financial support for my dissertation. Peter Reuter, who chaired my dissertation committee, along with Michael Kennedy and Dick Kaplan, the other members of my committee, aided me immeasurably in formulating, formalizing, and testing the ideas central to this book. A special acknowledgment must also be given to Barbara Williams who, as former co-director of the Drug Policy Research Center, made an early investment in my career development.

I was fortunate in the course of writing about a complex public policy problem to be able to draw on my friends' and colleagues' widely varying experiences, intellectual strengths, and expertise. During the writing process, I made frequent use of their knowledge of crime, criminal justice, and the law; health (both mental and physical); international relations and foreign policy; economics and modeling; military technology and tactics; and many other subject areas too numerous to name. Many thanks to Jonathan Caulkins, Cheryl Damberg, Michael Dardia, Susan Everingham, Christopher Leslie, C. Peter Rydell, Jeannette VanWinkle, Mitchell Wade, and Michael Wall for their substantial contributions to this work. In addition, others, such as Carole Simms and Barbara Neff, made the research easier by ensuring that I always got the materials I needed. Cindy Kumagawa, of RAND's commercial book program, supported this project at every stage, and provided invaluable encouragement during the moments when my confidence flagged. I am grateful to Darlene Thomson for ironing out the procedural and logistical issues that arose as part of being the school's first post-doctoral fellow. I am also indebted to Francisco Thoumi for his critical commentary, as well as numerous staff members at other organizations, including the Washington Office on Latin America, the Department of State, the Department of Defense, and the Office of National Drug Control Policy, who provided me with important sources and publications. Also, many thanks are due to Karen Yuhas for her support over the past two years. Without her, this book might not have been possible.

Several anonymous sources also contributed to this endeavor by providing insights into the workings of the drug trade and frank evaluations of drug policy research and government policies. Although they wish to remain anonymous, their contributions have not been forgotten. I must conclude by noting that despite the contributions others made to this book, I alone remain solely responsible for its contents and the inevitable errors therein.

Part I

The Combatants

1

We Have Met the Enemy...

This is a book about policies intended to control the production and export of cocaine from Latin America. These policies, their impact on drug trafficking, and their effects on U.S. drug control objectives are considered in three steps. Part I develops a theoretical approach, if you will, by combining cocaine consumption, cocaine production, and cocaine control strategies in an analytic framework. There are multiple purposes for juxtaposing consumption, production, and policies, and for developing and presenting an analytic framework. One of the primary reasons for this format is to give the reader sufficient context in which to interpret international drug control efforts. Source country control policies cannot be considered alone, without reference to treatment, prevention, and other control policies, because to do so is to foster the (false) impression that the only alternative to the current international drug control policy to apply it more (or less) vigorously. Similarly, while it might seem strange that a book about international cocaine control policies would begin with a discussion about the people who use cocaine and the consequences of their consumption choices, cocaine users are a vital part of the story. Understanding the underlying demand for cocaine lends to understanding how international control policies do, and do not, affect cocaine consumption. The analytic framework simulates policies' impact on both production and consumption markets. From this, the reader can gain a clearer understanding of how policies implemented in foreign countries affect cocaine's availability, price, and use, and for how source country policies fare relative to other policy options.

Part II examines international control policies in action. Over the last decade the United States has spent almost $17 billion on projects ranging from eradication and development assistance in Bolivia and Peru to judicial assistance in Colombia and interdiction in the Transit Zone.

3

Using the analytic framework established in part I, this rich history is probed to explore how cocaine control policies have been implemented, how the traffickers have adapted to evade the policies' effects, as well as how control policies have affected cocaine's availability and price in the United States. Equally important, however, part II evaluates source country policies' effects in the producing nations. Source country policies are implemented in a complex, potentially explosive environment that includes rising political tensions among Bolivian coca farmers, an ongoing guerrilla insurgency in Peru, systemic political violence in Colombia, and strained political institutions in Mexico. The extent to which these and other social, economic, and political problems exist in the source countries, combined with the size of the U.S. control effort and its importance to the producing nations, ensures that drug control programs will have significant effects on the source countries' most pressing domestic issues.

In part III, the focus turns to alternatives. Specifically, part III considers what would be gained and lost through changes in source country control policies. Alternative policies are evaluated not only in light of their probable effects on U.S. drug-control objectives, but for their probable impact in the source countries. This chapter will also addresses whether there is something particular about cocaine markets that limit the efficacy of source country control policies, or whether the policies' limits extend to other illicit drugs as well. Part III concludes with an examination of which elements of current source country policies should be retained, which should be discarded, and which policies might logically be substituted in their place.

The Use and Abuse of Cocaine

Who uses cocaine, how does cocaine use harm the user, and how does it harm the nation and society? These are the subjects of this chapter. As subsequent pages will reveal, the number of people using cocaine is large, perhaps even startlingly so. There are consequences to the fact that so many people choose to use cocaine, just as there are consequences to the fact that people smoke cigarettes or drink alcohol. Some of the costs of cocaine consumption might be lessened if cocaine were legalized, while other costs would likely be worsened. In general, this chapter seeks to avoid discussion of the morality of cocaine use or the wisdom of legalization, not only because such a discussion tends not to be very productive, but also because, like it or not, national drug policy will not be moving toward legalization in the near future.[1] Instead, the point is to gain an understanding of cocaine use patterns as they are *under the existing counternarcotics regime*.

How Cocaine Works

Under normal circumstances, the brain releases and absorbs neurotransmitters such as dopamine, norepinephrine, and serotonin in response to external signals and circumstances. Cocaine, however, is a stimulant that temporarily blocks the brain's ability to reabsorb the transmitters once they are released.[2] As a result, the transmitters accumulate in the synapses between nerve endings. Accumulated norepinephrine and serotonin arouse the body's adrenal system, while accumulated dopamine prolongs the transmission of signals between sending and receiving nerves.[3] Adrenal activation results in heightened awareness, energy, and similar sensations, while prolonged nerve stimulation results in euphoria and mood elevation that are linked to the dopamine transmitter. The high, which develops in five to fifteen minutes in the case of powder cocaine and eight to twelve seconds in the case of crack, gradually tapers off as the supply of transmitters is reabsorbed.

Unlike heroin, cocaine is not physically addicting. That is, people who cease cocaine use do not suffer from withdrawal symptoms such as "the shakes," nausea, and other physical symptoms that occur in heroin addicts when the level of heroin in their bloodstream falls below a threshold level. Despite the fact that cocaine is not physically addictive, it has addictive characteristics. Higher doses of the drug will yield increased mood-altering effects, and thus, while cocaine does not produce physical dependence akin to heroin, the high the drug produces encourages pursuit of more intense intoxication, thereby producing a form of psychological addiction. Cocaine is said to have positively reinforcing addictive characteristics to the extent that individuals, in the absence of any chemical, medical, or other stimulus, crave cocaine for its euphoric properties. Not all individuals who try cocaine will become "positively" addicted, and what causes this form of dependence in some individuals, but not others, is not entirely understood.[4] The positive addiction mechanism may be environmental ("bad friends"), genetic ("bad genes"), biological (corruption of neural mechanisms), psychological (addiction-prone personality), or some combination of these and other factors.

Negatively reinforcing addictive characteristics, which cocaine can have if users consume it in an effort to alleviate feeling "bad" or depressed, are thought to have a biological basis. Negative reinforcement appears to occur as a function of repeated use, and although there may be a number of factors that influence negative addiction, the most important appears to be the biological function of dopamine production.[5] Frequent cocaine consumption taxes the body's dopamine production capabilities, eventually to the point where the body can no longer maintain the production of the neurotransmitters. Continued consumption when the body cannot produce dopamine exhausts the supply and leads to dopamine depletion. When dopamine depletion occurs the user has little ability to maintain even a normal level of stimulation; the lack of dopaminergic activity leaves the user depressed, anxious, and craving more of the pharmacological stimulus. At such a point, consumption of cocaine will cause a user to become high, only to bypass feeling normal and become dysphoric, or understimulated, again.[6] In this type of negatively reinforcing cycle, users may go on binges, lasting days or weeks, during which cocaine is consumed repeatedly in an effort to dispel the dysphoria.

One important factor influencing the strength of the addiction is the form in which the cocaine is consumed. Generally, cocaine users either consume the drug as powder, in which case it is inhaled, or as crack, in which case it is smoked. Cocaine hydrochloride, or powder cocaine, dissolves in water-based mediums such as blood. A typical powder cocaine user will inhale or "snort" the cocaine through the nose, where it is absorbed through the blood vessels in the nasal passages. Powder cocaine is not smoked because it undergoes chemical changes when heat is applied that cause it to lose its euphoric properties.

Crack, or cocaine alkaloid, however, is not water soluble and thus cannot be absorbed into the bloodstream through direct contact. The chunks of crystals do, however, retain their pharmacological properties when heated. Crack is thus most effectively consumed by smoking, although the term "smoking" is a misnomer since heated crack does not actually burn, but rather releases a vapor. The vapors, which are soluble in water, are absorbed into the bloodstream through the network of capillaries that line the lungs. Other routes of administration, including intravenous injection, and other forms of cocaine, such as freebase, are available, but have not proven to be as popular or durable as powder and crack.[7]

Consumption of crack cocaine has proven to be much more addictive than powder cocaine. The speed with which neurotransmitter reuptake is blocked, and thus that the high develops, depends primarily on the rate at which cocaine is absorbed into the bloodstream.[8] Crack acts more quickly and intensely than powder cocaine because crack is absorbed through the myriad of capillaries lining the lungs, while powder is absorbed through the relatively few blood vessels found in the nasal passages. Crack is absorbed in a sharp burst in just a few seconds; powder cocaine is absorbed more slowly and evenly over a period of a few minutes. Crack is thus more positively addictive than powder cocaine because it offers greater euphoria and sharper contrast with normality.

Crack is also more negatively addicting than powder cocaine. The impact delivered through smoking crack, while rapidly felt, also rapidly fades.[9] Crack users thus typically experience the depressing return to sobriety in short order. More importantly, crack appears to affect and deplete the dopaminergic system more drastically and more rapidly than powder cocaine. Crack users may therefore come to experience the cycle of negative reinforcement in just a few sessions, whereas that cycle typically takes longer to develop, if at all, among powder cocaine users.

Consequences of Cocaine Dependence

The practical consequences of addiction, also called dependence and abuse, can be severe. Clinicians have developed criteria by which dependence can be measured.[10] A person is said to have a substance abuse problem, or more colloquially, to be addicted, if three or more of the following problems exist: the substance is used for longer than intended; numerous unsuccessful attempts to reduce or control use are made; a significant amount of time is spent obtaining, using, or recovering from use; use interferes with fulfilling responsibilities or with physical health; important social, work, and recreational activities are abandoned in favor of continued use; use continues despite the presence of adverse effects; tolerance to use develops; attempts to quit use bring on symptoms of withdrawal.

It is not clear what leads some individuals to become dependent on cocaine yet allows others to maintain their habit at a less destructive level. What is clear, however, is that dependent users can inflict significant harm on themselves and on others. Cocaine is a vasoconstrictor, meaning it operates to shrink, temporarily, the size of blood vessels with which it comes in contact. As a consequence, many of the most deleterious effects of cocaine consumption stem from its constrictive properties. Perhaps most seriously, cocaine can restrict the flow of blood to fetuses during pregnancy.[11] Blood shortages deprive fetuses of nutrients, and thus can result in low birthweight and arrested growth. Of particular concern is the probable relationship between cocaine use during pregnancy and microcephaly, or abnormally small brain development.[12] Research also suggests that cocaine during pregnancy impairs infants' respiratory and arousal responses, raising the risk that the infant will succumb to Sudden Infant Death Syndrome (SIDS).[13] Other known consequences of cocaine consumption during pregnancy include fetus malformations and growth abnormalities and behavior problems in the children after birth.[14]

The health consequences of cocaine consumption, however, are hardly confined to unborn children. The most common route of administration is nasal insufflation, or snorting. Frequent snorting can result in adverse health effects ranging from sinus problems relating to the frequent constriction and swelling of nasal passages to elevated risks of heart attack, stroke, and convulsions. Crack users can, in addition to the cardiovascular consequences associated with powder cocaine, develop medical complications such as "crack lung" (black expectoration), reduced pulmonary functioning, and psychiatric disorders such as schizophrenia, depression, and antisocial personality disorders. Prior to 1987 and the widespread use of crack, most hospitalizations from cocaine were related to complications from intravenous injection. After crack use became widespread, however, the majority of cocaine-related hospitalizations were for cardiovascular, central nervous system, or psychological problems.[15] Cocaine elevates blood pressure rapidly, and thus even novice users assume many of the health risks that chronic users undertake.

Frequent cocaine use, particularly crack consumption, often involves a culture and lifestyle that puts the user at risk. Heavy cocaine users often undertake risks and engage in practices detrimental to their well-being. For example, sexual favors are often exchanged for drugs, particularly crack, and cocaine is thought to stimulate sexual appetite.[16] Both of these factors lead to sexual practices in the heavy use community that leave the parties at a high risk for contracting sexually transmitted diseases. Other communicable infectious diseases, such as tuberculosis, are problematic in the cocaine-abusing community because of the poor conditions in which users are known to live and congregate. Often, heavy cocaine users abuse other substances such as cigarettes and alcohol, and such poly drug use further complicates their health picture. Dependent users may also more frequently jeopardize their physical security by venturing into unsafe neighborhoods and environments to obtain drug supplies, by forsaking adequate housing in favor of drug use, or by attempting to steal drugs from dangerous and vindictive suppliers out of desperation.

It is generally accepted that addicts are the most problematic users. That is, they are the least likely to be able to hold down jobs, but the most likely to resort to criminal means to support their habits and the most likely to cost the health care system because of complications from their drug use. As the pages progress to a discussion of the costs of cocaine use, it is useful to remember that much, but not all, of the impact that society feels is due to this relatively small group of dependent users.

Past Experience and Present Epidemiology

Contrary to popular perception, cocaine has had a long and prominent position in the history of American substance abuse.[17] As far back as the late 1800s, cocaine was commonly found in patent medicines and elixirs. Perhaps the most well-known of these tonics was *Vin Coca Mariani,* a drink touted for its ability to enervate those who drank it. Astonishingly, the earliest versions of *Coca Cola,* the soft drink developed by chemist John Pemberton, contained small, but nevertheless potent, doses of cocaine. In fact, the coca leaves used as a flavorant, and from which cocaine is still processed, gave *Coca Cola* its name. By 1885 cocaine was available not through products such as *Coca Cola,* but from pharmaceutical companies for maladies such as sinusitis, hay fever, and fatigue, in bars as an additive to mixed drinks, and door-to-door from salesmen.[18]

Eventually, the potency of cocaine was recognized and its purveyors came under gradual regulation. Part of the impetus for regulation arose from the concern that widespread cocaine consumption, particularly among southern blacks who were given the drug to increase their work effort, would incite violence against whites.[19] Similarly, the Progressive Movement gained strength and used its influence to shape public morality and federal legislation regarding cocaine and other substances of abuse. By 1900, cocaine was removed from soft drinks. Medicinal cocaine came under regulation with passage of The Pure Food and Drug Act in 1906. The law mandated that patent medicines include a label that detailed the drug content. Early efforts to control the distribution of narcotics came in 1912 and 1914, with the Hague Convention and the Harrison Act, respectively. The passage of the Harrison Act, which required registration with the Treasury Department and payment of taxes, and which required all dispensers of regulated narcotics to keep log books of transactions, spurred the opening of a number of narcotic clinics that treated people addicted to various drugs. Combined, these factors served to diminish, but not eliminate, cocaine consumption.

Events in the early 1930s further reduced cocaine consumption. Alcohol Prohibition was repealed in the 1930s, and individual consumption rates of spirits rebounded sharply. Also in the 1930s, amphetamines, which have effects similar to cocaine, became widely available and were significantly less expensive than cocaine.[20] The increase in alcohol consumption, the weak, indeed virtually nonexistent, regulation of amphetamines and barbiturates, and the increasing regulation of cocaine and heroin products combined to reduce the use of cocaine sharply by the beginning of World War II.

The consumption of, and the battle against, cocaine lay virtually dormant for several decades, until the extensive drug use of the 1960s once again sparked a national temperance movement and elevated the concern about substance abuse to the national level. The rapid spread of drug use in the 1960s has its roots in the confluence of several factors. A variety of national issues, most notably the Vietnam War and the civil rights movements, provoked tensions between younger and older Americans. Many of the post-World War II generation of parents could not understand their children's opposition to Vietnam, nor could they fully accept the consequences of the civil rights effort. For their children, drugs became a symbolic divide and a method of expressing opposition to government and to traditional social strictures. Huge numbers of children were born in the years immediately after World War II. The sheer size of the baby boomer population in the 1960s and that age cohorts' susceptibility to drug use, combined with the fact that many young adults of the 1960s were in the first generation to attend college in large numbers, helped ensure that drug use spread rapidly among young adults.

Throughout the decade of the 1960s, marijuana, amphetamines, sedatives, and psychedelic drugs such as LSD remained the drugs of choice. Federal authorities responded by attempting to better regulate production of amphetamines and sedatives, including implementation of Food and Drug Administration regulations that curbed nonmedicinal use, and Bureau of Dangerous Drug crackdowns on processing laboratories. The Nixon Administration responded to the wave of drug use by establishing the National Commission on Marijuana and Drug Abuse in 1971, and with that act drug use became a permanent part of national policy. Additionally, marijuana and heroin became the subject of federal attention, and U.S.-supported drug control programs were implemented in the source countries of Mexico, Colombia, and Turkey.

But while policy attention was devoted to bringing existing drug problems under control, cocaine was once again emerging as a problem. Development projects—particularly the completion of permanent roads—in Peru and Bolivia opened the interior of those countries to settlement, but also provided drug smugglers with easier trafficking routes. As key industries—such as Bolivian tin mining—in the Andes weakened, and as commercial agriculture in the interior failed to develop, coca farming and drug trafficking became attractive alternatives.

At the same time, existing Colombian trafficking organizations began to build cocaine markets. Colombian traffickers, who had been the high-cost marijuana suppliers because of the cost involved in shipping the bulky product from Colombia to the United States, soon found their business significantly curtailed when the U.S. government began to attack the marijuana traffic. But Carlos Lehder, who became one of the cocaine trade's leading traffickers for a time, saw an opportunity to use the existing resources of the marijuana trade and adapt them to develop the cocaine trade. Imprisoned in the United States for a brief time on a marijuana charge, Lehder, together with his cellmate, saw cocaine as a potentially lucrative venture.[21] The Colombian drug traffickers preserved the institutional knowledge and key personnel associated with marijuana trafficking and expanded the cocaine trade while U.S. counternarcotics efforts concentrated on marijuana, LSD, and heroin.[22] Among the remnants of the marijuana trade were trafficking routes and distribution networks, including contacts in transshipment nations such as the Bahamas.[23] Other Colombians were well capitalized from the profits earned by emerald, cattle, and other smuggling operations. The Ochoa family, for example, ran a small import-export firm in Miami that served as a cover for smuggling operations.[24] The large expatriate population of Colombians in the United States simplified the distribution of the drugs to American markets.

As the cocaine epidemic in the United States matured in the early and mid 1980s, a variation of the drug called crack began to appear with increasing frequency. As discussed previously, crack offers a rapid and intense high, and this factor alone might well have been sufficient to guarantee its popularity. However, crack also proved to deliver its high at a very economical price. A crack user could get high for as little as five dollars, less than a tenth the cost of a typical gram of powder cocaine.[25] From the dealers' perspective, crack was a godsend as well: a gram of pure powder might yield twenty-five or more rocks of crack, or nearly twice the revenue of pure powder cocaine.

Just why crack became popular when it did from 1985 through 1987 is not entirely clear. *Basuco,* an intermediate product of the cocaine production chain that is very similar to crack, had been commonly applied to cigarettes in cocaine producing regions of Latin America as far back as the 1950s. These cigarettes, called *pitillos,* remained popular in the region for decades. More recently, freebase cocaine, again a product similar to crack, had enjoyed relative prominence among cocaine aficionados as recently as the early 1980s. *Basuco,* however, was often contaminated with the chemicals used to make powder cocaine, and use of it became associated with severe medical consequences. Freebase, too, had its drawbacks, not the least of which was the fact that most users manufactured their own product, a process that required the use of dangerous and explosive chemicals. Eventually crack, which presented few of the difficulties associated with *basuco* and freebase, was introduced to U.S. markets and became very popular in short order.

Who Uses Cocaine?

There are a number of different methods from which a picture of cocaine use and abuse can be drawn. Perhaps the most useful tools are the prevalence data that give estimates of the numbers of cocaine users and the frequency with which they use cocaine. These data have been instrumental not only as a mechanism for shaping public opinion about cocaine use, but as a guide for allocating drug control resources and designing appropriate drug policies.[26]

The population of cocaine users has changed substantially over time. In 1972, the first year in which the National Household Survey on Drug Abuse (NHSDA) asked respondents about cocaine use, approximately five million Americans reported having tried cocaine at least once in their lifetime.[27] By 1977, lifetime prevalence, as the measure of the number of people having tried cocaine least once in their lifetime is known, climbed to 10 million, and by 1979 the number reached 15 million. The rate of growth in lifetime prevalence began to slow in 1981, but only after lifetime prevalence had reached over 22 million. Since 1981, the number of lifetime users has continued to climb, but at a much slower annual rate.

The total number of people who have tried cocaine, while large and perhaps cause for concern, is not necessarily the best indicator of the nation's cocaine problem. A survey of lifetime prevalence does not reveal much about how many people *currently* use cocaine, nor about how many people for whom cocaine use represents a problem. Thus, the NHSDA also asks respondents about their cocaine use over the past year and the past month. Categories of more frequent cocaine use show patterns similar to that of lifetime prevalence, but with some important differences. Past-year cocaine use was at approximately 3 million people in 1972, but had climbed to roughly 12 million ten years later. In other words, the number of people reporting cocaine use over the last year quadrupled between 1972 and 1982. However, unlike lifetime prevalence, which kept rising after 1982, past-year prevalence appeared to have peaked in the early 1980s. By the time of the next survey in 1985, past-year prevalence had declined slightly, and by 1988 had fallen to around 7.5 million people.

Past-month consumption is typically regarded as a proxy for the number of heavy users, and the number of heavy users is in turn often regarded as a rough indication of the nation's cocaine problem. Past-month use peaked at about 4.5 million users in 1985, but had declined to approximately 1.5 million users by 1990, before climbing again in 1991. Figure 1.1 summarizes the national trends from household surveys of adults.

When individual demographic groups are examined for their cocaine consumption patterns, a number of results that are contrary to public

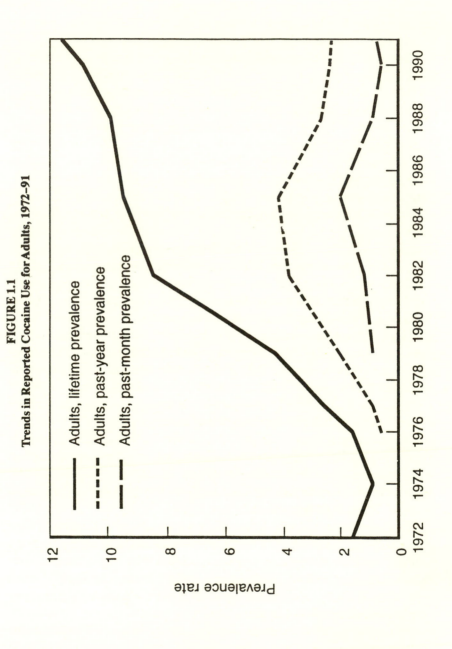

FIGURE 1.1

Trends in Reported Cocaine Use for Adults, 1972–91

Adults, lifetime prevalence
Adults, past-year prevalence
Adults, past-month prevalence

Prevalence rate

TABLE 1.1
Lifetime Prevalence of Cocaine Use by Ethnicity for 1991

	Ever used cocaine (%)	Estimated lifetime users
White	12.0	18,805,000
Black	11.3	2,594,000
Hispanic	11.2	1,814,000

Note: NHSDA (1993) and NHSDA Population Estimates (1991).

perception about cocaine abuse emerge. Lifetime prevalence figures for 1991 reveal that the majority of people who have ever used cocaine are white. In contrast, a disproportionate share of prisoners serving time for cocaine-related offenses are black, a fact that has helped anchor the public's perception of the cocaine problem to the black community. In fact, a greater percentage of whites than blacks report lifetime use across every age group except those over thirty-five. Similarly, whites report lifetime use at higher rates than Hispanics in total, although Hispanics report higher rates for the twelve through seventeen and over thirty-five age groups. Thus, whites constitute the largest block of lifetime cocaine users not only because they are, by far, the largest demographic group, but because they report use at higher rates than blacks and Hispanics (see table 1.1 for detail).

When more recent use is considered, however, the situation is reversed: blacks and Hispanics report significantly higher rates of current use, often two and three times the rates of whites. Using these figures, whites still outnumber black and Hispanic current users, but the gap is much closer than with lifetime prevalence (see table 1.2). Past-month use figures clearly indicate that there is substantial problem cocaine use in white, black and Hispanic communities.

Not surprisingly, cocaine use varies with age as well. Generally, the highest rates of use of illegal substances can be found among the young. Annual data from the Monitoring the Future (MTF) study, a survey of high school students supported by the National Institute on Drug Abuse, show that lifetime, annual, and monthly cocaine use peaked among twelfth graders in 1985 (see figure 1.2).[28] Annual data on crack use were not available until 1987, but a lower percentage of high school students have reported using crack each year since questions regarding crack use

TABLE 1.2
Past-Month Prevalence of Cocaine Use by Ethnicity for 1991

	Used cocaine in past month(%)	Estimated 1991 past-month users
White	0.7	1,096,000
Black	1.8	413,000
Hispanic	1.6	258,000

Note: NHSDA (1993) and NHSDA Population Estimates (1991).

were added (figure 1.2). Similar declines in reported cocaine and crack use are evident among young adults and college students who have been out of high school one to four years.[29] Interestingly, the decline in use among young adults was *not* related to any perceived decline in the availability of cocaine.[30] Indeed, survey results report *increases* in the perceived availability of cocaine from 1982 to 1990.[31]

Enthusiasm about the reported declines in cocaine and crack use among youth is tempered by an important and recent shift in factors that are thought to influence drug use patterns. Until recently, social opprobrium against cocaine use had been climbing, but now attitudes and perceptions regarding cocaine and crack appear to be changing in directions that portend future increases in their consumption.[32] Survey results show that the perceived harmfulness of regular cocaine use and peer disapproval of regular cocaine and crack use rose steadily throughout the 1980s. However, beginning with the survey of the graduating class of 1991, the rates of perceived harmfulness and disapproval for cocaine began to decline, as did the rate for perceived harmfulness of crack (see figure 1.3). Peer disapproval of crack rose slightly between 1990 and 1992.

Previous analysis has indicated that declines in reported cocaine use among young adults have been driven by shifts in these attitudinal factors. That is, as cocaine was increasingly thought to be harmful and as it lost peer approval, consumption of the drug declined.[33] Figure 1.4, which combines portions of figures 1.2 and 1.3, illustrates that increases in disapproval and perceived harmfulness were accompanied by declining annual prevalence rates among high school students.

To date, the shifts in declines in perceived harmfulness and disapproval have been slight, but there is concern that the social forces which

FIGURE 1.2
Lifetime, Annual, and Monthly Prevalence for Cocaine Among Twelfth Graders, 1978–92

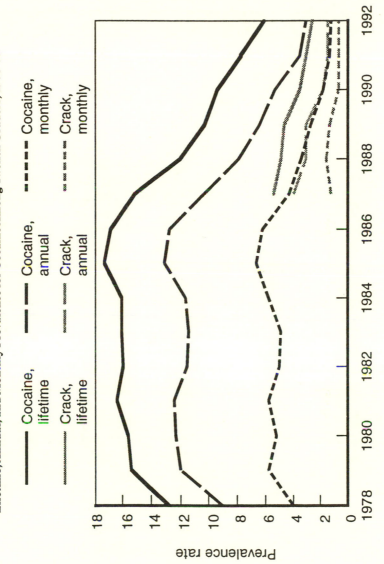

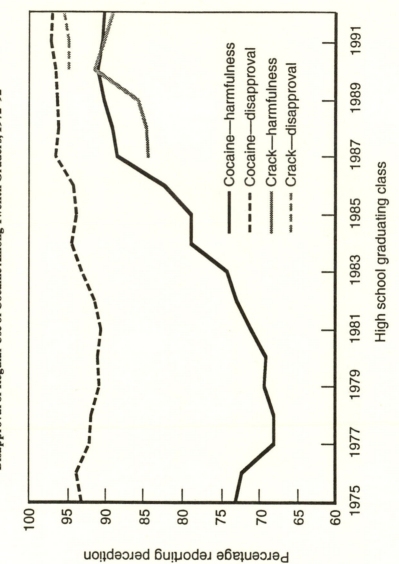

FIGURE 1.3

Trends in Perceived Harmfulness of Regular Use, Availability, and Disapproval of Regular Use of Cocaine Among Twelfth Graders, 1972–92

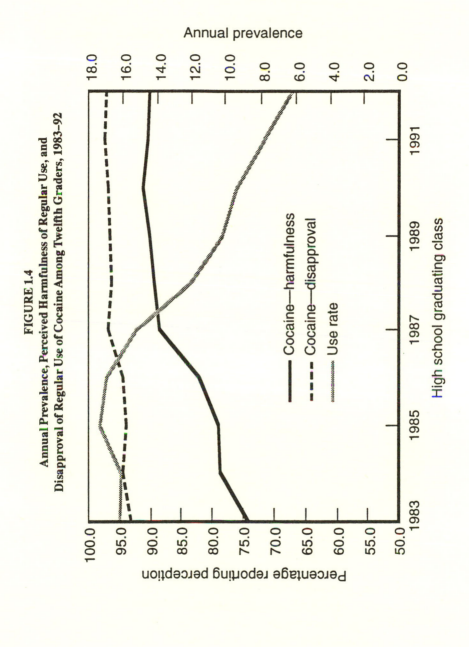

FIGURE 1.4

Annual Prevalence, Perceived Harmfulness of Regular Use, and Disapproval of Regular Use of Cocaine Among Twelfth Graders, 1983–92

Annual prevalence

High school graduating class

Percentage reporting perception

Cocaine—harmfulness

Cocaine—disapproval

Use rate

shape these perceptions have themselves eroded. In particular, in recent years some of the factors thought to be responsible for creating increased perceptions of harmfulness and disapproval, including national political attention, press coverage, and national priorities, have become less focused on drugs. Ironically, these factors are thought to be even more important in times of declining reported use among youth, such as the latter 1980s, because as the young adult user population declines younger students have fewer negative examples from which they can learn vicariously about the dangers of drug abuse.[34]

Interpreting Data

Estimates of prevalence are important because they provide policy-makers with the information they need to understand the breadth and depth of a drug problem, provide a crude method of allocating drug control resources, and provide a convenient scorecard for judging the strengths and weaknesses and the successes and failures of drug control policies. Indeed, prevalence estimates are one of the primary tools in use at the national level. But there are two potential weaknesses of prevalence data that need to be addressed. The first is that the data may be incomplete or inaccurate, and policy decisions may be accordingly adversely affected. The second shortcoming is that prevalence data are often of limited use for determining how drug problems are changing, except over very long periods of time.

Prevalence Data: An Incomplete Picture?

The ethnic and age breakdowns of cocaine use figures were presented, in part, to demonstrate the limited ability of such data to completely characterize the cocaine problem. The NHSDA and MTF surveys omit population subgroups that are extremely likely to use drugs, including the homeless and prisoners in the case of the NHSDA and school drop outs in the case of MTF. These are precisely the population groups likely to have higher levels of drug consumption than those reported in the surveys. More generally, NHSDA and MTF are likely to under count heavy users because such users are less likely to be willing or able to participate in the interview. NHSDA and MTF thus might not only distort the overall picture of cocaine use and abuse, but might also lead to an underestimation of cocaine use among groups that are of particular policy interest.

Despite not including several hard-to-reach populations, the NHSDA survey reaches a sample that represents a very high proportion of the U.S. population, 99 percent by one estimate.[35] The representativeness is so high because the omitted groups constitute such a small proportion of the overall population. To some extent, supplemental data sources can compensate for some weaknesses of the NHSDA. One example is the Drug Use Forecasting (DUF) system, which monitors trends among the offender populations. Established in 1987, DUF tracks drug use trends in arrestees in twenty-three large U.S. cities. Pilot studies, which became the basis of DUF, revealed that a large percentage of arrestees, 42 percent in 1984 and up to 83 percent in 1986, tested positive for cocaine.[36] DUF results indicate that a substantial portion of the arrestee population has consumed cocaine in the two to three days immediately prior to arrest.

By several estimates, the size of the past-month use population might double or triple the current estimate if the omitted population groups were included in the count.[37] The discrepancies among prevalence figures point to the difficulty in deriving estimates about illegal behavior, and the hesitance that one should have in using any one estimate or set of numbers to describe "the" cocaine problem. From a public policy perspective, the variance in estimates also underscores how difficult it is to design and implement drug control policies when basic information is scarce and contradictory.

Prevalence Data, Quantities Consumed, and Shifting Trends

Another component of the national picture is the amount of cocaine users consume. While NHSDA surveys respondents about the amounts they use, the data are again fraught with difficulty. It is difficult to elicit accurate responses about the *quantities* of cocaine consumed, but not necessarily because respondents are being deceptive. Whether in the powder form as lines of cocaine or the crystallized form as rocks of crack, users do not necessarily weigh out a given amount of cocaine for use in a session. Additionally, many sessions of cocaine use involve pooling and sharing the drugs, again making it difficult for users to keep track of the amount they have used. Finally, while the purity of cocaine can vary considerably, the respondent's ability to distinguish, let alone report, such matters is limited at best.

As a result of the complications in measuring quantities, survey instruments often are not a good tool for determining the quantities of cocaine used. In terms of the public policy dimension of cocaine use, it is often the frequency of use that is used to distinguish between "problem" and "casual" users. Of course, the correlation between frequency and quantity is not perfect, but it is perhaps the best indicator available under the circumstances. On the basis of frequency of cocaine use, those that have consumed cocaine in the past month at the time of the survey are considered heavy users, while those that have used it in the last year (less the overlap from past-month use) are considered light users. On the basis of a similar construct, Everingham and Rydell estimate that only about 22 percent of cocaine users are heavy users, and about 78 percent are casual users.[38] By the same estimate, however, heavy users consume about 70 percent of the cocaine, and light users consume about 30 percent. In other words, a relatively small portion of the drug-using population consumes a relatively large amount of the cocaine.

The available data do indicate that the decline in the number of current users has been offset by an increase in the quantities of cocaine consumed by the remaining users. The amounts of cocaine reaching U.S. domestic markets have remained steady or increased[39] and, thus, the resulting tradeoff for fewer initiates into cocaine use is an increase in the number of heavy, or problem, users. The problem with the prevalence data, however, is that they do not provide much early warning but rather reflect changes in the nature of cocaine use patterns only when many years of data are compared.

To provide policymakers with more timely information, an early warning system called the Drug Abuse Warning Network (DAWN) was established. DAWN records drug-related emergency room admissions and medical examiner records. Although DAWN data are problematic in many respects, information from the reports provided early indication that an increasing proportion of drug consumption was occurring among hard-core users.[40] A similar set of early warning indicators is built into the MTF survey, which monitors teenagers' and young adults' perceptions about drug use. Shifts in these attitudinal factors, as discussed earlier, may signal that changes in consumption patterns are on the horizon.

The purpose of discussing the shortcomings of the various data sources was not to criticize them as sources of data, but rather to illustrate how difficult it is to understand the various components of cocaine use in the United States. Drug use in the United States is a dynamic problem that ebbs and flows constantly, not only in response to drug control efforts, but because of demographic, socioeconomic, and other forces that are beyond direct control. Additionally, cocaine consumption is an issue with multiple dimensions and, thus, progress in one direction will not always mean equal progress in all directions, and in fact, may foretell retreats from other objectives.

National Costs of Cocaine Use

No matter how it is dissected, drug abuse is an expensive problem in the United States. A 1991 study estimated that Americans spent approximately $40 billion on illegal drugs in 1990, almost $18 billion of which was spent on cocaine.[41] Federal authorities spent approximately $12 billion on counternarcotics programs, and state and local authorities perhaps twice as much again to combat drug consumption.[42] Combined, federal, state, and local authorities dedicated perhaps $36 billion of resources against drug abuse, with most of the spending being used interdict drugs, or to arrest and prosecute traffickers and users.[43] Only about one-third of federal resources, and an even smaller share of state and local resources, are mobilized in support of treatment and prevention programs. An unknown, but substantial, portion of these government expenditures are related to cocaine.

The amounts spent obtaining illicit drugs and on government counternarcotics programs represent only a fraction of much larger costs that society bears because of drug abuse. Society feels the impact of drug abuse in many ways. Increased hospitalization and medical care bills, reduced and impaired productivity, and increased criminal activity are a few examples. Equally important, the steps society takes to combat drug use raise the social costs associated with drug consumption. For example, law enforcement efforts against drug markets are thought to contribute to the level of violence encountered in those markets, and are also thought to have partially caused an increase in the purity of the drugs marketed.[44] It is impossible to quantify these costs precisely, but the sections below explore some of the subjects in more detail.

Aggregate Medical Costs of Drug Abuse

Recent estimates indicate that all forms of substance abuse, including substances such as cocaine, tobacco, and alcohol, account for nearly $4.2 billion of $21.6 billion in 1991 Medicaid hospitalization costs.[45] Illicit drugs represent about 41 percent of the $4.2 billion, tobacco another 41 percent, and alcohol the remaining 18 percent. Thus, approximately $2 billion of Medicaid hospitalization costs can be attributed to all forms of illegal substance abuse. Tobacco and alcohol, however, are consumed on a regular basis by a much larger number of people than are illicit drugs. Thus, the implication is that drugs are, on a *per capita* basis, more damaging in terms of hospital stays than tobacco and alcohol. In other words, while illicit drugs pale in comparison to the effects of alcohol and cigarettes in terms of aggregate effects on national health, they do so only because both alcohol and tobacco are much more widely abused.[46] In 1993, cocaine was a factor in 123,317 DAWN emergency room admissions, a 3 percent increase over 1992.

While $2 billion in excess costs does not seem to be all that high, the Center on Addiction and Substance Abuse (CASA) analysis only addressed the Medicaid hospitalization component of drug abuse. Yet to come are analyses of drug abuse's impact on outpatient care, private insurers, and other components of the medical care community. If the other studies reveal that drug abuse raises costs by the same proportion it did with Medicaid hospitalization, the total cost of drug abuse in the United States' nearly $1 trillion medical economy could approach $80 billion.

Cocaine and the Workplace

One of the ways that cocaine is thought to disrupt the social fabric is by impairing or limiting users' productivity. More than 6 million people were thought to have used cocaine at least once in 1991. If, on average, those 6 million people were 10 percent less productive than they would have been if they had not used cocaine, the cost to society of "criminal" cocaine consumption would again be in the billions of dollars. And indeed, with lifetime prevalence over 20 million and past-year prevalence over 6 million, it is inconceivable that cocaine use has not affected national work performance. But cocaine's effects on productivity are not all that clear. Certainly, there are classes of dependent cocaine users who are unable to hold down jobs and unable to perform employment obligations, just as there are alcoholics and smokers who miss work as a result of their consumption patterns. Users who are not dependent, however, might not suffer from these problems and in fact may experience increased productivity through cocaine's stimulative effects.

One measure of the extent to which workplace drug use has become a concern can be derived from changes in employee drug testing patterns. Since 1986, when President Reagan signed an executive order that mandated drug-free federal working conditions, and since 1987 when widespread testing of federal employees was authorized, drug testing has spread significantly in the public and private sectors. For example, the Department of Transportation now conducts random drug tests of truckers, aviation industry personnel, and merchant seamen, and the military screens applicants for drug use. In the private sector an estimated 30 to 40 percent of companies tested employees in 1990, up from 5 percent in 1982.[47] Combined, productivity losses from all forms of substance abuse were projected to reach $160 billion by 1995.[48] Most of that projected total, however, can be attributed to alcohol; cocaine's share cannot be determined.

In any event, the utility of drug testing as a mechanism for curbing productivity losses related to substance abuse has been questioned. Testing itself is relatively expensive to conduct and signifies only that drugs have been used, but not amounts or frequency of use. Because of these limitations and because the correlation between substance use and job performance is not clear, current testing methods cannot impart definitive information about the impact of drug use on job performance. Thus, whether the potential benefit of identifying people who have used drugs and who thus might be endangering colleagues or who might suffer from impaired performance exceeds the potential cost of drug testing, including potential harms to civil liberties, is not clear.[49]

Crime and Cocaine

In 1991, NHSDA added questions to the survey that addressed criminal activity. Subsequent analysis of the NHSDA data shows that a strong relationship between criminal activity and drug use, particularly cocaine use, exists.[50] The NHSDA data thus support the findings of previous research on drugs and crime.[51] Evidence of a relationship, however, is not evidence of causality. It is not clear whether criminals are more likely to engage in other forms of deviant behavior, such as drug abuse, or whether drug abuse causes criminal behavior. Moreover, selling and consuming cocaine are criminal offenses, and these two activities constitute the bulk of the crimes that drug users commit.[52] Selling drugs, for example, is a common method for financing a drug habit.[53] The crimes of buying and selling drugs have led to an explosion in the number of arrests and convictions for these offenses. Prison populations have increased steadily in the last decade in large part due to drug cases. Once these crimes are factored out, the relationship between drug use and crime becomes more muddled.

The costs associated with the crimes of dealing and consuming cocaine are probably not trivial. Perhaps 600,000 individuals are engaged in the wholesaling and retailing of cocaine in the United States. Assuming these individuals could all find legal employment, the opportunity cost, or the amount of legal economic activity that society loses out on as a result of cocaine dealing, would total more than $10 billion.

Beyond the illegal acts of buying and selling drugs, there are three other main categories of crime connected to cocaine—or more generally, drug—use. The first are economic crimes committed to maintain consumption of drugs. Such crimes might be motivated by the high cost of the drugs, or by the user's inability to maintain other types of employment, but they have as their common characteristic the goal of financing more drug purchases. DUF data show that in most large cities more than 50 percent of those arrested for crimes such as larceny, robbery, and burglary tested positive for cocaine.[54] Again, however, the matter of causality in these crimes is not clear, but some portion of predatory and property crimes can probably be attributed to economic need.[55] A better example of cocaine-related criminal behavior might be found among crack addicts who exchange sexual favors for drug supplies. In this case, the criminal act of prostitution is used to finance more drug purchases.

A second category of drug-related crimes are those that are induced by the pharmacological effects of the drug. Alcohol, for example, is known to contribute to violent behavior in some people.[56] Numerous studies have suggested links between cocaine and violent behavior.[57] In particular, the evidence suggests that a link between acute cocaine intoxication and violence does exist. Nevertheless, the majority of deaths classified as cocaine-related cannot be attributed to the pharmacological properties of the drug, but rather to the market structure.[58] Cocaine may be culpable in other crime categories, such as impaired driving offenses, but evidence in this area is far from plentiful.

Finally, a good number of crimes, particularly violent crimes, are committed as part of managing and operating the drug business. Violence is used as a mechanism of control over subordinates and rivals, as a method of resolving disputes, as a means of regulating market share and as an act of retribution.[59] While it has been suggested that law enforcement against the drug industry provokes some of this violence, it is also clear that the drug industry would utilize violence even in the absence of law enforcement pressure.[60] Other criminal activities related to the structure of the cocaine trade include bribery and corruption of public officials. A recent supplement to DUF asked arrestees about their use of firearms. Preliminary survey results found that a sizeable fraction of those participating in drug markets are armed, that drugs, gang membership, and firearms are linked in significant ways, and that many juvenile arrestees indicated that they had access to, and had used, guns. Perhaps most disturbingly, many arrestees (juvenile and adult) indicated that guns and violence were acceptable methods for garnering respect, protecting oneself, and seeking revenge. More complete results of this study will be available in late 1996.

What these drug-related criminal activities cost society is anybody's guess, although the total is likely to be substantial. The criminal costs of cocaine abuse are visible across a number of dimensions. Society pays for trials, legal fees, and incarceration. Additional social losses accrue from premature deaths that can be attributed to the violence of cocaine markets.

But the costs of cocaine-related crime clearly exceed these estimate of direct costs. There are implicit, unmeasurable costs that drug trafficking and drug violence have on neighborhoods. Fear of drug-related crime causes businesses to relocate and private citizens to move to safer neighborhoods. The exodus of capital and families from neighborhoods contributes to further blight and weakening of the social structure. In short, both the reality and fear of drug-related crime exact a toll on society.

Summary

In many respects, cocaine does not differ from other substances that are widely abused, including alcohol and tobacco. That is, abuse of cocaine can have significant health consequences for the user, is related to workplace performance, and is linked to certain types of criminal activity. At the same time, however, there are gaps in our knowledge about cocaine use that lead to gaps in our knowledge about the consequences of cocaine use and abuse. There is general agreement on the health consequences of cocaine use, particularly heavy consumption, but there is much less agreement on the likelihood of progressing from light use to dependence and abuse. Similarly, while there is some agreement that cocaine use and abuse may affect workplace performance, there is no measure like a blood alcohol test that informs about the degree and consequences of cocaine impairment. Finally, while cocaine has been linked to crime, it is not at all clear that cocaine use *causes* criminal activity, particularly when the crimes of cocaine use and possession, and the crimes encouraged by the enforcement regime itself, are factored out.

As will be evident in chapter 2, the fundamental gaps in knowledge about cocaine make it difficult to formulate an effective cocaine control policy. Among other factors, the holes in knowledge complicate the resource allocation process. It is difficult to get agreement about how to attack the problem when there is little agreement on the nature and consequences of the problem itself.

Notes

1. Daedalus, "Political Pharmacology: Thinking About Drugs," vol. 121, no. 3 (Summer 1992) provides several views on drug control regimes.
2. Strictly speaking, the term *narcotic* is inaccurate in reference to cocaine. Narcotics are drugs that act to sedate the user; cocaine acts to stimulate the user.
3. Gawin and Ellinwood (1988); Volpe (1992); Allen and Jekel (1991).
4. For a range of analyses on drug addiction see Glantz and Pickens (1992); Wise (1988); Deminiere, Piazza, Le Moal and Simon (1989); and NIDA Research Monograph 110 (1991).
5. King, Curtis, and Knoblich (1992).
6. Volpe (1992); Khalsa, Tashkin, and Perrochet (1992).
7. Injection, for example, requires surmounting the "needle barrier," or users' reluctance to insert a needle into their arms. Freebase is distinguishable from crack only in that the former is a product prepared by the user, and the latter purchased from a retailer.
8. Allen and Jekel (1991).
9. Gawin and Ellinwood (1988); Siegel (1992).
10. American Psychiatric Association (1987).
11. Woods, Plessinger, and Clark (1987).
12. Volpe (1992).
13. Bauchner et. al (1988).

14. Zellman et. al. (1992), 3.
15. Rubin and Neugarten (1992).
16. Inciardi (1992) covers these matters in detail.
17. Musto (1987) provides and in-depth view. See also Inciardi (1992) and Zimring and Hawkins (1992).
18. Musto (1987).
19. Musto (1987); Brecher (1972).
20. Ibid.
21. Eddy et al. (1988), 131–48, especially 132–33.
22. Gugliotta and Leen (1989), 30–31 and 74–76.
23. Eddy et al. (1988), 99–108.
24. Ibid., 32–33.
25. Inciardi (1992).
26. Reuter (1993) provides a discussion of the role these have, and should have, in formulating national drug control policy.
27. In general, cocaine use figures can be obtained from the National Household Survey on Drug Abuse (NHSDA) conducted by the National Institute on Drug Abuse (NIDA). These figures are taken from "Overview of the 1991 National Household Survey on Drug Abuse" (December 1991).
28. Johnston, O'Malley, and Bachman (1993a).
29. Johnston, O'Malley, and Bachman (1993b).
30. Bachman, Johnston, and O'Malley (1990).
31. Bachman, Johnston, and O'Malley (1990) report on the perceived availability of cocaine.
32. Johnston, O'Malley, and Bachman (1993a).
33. Bachman, Johnston, and O'Malley (1990).
34. Johnston, O'Malley, and Bachman (1993a).
35. Everingham and Rydell (1993).
36. Wish and O'Neil (1991).
37. Staff Report, Committee on the Judiciary, United States Senate (1990); Mullen and Arbiter (1992).
38. Everingham and Rydell (1993).
39. INCSR (various years) reports on estimates of cocaine production.
40. Ebener et al. (1994) discuss DAWN data in detail in Appendix F. For heroin, the increase in heavy use became clear because of a steady increase in the age of heroin emergency room patients. The raw number of DAWN emergency room mentions themselves, however, are not necessarily indicative of trends in drug use. As Ebener et al. report, numerous factors influence the decision to seek emergency attention, such that there is no reason to believe the ratio of heavy users to emergency room admissions is constant. To take one example, IV drug users who have AIDS are likely to have greater emergency needs than IV drug users that do not have AIDS. Thus, as AIDS prevalence in the IV drug using community increases, the need for emergency care might increase as well, even though the underlying size of the drug using population remains steady or falls as community members succumb to AIDS. Among DAWN's other limitations, the system only records emergency room admissions and excludes certain hospital systems from the census. Thus, DAWN is not appropriate for estimating other drug-related health issues, such as chronic illnesses, and it omits drug-related events in other large medical systems such as Veteran's Administration hospitals.
41. "What America's Users Spend on Illegal Drugs" (1991).

42. See *National Drug Control Strategy: Budget Summary* (1992).
43. Reuter (1993) makes this estimate.
44. Goldstein et al. (1991) and Goldstein, Brownstein, and Ryan (1992) address the issue of drug market violence. Reuter and Kleiman (1986), among others, discuss the issue of law enforcement induced increases in purity. See also Prohibition article.
45. CASA (1993). Drugs account for 41 percent of the estimated 19.2 percent of Medicaid inpatient hospital costs that are attributed to substance abuse. No breakdown of cost increments is available for individual drugs.
46. NIDA (1987), 6; Kleiman (1992), 290–91.
47. West and Ackerman (1993).
48. Ibid.
49. See Harris (1993) and Hartman and Crow (1993).
50. Harrison and Gfroerer (1992). Again, the NHSDA data are subject to the same problems discussed earlier. That is, the survey excludes certain populations. Their inclusion might not only change perceptions of drug use, but the relationship between criminal activity and drug use as well.
51. See in particular Anglin and Speckart (1988), Speckart and Anglin (1985), and Wish and Johnson (1986).
52. Harrison and Gfroerer (1992).
53. MacCoun and Reuter (1992).
54. Wish and O'Neil (1991).
55. Hunt (1991).
56. For an overview, see De La Rosa, Lambert, and Gropper (1990).
57. Brody (1990) provides an overview.
58. Goldstein, Brownstein, and Ryan (1992) and Goldstein, et al. (1991).
59. Ibid.
60. Ibid.; Moore (1990); and Fagan and Chin (1990).

References

Allen, David F., and James F. Jekel, *Crack: The Broken Promise* (New York: St.Martin's Press, 1991).

American Psychiatric Association, *Diagnostic and Statistical Manual of Mental Disorders*, 3rd. ed., revised (Washington, D.C., 1987).

Anglin, M. Douglas, and George Speckart, "Narcotics Use and Crime: A Multisample, Multimethod Analysis," *Criminology* 26 (1988): 197–233.

Bachman, Jerald G., Lloyd D. Johnston, and Patrick M. O'Malley, "Explaining the Recent Decline in Cocaine Use among Young Adults: Further Evidence that Perceived Risks and Disapproval Lead to Reduced Drug Use," *Journal of Health and Social Behavior* 31 (June 1990): 173–84.

Bauchner, H., B. Zuckerman, M. McClain, D. Frank, L. E. Fried, and H. Kayne, "Risk of Sudden Infant Death Syndrome among Infants with in Utero Exposure to Cocaine," *Journal of Pediatrics* 113 (1988): 831–34.

Brecher, Edward M., *Licit and Illicit Drugs* (Boston, Mass.: Little, Brown, 1972).

Brody, Steven L., "Violence Associated with Acute Cocaine Use in Patients Admitted to a Medical Emergency Department," in *Drugs and Violence: Causes, Correlates and Consequences*, National Institute on Drug Abuse Research Monograph Series, (Washington, D.C.: U.S. Department of Health and Human Services, 1990).

Center on Addiction and Substance Abuse at Columbia University, *The Cost of Substance Abuse to America's Health Care System, Report 1: Medicaid Hospital Costs* (New York: CASA, 1993).

De La Rosa, Mario, Elizabeth Y. Lambert, and Bernard Gropper, "Introduction: Exploring the Substance Abuse-Violence Connection," in *Drugs and Violence: Causes, Correlates and Consequences,* National Institute on Drug Abuse Research Monograph Series,(Washington, D.C.: U.S. Department of Health and Human Services, 1990).

Deminiere, J. M., P. V. Piazza, M. Le Moal, and H. Simon, "Experimental Approach to Individual Vulnerability to Psychostimulant Addiction," *Neuroscience & Biobehavioral Reviews* 13 (1989): 141–47.

Ebener, Patricia, Jonathan Caulkins, Sandy Geschwind, Daniel McCaffrey, and Hilary Saner, *Improving Data and Analysis to Support National Substance Abuse Policy* (Santa Monica, Calif.: RAND, 1994).

Eddy, Paul, with Hugo Sabogal, and Sara Walden, *The Cocaine Wars* (New York: W. W. Norton, 1988).

Everingham, Susan S., and C. Peter Rydell, "Modeling the Demand for Cocaine," DRR-390-ONDCP/A/DPRC (Santa Monica, Calif.: RAND, 1993).

Fagan, Jeffrey, and Ko-lin Chin, "Violence as Regulation and Social Control in the Distribution of Crack," in *Drugs and Violence: Causes, Correlates and Consequences,* National Institute on Drug Abuse Research Monograph Series (Washington, D.C.: U.S. Department of Health and Human Services, 1990).

Gawin, Frank H., and Everett H. Ellinwood, Jr., "Cocaine and Other Stimulants: Actions, Abuse and Treatment," *New England Journal of Medicine* 318, 18 (1988): 1173–82.

Glantz, Meyer, and Roy Pickens, eds., *Vulnerability to Drug Abuse* (Washington, D.C.: American Psychological Association, 1992).

Goldstein, P., Henry Brownstein, and Paul Ryan, "Drug-Related Homicide in New York: 1984 and 1988," *Crime and Delinquency* 38, 4 (1992): 459–762.

Goldstein, P., H. Brownstein, P. Ryan, and P. Belluci, "Crack and Homicide in New York City in 1988," *Contemporary Drug Problems* 16, (1991): 651–58.

Gugliotta, Guy, and Jeff Leen, *Kings of Cocaine* (New York: Simon and Schuster, 1989).

Harris, Michael M., "Drugs in the Workplace: Setting the Record Straight," *The Journal of Drug Issues* 23, 4 (1993): 727–32.

Harrison, Lana, and Joseph Gfroerer, "The Intersection of Drug Use and Criminal Behavior: Results from the National Household Survey on Drug Abuse," *Crime & Delinquency* 38, 4 (1992): 422–43.

Hartman, Sandra J., and Stephan M. Crow, "Drugs in the Workplace: Setting Harris Straight," *The Journal of Drug Issues* 23, 4 (1993): 733–38.

Hunt, Dana, "Stealing and Dealing: Cocaine and Property Crimes," in *The Epidemiology of Cocaine Use and Abuse,* National Institute on Drug Abuse Research Monograph Series (Washington, D.C.: U.S. Department of Health and Human Services, 1991).

Inciardi, James A., *The War on Drugs II* (Mountain View, Calif.: Mayfield Publishing Company, 1992).

International Narcotics Strategy Report (INCSR), United States Department of State, Bureau of International Narcotics Matters (Washington, D.C.: USGPO, various years).

Johnston, L. D., P. M. O'Malley, and J. G. Bachman, *National Survey Results on Drug Use from the Monitoring the Future Study, 1975–1992, Volume I: Secondary School*

Students, National Institute of Health Publication 93-3597, (Rockville, Md.: National Institute on Drug Abuse, 1993a).

―――, *National Survey Results on Drug Use from the Monitoring the Future Study, 1975–1992, Volume I: College Students and Young Adults,* National Institute of Health Publication 93-3598, (Rockville, Md.: National Institute on Drug Abuse, 1993b).

Kandel, Denise B., "The Social Demography of Drug Use," *The Milbank Quarterly* 69, 3 (1992): 365–414.

Khalsa, M. Elena, Donald P. Tashkin, and Brian Perrochet, "Smoked Cocaine: Patterns of Use and Pulmonary Consequences," *Journal of Psychoactive Drugs* 24, 3 (1992): 265–72.

King, Roy, Deborah Curtis, and Guenther Knoblich, "Biological Factors in Sociopathy: Relationships to Drug Abuse Behaviors," in Meyer Glantz and Roy Pickens, eds., *Vulnerability to Drug Abuse* (Washington, D.C.: American Psychological Association, 1992).

Kleiman, Mark A. R., *Against Excess: Drug Policy for Results* (New York: Basic Books, 1992).

MacCoun, Robert, and Peter Reuter, "Are the Wages of Sin $30 an Hour: Economic Aspects of Street-Level Drug Dealing," *Crime and Delinquency* 38, 4 (October 1992): 477–91.

Moore, Joan, "Gangs, Drugs and Violence," in *Drugs and Violence: Causes, Correlates and Consequences,* National Institute on Drug Abuse Research Monograph Series (Washington, D.C.: U.S. Department of Health and Human Services, 1990).

Mullen, Rod, and Naya Arbiter, "Against the Odds: Therapeutic Community Approaches to Underclass Drug Abuse," in Peter H. Smith, ed., *Drug Policy in the Americas* (Boulder, Colo.: Westview Press, 1992).

Musto, David F., *The American Disease: Origins of Narcotic Control* (New York: Oxford University Press, 1987).

National Drug Control Strategy: Progress in the War on Drugs, The White House, January 1993.

National Drug Control Strategy: Budget Summary, The White House, January 1992.

National Drug Control Strategy, The White House, January 1991.

National Drug Control Strategy: A Nation Responds to Drug Use, The White House, January 1992.

National Institute on Drug Abuse, *The Epidemiology of Cocaine Use and Abuse,* NIDA Research Monograph 110 (Washington, D.C.: U.S. Department of Health and Human Services, 1991).

―――, *National Household Survey on Drug Abuse: Population Estimates 1991* (Washington, D.C.: U.S. Department of Health and Human Services, 1991).

"Political Pharmacology: Thinking About Drugs," in *Daedalus* 121, 3 (Summer 1992).

Reuter, Peter, "Prevalence Estimation and Policy Formulation," *Journal of Drug Issues* 23, 2 (1993): 167–84.

Reuter, Peter, and Mark A. R. Kleiman, "Risks and Prices: An Economic Analysis of Drug Enforcement," in Michael Tonry and Norval Morris eds., *Crime and Justice: An Annual Review, Volume 7* (University of Chicago: 1986).

Rubin, Rhonda, and Joel Neugarten, "Medical Complications of Cocaine: Changes in Pattern of Use and Spectrum of Complications," *Clinical Toxicology* 30, 1 (1992): 1–12.

Siegel, Ronald K., "Cocaine Free Base Use," *Journal of Psychoactive Drugs* 24, 2 (April-June 1992): 183–212.

Speckart, George, and M. Douglas Anglin, "Narcotics and Crime: An Analysis of Existing Evidence for a Causal Relationship," *Behavioral Sciences and the Law* 3 (1985): 259–82.

Staff Report, Committee on the Judiciary, United States Senate, *Hard-Core Cocaine Addicts: Measuring—and Fighting—the Epidemic* (Washington, D.C.: USGPO, 1990).

Substance Abuse and Mental Health Services Administration, *National Household Survey on Drug Abuse: Main Findings 1991* (Washington, D.C.: U.S. Department of Health and Human Services, 1993).

U.S. Department of Health and Human Services, Public Health Service, Alcohol, Drug Abuse and Mental Health Administration, *The Economic Cost of Alcohol and Drug Abuse and Mental Illness: 1985* (Washington, D.C.: U.S. Department of Health and Human Services, 1989).

Volpe, Joseph J., "Effect of Cocaine Use on the Fetus," *New England Journal of Medicine* 327, 6 (1992): 399–407.

What America's Users Spend on Illegal Drugs, an Office of National Drug Control Policy Technical Paper (Washington, D.C.: Office of National Drug Control Policy, 1991).

West, Louis Jolyon, and Deborah L. Ackerman, "The Drug Testing Controversy," *The Journal of Drug Issues* 23, 4 (1993): 579–95.

Wise, Roy A., "The Neurobiology of Craving: Implications for Understanding and Treatment of Addiction," *Journal of Abnormal Psychology* 97, 2 (1988): 118–32.

Wish, Eric D., and Bruce D. Johnson, "The Impact of Substance Abuse on Criminal Careers," in *Criminal Careers and "Career Criminals,": Volume 2,* A. Blumstein, J. Cohen, A. Roth and C. A. Visher eds. (Washington, D.C.: National Academy Press, 1986).

Wish, Eric, and Joyce O'Neil, "Cocaine Use in Arrestees: Refining Measures of National Trends by Sampling the Criminal Population," in National Institute on Drug Abuse, *The Epidemiology of Cocaine Use and Abuse,* NIDA Research Monograph 110 (Washington, D.C.: U.S. Department of Health and Human Services, 1991).

Woods, J. R., Jr., M. A. Plessinger, and K. E. Clark, "Effect of Cocaine on Uterine Blood Flow and Fetal Oxygenation," *Journal of the American Medical Association* 257 (1987): 957–61.

Zellman, Gail L., Peter D. Jacobson, Helen DuPlessis, and M. Robin DiMatteo, *Health Care System Response to Prenatal Substance Abuse: An Exploratory Analysis,* N-3495-DPRC (Santa Monica, Calif.: RAND, 1992).

Zimring, Franklin E., and Gordon Hawkins, *The Search for Rational Drug Control* (Cambridge University Press, 1992).

2

...And it is the U.S.

At one point in the not-too-distant past, drug abuse ranked near the top of public opinion polls in which respondents classified the largest problems facing the United States.[1] Drugs first emerged prominently in 1986 when 3 percent of the public listed drugs and crime as the most important issues facing the country. By the next year, after intensive media coverage of cocaine-related problems, including the death of basketball star Len Bias, 15 percent reported drugs as the most important problem. That proportion was sufficient enough to put substance abuse at the top of the list. Concern about drugs peaked in 1989, when a full one-third of the public reported drugs as the primary problem facing the United States. Since 1989, however, public concern about drugs has been supplanted by a variety of other concerns, including the economy, jobs, and now, health care. At present, only a small portion of the public considers drugs to be a major public concern, although crime, which the public closely associates with drugs, is more frequently mentioned.

A variety of factors fueled the public's concern about drug abuse. Perhaps most importantly the rapid expansion of the drug trade, particularly cocaine markets, was closely linked to spasms of violence in many U.S. communities. In Miami, Colombian trafficking organizations waged war against each other, resulting in countless bloody shootouts and murders. Much of this carnage was not only indiscriminately carried out in public, but was deliberately shockingly violent and gory as part of an effort to intimidate rival dealers. In Los Angeles the violence was centered around urban street gangs, which became synonymous with drug trafficking. By the late 1980s the "drive-by" shooting, in which gunmen shoot at a target from a moving car, had become a standard part of the urban lexicon. Los Angeles also earned the dubious distinction of being an exporter of gang violence as refugees from Los Angeles established gangs in other communities, including cities such as Wichita, Kansas and Portland, Oregon.[2]

A second explanation for public concern was that drug consumption, particularly of cocaine, spread rapidly and visibly. Drug marketing and consumption confronted the public on a daily basis. Aggressive dealers hawked their wares throughout the cities as strained police resources attempted to keep up. Parks were no longer available for family use, but instead became open-air drug markets. Entire neighborhoods were virtually abandoned to the crack trade. Escape from the drug trade seemed virtually impossible, particularly as retailers expanded their operations to suburban and rural markets.

Other factors contributed to public concern as well. For example, prevalence data provided support for the realization that drug use was increasingly common among children. In many cases, drugs were readily available on high school and junior high school campuses, much to the shock of many parents. Drug use also threatened to mutate into a public health crisis as HIV spread through the use of intravenous drugs and the dangerous sexual practices associated with heavy drug use.

Combined, these factors engendered a climate that was hostile to drug use and its perceived consequences. The political system was compelled to respond, and it did so in relatively short order. The Reagan administration announced in 1986 that the federal government would expand its counterdrug efforts significantly. The "War on Drugs" and policy of "zero tolerance" resulted in numerous policy measures that both drew from previous national drug control efforts and featured new approaches. An Office of National Drug Control Policy was established, widespread drug testing of federal and private sector workers became common, and a stricter legal regime, including use of mandatory minimum sentences for drug offenders, was put in place. As a result of these and other policy measures, drug control became a part of the fabric of American life.

U.S. Drug Control Policy

The Office of National Drug Control Policy (ONDCP) maintains responsibility for coordinating and monitoring the nation's approach to counternarcotics policy. Created in 1989 after the passage of the Anti-Drug Omnibus Control Act a year earlier, ONDCP had a staff of about 110 officials who established national drug control priorities and objectives and communicated those objectives to the myriad federal departments, agencies, and bureaus that implement national drug programs. President Clinton reduced the staff to about twenty-five early in his administration. Personnel strength has since climbed from this low, but is still well below the 1989 level. ONDCP's existence has been threatened at various other points, including 1995, when the Senate briefly considered eliminating the office. ONDCP annually articulates the nation's goals and objectives with respect to drug abuse through the National Drug Control Strategy (NDCS). The NDCS document not only summarizes the nation's strategy with respect to drugs, but acts as a blueprint in the war on drugs by guiding the allocation of resources in broad functional categories, suggesting changes in state and local strategies to support the national agenda, and providing a set of criteria by which progress in stemming drug abuse can be measured.

Responsibility for coordination and monitoring, however, is not the same thing as control. ONDCP actually controls very little of counter narcotics policy directly because it has very little direct budgetary authority. Except for small amounts available for grants and research, ONDCP does not disperse counterdrug resources.[3] Instead, ONDCP's annual report is the President's official request for drug control resources, and represents the administration's best estimate of what is needed to control drug abuse. Congress, however, funds the drug control program in pieces by approving a series of appropriations bills. Thus, although the drug control program is submitted in one report, Congress does not consider the drug control "budget" in one comprehensive package, but rather in a diffuse conglomeration of spending bills. These spending bills are typically constructed from the work of specialized committees and subcommittees, which are organized around broad functions such as national security, foreign affairs, and so forth. Because these functional categories have their appropriations enacted at different points during the year, there is little opportunity to compare explicitly supply and demand control alternatives.

By law, agencies and departments with counterdrug responsibilities are required to address ONDCP's strategic program in their budget request. One of ONDCP's tasks is to certify that the agencies' budget requests are sufficient for fulfillment of counterdrug responsibilities. For many government entities, drug control is of secondary—or even tertiary—concern. Their departmental priorities may provide organizations with the incentive to maximize the appearance of complying with ONCDP mandates, while minimizing actual participation in low-priority drug control missions.[4] The accounting process is further complicated by the subjective nature of drug control activities. Many organizations, such as Customs and the Coast Guard, essentially compute the drug control effort by estimating the fraction of the organization's time devoted to drug control and multiplying that fraction by the overall budget. It is obvious that organizations can manipulate their estimate of the proportion of time spent on drug control to feign compliance with ONDCP's mandates. Giving the appearance of devoting enough resources to the drug control is particularly important since ONDCP cannot readily assess the policy effectiveness of organizations' efforts. In some cases, organizations will go to absurd lengths to have activities counted as drug related. In one notorious example, the Secret Service sought to count time spent guarding First Lady Nancy Reagan, who was heavily involved in promoting an anti-drug message, as part of its counterdrug effort.[5] Such tactics preserve the size of an agency's budget without increasing its mission requirements.

One consequence of ONDCP's lack of budgetary authority is that the organization cannot respond as rapidly to changes in the nature of the drug problem as it might be able to if it controlled the budget process. Since there is no communal or common counterdrug budget, cuts in one program—the Defense Department's interdiction assistance budget, for example—cannot immediately be applied to another function where resources might be more effectively used, such as Health and Human Services' treatment and prevention programs. Indeed, departments facing cutbacks in one drug mission will have the incentive to keep the money within the department by expanding other missions that may not be as relevant to counterdrug goals. Such maneuvers, while useful at preserving the size of individual departments' budget slices, do not necessarily make for the most efficient and rational allocation of budget resources.

Controlling Supply and Demand

Since ONDCP's inception, the strategy set forth in the NDCS has embraced two main elements: controlling the supply of and demand for drugs. As a consequence, national drug control programs are typically categorized as either supply control or demand control. In general, supply control programs target the people who manufacture, transport, and distribute drugs, and demand control programs target the people who use drugs. In practice, this distinction is somewhat artificial because supply and demand are mutually reinforcing and mutually interacting concepts, and because some programs affect both traffickers and users. To take but one example, consider what happened when Mexican marijuana plants were sprayed with Paraquat in an effort to control supply. Shortly afterward, demand for marijuana fell temporarily out of concern that the treated cannabis might be poisonous. Nevertheless, from the perspective of organizing and dispersing federal resources, the distinction between supply and demand programs has proven useful.

Demand and supply control programs can be further subdivided into categories that describe functional operations, and it is here that the role of source country control programs in the national drug control strategy becomes clearer. Source country control policies are a subset of a larger category of programs known as *international and border control.* International and Border Control policies are aimed at stemming the production and export of all drugs, not just cocaine. Moreover, these policies are aimed at preventing the drugs from ever entering the United States. Once the drugs cross the border into the United States they become subject to another set of supply control strategies, known as *domestic enforcement.* Domestic enforcement is aimed at curbing the distribution and retail sale of drugs in the United States. Unlike international and border control programs, which are operated by the federal government (or by foreign governments), a large portion of domestic enforcement is conducted by state and local organizations such as police forces and sheriffs departments.

Treatment and prevention programs constitute the main components of demand control. Treatment services target those with an existing (or past) drug abuse problem. In contrast, prevention programs, as the name implies, seek to prevent individuals from experimenting with, or becoming dependent on, drugs. As with domestic enforcement, nonfederal organizations maintain a prominent role in treatment and prevention programs. In the case of treatment, federal authorities provide approximately one-fifth of the treatment slots, with the balance provided through other sources.

The subsequent sections of this chapter acquaint the reader with the elements of national drug control strategy, starting with the focus of this book, source country cocaine control programs and their broader parent category, international and border control. The other elements of national drug control strategy are included to provide a better understanding of the complex relations and interactions between elements of federal drug control strategy.

International and Border Control

In recent years, the drug war has again taken on a distinctly international flavor. The United States spends approximately $3 billion on *international and border* drug control programs, or one quarter of the federal drug control budget.[6] Source country control policies are a subset of international and border control, and marijuana, heroin, and other drugs are subject to control, so that the actual spending on source country cocaine control programs is less than the total for international and border control programs.

Responsibility for implementing and executing international and border control programs is divided between a number of agencies. As noted before, ONDCP maintains the role of overall strategic planning and guidance. In terms of implementation, the lead role belongs to the State Department and, more specifically, the Bureau of International Narcotics and Law Enforcement Affairs (INL).[7] INL maintains responsibility for program management, international drug policy formulation, and drug diplomacy initiatives. Much of INL's own $160 million 1994 budget was devoted to strengthening various aspects of Bolivian, Colombian, and Peruvian police and counternarcotics capabilities through provision of aviation support, vehicles, and communications equipment. More than $150 million of the $213 million request for 1996 is earmarked for Latin American nations; less than $12 million was requested for Asia, Africa, and Europe combined.

Although coordination of international drug control policy belongs to INL, the Customs Service, the Department of Defense (DOD), and the U.S. Coast Guard actually have much larger operational budgets for international and interdiction programs than does INL (see figure 2.1 for an overview). Since 1987, the first year for which total international and interdiction spending exceeded $1 billion, Defense, Coast Guard, and Customs have consistently ranked among the four largest international and interdiction programs.

FIGURE 2.1
International and Interdiction Budgets, 1987–96

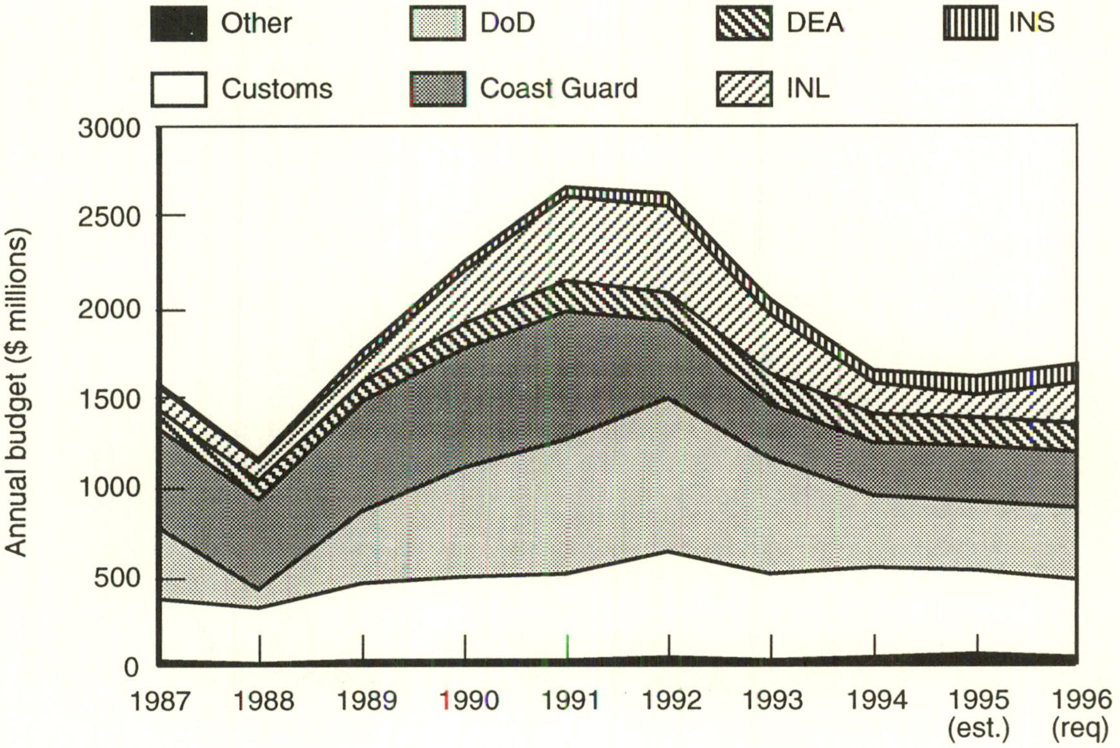

The Coast Guard and the Customs Service ranked first and second in 1988, 1989, and 1990, primarily because of the strong emphasis on border integrity, protection of territorial limits, and transit zone interdiction. The Coast Guard's interdiction budget reached its highest point in 1991, at $714 million. The most significant component of the Coast Guard's counter-drug budget is operations and maintenance. Managing, recruiting, training, and sustaining the drug-related portion of the Coast Guard force cost an estimated $258 million in 1994, fully 82 percent of the estimated counter-drug budget. That budget supported the equivalent of just over two-thousand personnel. A large portion of the remainder was spent on procuring vessels and equipment. Since 1991, the Coast Guard's interdiction budget has declined more than 50 percent to $320 million. This decline is explained by two factors. First, the Coast Guard completed much of its procurement and construction program in the latter 1980s and early 1990s, resulting in smaller capital budgets in recent years. Second, operational budgets for drug control have been taxed by the Coast Guard's heavy involvement in controlling the flow of Haitian refugees.

The Customs Service's drug control budgets rose through 1992 to $588 million, and have since stabilized at a level about 17 percent below the 1992 peak. Generally, Customs' international drug control budget has grown in parallel with the estimated increases in drug trafficking. Although 1992 proved to be the high point of Customs' drug control budget, Customs' international drug control budget still reflects not only the continued high level of international drug trafficking, but the growing volume of legitimate commerce and trade that Customs must regulate.

The U.S. Customs Service is charged with maintaining the integrity and security of U.S. borders through regulation of commercial and tourist traffic that comes over U.S. borders. Customs' primary regulation method is cargo and vehicular inspections at major ports, airports, crossings, and other entry locations. Customs annually inspects approximately 4 percent of all containers entering the United States, and approximately 20 percent of the containers entering the United States from the drug-producing nations of Latin America. Customs' second major task is interdiction at unofficial land, air, and sea points of entry and in the territorial waters and airspace off the U.S. coast. For 1993, approximately 25 percent of Customs' inspection and control programs, and 60 percent of its operations and investigations programs, were scored as drug related. Customs' counter-drug effort involves the equivalent of an estimated 5500 full-time personnel.

As DOD's drug war missions, including detection and monitoring, communications integrations, and disposition of excess military equipment, became fully operational, DOD rose in the international and interdiction spending rankings. DOD reached second place in 1990, and first place in 1991, where it remained through 1993. DOD's international and interdiction budget peaked in 1992 at more than $850 million, but has since declined to slightly less than $400 million.

DOD's participation in international drug control is largely confined to assisting U.S. and foreign law enforcement and drug control agencies with detecting and monitoring the flow of drugs. Of the nearly $400 million DOD contributed to international and interdiction efforts in 1994, more than 53 percent was devoted to detection and monitoring in the Caribbean Basin, and more than 13 percent to detection and monitoring support within the primary cocaine-producing nations. The remaining third of DOD's international and interdiction budget was used to support source country law enforcement initiatives, provide intelligence, host joint exercises, and assist with communications.

The Drug Enforcement Administration (DEA) and the Immigration and Naturalization Service are two other federal organizations with significant participation in international and border control programs. DEA has extremely broad drug control responsibilities, the majority of which do not involve international programs. With respect to international programs, DEA's primary responsibilities are investigations, case preparation, enforcing the Controlled Substances and Chemical Diversion Trafficking Acts, managing the National Narcotics Intelligence System, providing forensic and investigative training, and supporting the Targeted Kingpin Organization (TKO) strategy. DEA's international programs cost approximately $170 million in 1994, or approximately the size of INL. Beginning with 1994, chemical diversion control was to be funded entirely from registration fees levied on producers.

The Immigration Service's primary responsibility is to control the alien population in, and wishing to enter, the United States. A significant portion (estimated to be 16 percent in 1993) of INS's alien control operations involves aliens suspected of drug trafficking. INS's international and interdiction budget surpassed $74 million in 1994. This total was divided among border patrol operations, other inspections, investigations, detention and deportation operations, and intelligence, training, communications, and R&D.

International and Source Country Programs in History

The focus on controlling foreign sources of drug supplies is not a departure from the historical norm, but rather represents a consistent pattern in the history of U.S. drug policy.[8] Consumption of illicit drugs in the United States has long been ascribed to unsavory societal elements, many of which were considered unsavory because or their foreign origins. Chinese immigrants, for example, were linked in the public's perception to the opium trade, and Mexicans to the marijuana trade.[9] As far back as 1909 and the Shanghai Opium Commission and 1912 and the Hague Opium Convention, the United States contemplated methods for controlling drug production at the source. Source country control is also fueled by the perception that the drug business is controlled by foreigners and by the belief that weak and corrupt foreign governments support the drug trade. In this sense, the "War on Drugs" takes on a national security dimension.[10]

In contrast to strict domestic enforcement, programs aimed at controlling drug production in, and exports from, foreign countries offer a number of seeming advantages. The conflict, if any, takes place well beyond the confines of American borders. Source country policies appear to generate results: drugs are seized, drug kingpins are arrested, and drug-producing crops are destroyed. The drug problem may also appear easier to control from overseas. Foreign drug control is a problem of thousands of traffickers and growers; domestic drug control is one of millions of consumers. In addition, since there is no indication that there has been a coalescence of national sentiment around more radical regimes, such as legalization, or less punitive programs, such as "grudging toleration,"[11] source country control programs serve as a convenient interim policy. Finally, there is little evidence that either *domestic* supply or demand reduction programs alone can reduce the production and consumption of cocaine.[12]

There are, however, externalities, or costs beyond budget expenditures, associated with source country control programs. Perhaps the most tangible consequence is that drug policy is made immeasurably more complicated since source country control programs must be coordinated across international boundaries beyond which the United States does not have jurisdiction. With relatively few exceptions the source countries, rather than the United States, are responsible for the operation of drug control programs. The United States provides funding and trains source country forces for their missions, but except for these operations, it does not control source country programs directly.

Yet, by virtue of supporting the Andean nations' law enforcement and military institutions, the United States runs the risk of becoming entangled in the domestic problems that the security institutions are empowered and obligated to address. In Colombia, the U.S. assistance has been used not only to prosecute counternarcotics aims, but to augment Colombia's capacity to defend itself against domestic threats to its political structure, raising fears that the outcome may parallel U.S. involvement in Vietnam.[13] In contrast, in Peru the United States has abandoned many counternarcotics objectives because of the threat posed by the *Sendero Luminoso,* an intense rivalry between the Peruvian national police and the military, President Fujimori's 1992 "self-coup," the Peruvian military's April, 1992 shootdown of a U.S. C-130 Hercules aircraft that killed one U.S. soldier, and fears of potential human rights abuses.[14] In either case, U.S. counternarcotics policy directly affects domestic issues in Colombia and Peru.

Finally, source country control programs are not without their domestic consequences. It is asserted that attempts to control production of drugs in foreign countries can lead to adverse consequences in the consuming nation. In one striking example, the high potency of marijuana now available across the United States is largely the result of traffickers' efforts to reduce the bulk of their contraband and evade intense interdiction programs that operated in Mexico and Colombia in the 1970s and 1980s.[15] Crackdowns in foreign countries also contributed to a rise in domestic U.S. marijuana farming. Similarly, a crackdown on cocaine markets in Colombia in the early 1980s may have augmented the spread of crack by temporarily restricting the supply of chemicals needed to convert base, a cracklike substance, into cocaine.[16] Eventually, crack proved to be a durable phenomenon, popular in the drug-using community. Both the marijuana and crack cases may be examples of the "Iron Law of Prohibition," which notes that as law enforcement efforts increase, so does drug potency.[17]

Policies and Goals

In general, source country policies are designed to accomplish one of three goals: create scarcity by preventing the movement and sale of drugs, prevent production by destroying the inputs to production, and provide employment alternatives to lure people away from the business of drug trafficking. Interdiction, eradication, and development assistance, respectively, are existing policies that correspond to these objectives. Other policies exist that are variations of these three main approaches, or which represent them in combination. For example, the destruction of cocaine processing laboratories is, in some sense, a variation of eradication because the intent is to destroy one of the primary inputs of cocaine production. Similarly, the "kingpin" strategy is a philosophical cousin of eradication to the extent that labor, or more accurately, leadership, are inputs into the production of cocaine.

Interdiction, eradication, and crop substitution will be the focus of the remainder of this book, in part because the policies have been rigorously examined in other works, in part because most other policy options are variations on these three choices, and in part because they are the strongest forms of scarcity, prevention, and alternative-based approaches.[18] These points will be clarified in the next chapter when the economic framework for analysis is presented, but for now it is important to remember that scarcity, prevention, and alternative-based approaches operate on the same principles no matter what policy name they are given. Interdiction, eradication and crop substitution and their accompanying objectives are presented briefly below. They will be considered formally in the context of the analytic framework in the next chapter.

Interdiction and Scarcity

A fundamental tenet of economics states that as a good in demand becomes scarce, its price will go up. The logical extension of such a price increase is that people will consume less of the more expensive product. In a very broad sense, interdiction is an effort to make cocaine more expensive and price consumers out of the cocaine market.[19] In theory, every time police forces intercept a cocaine shipment, a portion of the demand for cocaine goes unmet and retail cocaine prices increase. There is no particular reason that interdiction has to occur in the source countries. Indeed, a substantial amount of interdiction occurs both inside and beyond the borders of the United States. In theory the timing of the seizure can matter because the value of drugs increases as the shipment nears retail markets. The increase in prices, which is primarily due to the risks that the traffickers face and perceive, will be discussed in much greater detail in the chapter on the economic framework of cocaine trafficking. For now it is sufficient to point out that seizures made at the lower-risk stages of production will affect drug prices less than seizures made at the higher-risk stages of shipment and retailing.

According to official figures, the federal government spent almost $1.7 billion on international and interdiction programs in 1994, more than $1.3 billion of which was spent on interdiction activities. By law, DOD's role is limited. Military personnel cannot arrest traffickers and cannot participate in interdiction operations. Instead, DOD operates solely in the capacity of providing information to other organizations, both foreign and domestic, as well as providing training and equipment. Thus, since 1988 the Department of Defense has been the lead agency for detection and monitoring of aerial and maritime transit drug shipments. In addition, DOD provided millions of dollars of equipment and training to Bolivia, Colombia, and Peru to assist them in developing interdiction and other counterdrug capabilities. DOD concentrates its detection and monitoring activities in the Caribbean Basin and the Andean Ridge, which means that most of its efforts are directed against cocaine smuggling.

The actual physical interception of the drugs is accomplished by the Coast Guard and the Customs Service. These organizations, unlike the U.S. military, have law enforcement powers. The Coast Guard spent nearly $300 million to counter drug trafficking in 1994, most of which was spent on operations. The Customs Service estimates that about 25 percent of its border inspection and control activities are drug related, resulting in expenditures (for salaries and expenses) of over $500 million in 1994. Similarly, the Immigration and Naturalization Service (INS) counts 15 percent of border patrol and 25 percent of detention and deportation services as drug related for a total of $66 million in interdiction efforts. Again a large portion, but not all, of these organizations' efforts are cocaine related.

According to available records, more than 200 metric tons of cocaine were seized in 1994 before they reached the interior United

TABLE 2.1
International and Border Seizures of Cocaine, 1994
(metric tons)

Customs	92.7
Coast Guard	28.2
INS/Border Patrol	16.6
In-Country[1]	89.2[2]
Total	226.7

Note: [1]Figure for South and Central America, plus the Dominican Republic. [2]Colombia (30 mt), Mexico (22.1 mt) and Brazil (11.6 mt) account for more than 70 percent of this total.

States.[20] Again, the Department of Defense did not execute any of these seizures itself, but it did play a fundamental role by assisting other law enforcement organizations in the identification and monitoring of clandestine drug shipments. Table 2.1 summarizes the interdiction effort.

Eradication and Prevention

Without coca, drug traffickers could not make cocaine. Any input that is vital to the production of cocaine can be targeted for control, and as a consequence authorities have made efforts to control such factors as processing chemicals and cartel leadership. The 1988 Chemical Diversion and Trafficking Act instituted a variety of control mechanisms, including vendor restrictions and reporting requirements, in an effort to stem the flow of processing chemicals, sometimes known as precursor chemicals, to the cocaine industry. Similarly, Colombian law enforcement organizations have pursued "decapitation" and "kingpin" strategies, which target high-level cartel leaders in an effort to deprive the trafficking industry of its leadership.

Still, coca eradication in many respects remains the most attractive preventative measure. Coca plants represent fixed capital, and thus are easier to locate and destroy than more mobile input factors such as chemicals and labor. Throughout the last decade, the United States has supported various forms of coca eradication programs. In Peru, the United States supported a forced eradication, while in Bolivia it relied on a voluntary program. Colombia has used eradication programs as well, although until recent years its programs have been aimed primarily against poppies and marijuana.[21]

Eradication can take one of two forms: manual and herbicidal. Manual eradication offers greater political acceptability with the producing nations and has been experimented with in the past. The difficulty with manual eradication lies in the fact that men and equipment must be moved in large numbers to remote growing areas. Once there, the coca plant itself proves resilient to eradication efforts. It takes perhaps twenty man days of effort to pull up an entire hectare of coca plants by their roots.[22] Once pulled up, the plants themselves must be destroyed or burned so that processors and traffickers do not retrieve the plants once the eradication teams leave the area. In contrast, herbicidal eradication promises greater ease of implementation but conjures up visions of chemical contamination, environmental destruction, and other ecological, political, and social problems. Recent studies point to potentially effective herbicidal treatments for coca plants.[23] At least three herbicides—glyphosate, tebuthiuron, and hexazinone[24]—demonstrate the ability to kill coca plants. Questions persist, however, as to whether these chemicals are appropriate for use in the tropical environment in terms of soil persistence, damage to other crops, and the health hazard posed to humans in the area.

In recent years a natural form of eradication has been occurring in Peru's Upper Huallaga Valley.[25] A fungus, *fusarium oxisoporum*, has killed off thousands of hectares of coca plants. The fungus's effects on coca were noted in 1987, and since then *fusarium* has spread throughout the valley. At the same time the fungus has been detected spreading throughout the Upper Huallaga Valley, reports are surfacing that the coca trade is dispersing more widely throughout the region, including the Central and Lower Huallaga valleys.

Currently, the largest component of coca eradication programs is compensation given to Bolivia for meeting voluntary eradication targets. Under the terms of the agreement, the United States provides debt relief in exchange for progress toward eradication. This agreement, which was made possible by passage of a coca farming regulation act in 1988, annually results in approximately 5000 hectares of coca eradication. The aid, which is administered by the U.S. Agency for International Development, totals approximately $60 million per year. Direct funding for eradication programs stood at $17 million in 1993 and $16.5 million in 1994.

Crop Substitution and Alternatives

Crop substitution, or more generally, alternative development and development assistance, is premised on the assumption workers in cocaine production are not predisposed to illegal activity. Assuming a legal form of employment can be found that would replace their cocaine income, cocaine industry laborers would be willing to undertake employment in the legal sector of the economy. There are any number of ways that opportunities and incomes in the legal sectors can be bolstered to siphon labor away from cocaine production, but subsidization of agriculture, or crop substitution, is thought to be particularly appropriate because the early stages of cocaine production are agriculturally based (coca farming) and because most cocaine production takes place in rural areas where options other than agriculture are impractical.

The United States has supported a number of programs intended to pull farmers away from coca farming. U.S.AID/Bolivia, for example, provides marketing and export assistance, agricultural extension and research services, credit, and infrastructure development programs.[26] Under these programs, some coca farmers are provided technical expertise, loans, and services in an effort to increase the agricultural diversity of the region. Through these programs more than 1,000 Bolivian farmers in the Chapare region have received $5.6 million in loans; 4,000 farmers have received training; and exports of local crops to Argentina, Chile, and Venezuela have been established.[27]

Also, a number of development programs have been implemented over the past decade in Peru, most aimed at controlling the coca trade in Peru's Upper Huallaga Valley. This area was targeted for assistance as early as 1981 with the commencement of the Upper Huallaga Area Development Program (UHADP). UHADP consists of three parts: eradication, development and commercialization, and control of coca commerce. CORAH, Peru's national coca eradication authority, was given responsibility for the eradication programs; PEAH (Special Project for the development of the Alto Huallaga) was directed to establish and implement a regional development program; UMOPAR (Mobile Rural Police Unit) agents became responsible for regulating coca commerce in the UHV.

In addition to attempting to reduce coca farming directly in the Andes through eradication, the United States has also supported projects designed to stem the flow of labor to coca growing regions in an effort to limit the labor pool available for coca farming. Migrant labor, particularly from the highland valleys in Bolivia, supplies the cocaine trade with the work force it needs to produce coca. In Bolivia, the largest attempt to control migration is the Associated High Valleys (AHV) project. The AHV is an area adjacent to the Chapare that not only supplies the coca zone with some of the migrant and seasonal labor needed for coca production, but is also the origin of many of the homesteaders who have settled in the Chapare. The AHV projects entail a series of development projects designed to increase opportunities in the AHV in hopes of both stemming the flow of seasonal and migrant labor to the Chapare, and attracting back some of the migrants who have moved to the Chapare.

Beyond International Programs

For fiscal year 1994, international and interdiction programs represented more than 13 percent of all federal spending on drug control. The $1.3 billion spent on interdiction consumed almost 11 percent of the federal drug control budget, while the $329.4 allocated to international programs equalled slightly less than 3 percent of the federal total.

The balance of federal drug control spending, more than $10.5 billion, is divided among two other strategic elements of the national drug control strategy: domestic enforcement and demand control (treatment and prevention). Figure 2.2 shows that federal spending on each element of the national strategy has increased substantially over the past decade. But while all components of the drug strategy have experienced growth, the increases have not been balanced, nor has the historical distribution of spending among the components been balanced. In 1981, just over 40 percent of federal funds were devoted to treatment and prevention programs, but that ratio had declined to almost 32 percent by 1993. Since 1993, demand control's share has increased slightly, and is currently at about 64 percent of the federal drug control budget.

Domestic Enforcement

By all conventional measures, domestic enforcement against cocaine use and cocaine trafficking has increased substantially over the past

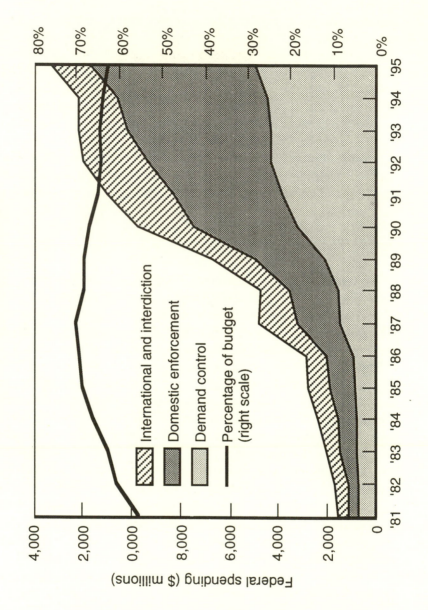

FIGURE 2.2
Federal Drug Control Spending, 1981–95

decade.[28] The number of people *arrested* for cocaine-related offenses (buying and selling) rose more than twelvefold between 1979 and 1988, and has continued to rise in intervening years.[29] Rising arrest rates in conjunction with a higher number of convictions, the implementation of sentencing guidelines (including mandatory minimum sentences), and the abolition of federal parole for drug offenses has led to an increase in average sentence length. Cocaine dealers' punishment risks are thought to have increased in the 1980s as a result of these enforcement efforts.[30]

Other elements of more stringent domestic enforcement abound. Law enforcement agencies, for example, now benefit economically from their counterdrug activities through forfeiture laws. Assets seized from drug traffickers are now routinely sold to provide law enforcement organizations with revenue, or retained for use in counterdrug operations. The revenue from such operations, which in the case of the Justice Department's Assets Forfeiture Fund reached $645 million in 1991, has grown so rapidly that federal, state, and local law enforcement organizations have established revenue sharing regulations for the dispensation of assets in instances where multiple law enforcement agencies are involved.[31]

At the workplace, employer testing of employees for drug use has become commonplace. In some cases the testing is paid for out of public funds, while in an increasing number of cases, the cost is absorbed by the private sector. Concomitant with the increase in testing has been the development of a variety of punitive regimes. In some cases, a positive test for an illicit substance is grounds for immediate termination, while in other instances follow-up counseling and treatment are required before termination is allowed.

Responsibility for domestic enforcement at the federal level is divided among a variety of departments and agencies, including DEA, FBI, the Federal Judiciary, the Department of Treasury, and the Department of Defense. DEA and FBI resources tend to be concentrated on trafficking investigations, Judiciary expenditures on incarceration and court operations, and Treasury resources on drug crimes related to money laundering, finance, and weaponry. DOD provides significant assistance to domestic enforcement efforts by delivering excess equipment (such as vehicles and helicopters) to DLEAs (Domestic Law Enforcement Agencies), providing air transportation to DLEAs, and by using National Guard forces to assist DLEAs in domestic eradication and seizure operations.

Much of the federal effort also involves coordination with local, municipal, and state enforcement efforts. As a result, a large portion of the domestic enforcement effort does not appear in federal statistics because it is carried out by state and local law enforcement organizations. No definitive estimate of state and local law enforcement efforts against drugs exists, but these efforts may be two to five times the federal domestic enforcement effort, and perhaps larger than the entire federal drug budget.[32]

Treatment

On any given day, there are more than a quarter of a million people being treated for all types of illicit drug abuse, but perhaps six times that many are in need of treatment services.[33] Some choose not to seek treatment, while others cannot find open treatment slots. The relative size of these two fractions is subject to much debate, although there is a consensus that "treatment on demand" does not exist.

Total federal spending on treatment, again for all types of illicit drugs, approached $2.4 billion in 1994. The Substance Abuse and Mental Health Services Administration (SAMHSA), the Department of Veterans Affairs, and the Health Care Financing Administration (HCFA), which provide $927.2 million, $850.6 million and $231.8 million in treatment services respectively, account for more than 80 percent of federal treatment spending. Combined, the federal government operated or administered over 125,000 treatment slots in a national network of over 633,000 slots, which served over 1.75 million people in 1992.[34]

Although the term *treatment* conveys a unitary sense, the drug treatment system in fact consists of several different approaches to drug dependence. For cocaine abusers the major types of treatment environments are therapeutic communities (TC), outpatient nonmethadone treatment (ON), chemical dependency (CD) treatment, detoxification, and correctional treatment programs.[35]

The therapeutic community approach to treatment involves a residential setting to which the user is committed for an extended period of time, including periods of a year or more. Because the user is in a residential environment where drug use is likely to be easily detected, TCs offer a substantial *incapacitation effect*. That is, while the clients are enrolled in a TC, their drug use is likely to be curtailed or incapacitated either because of the threat of detection, because of lower drug availability, or both. The length of the stay in the program is very highly inversely correlated with relapse. Clients who commit and complete longer stays are much less likely to resume drug use. However, the length of commitment necessary to achieve this effect can prove problematic for significant sections of the drug-abusing population. Few heavy users have the resources, willingness, or ability to enter a program that would isolate them from their job, family, and social structure for months on end.

In many respects, outpatient programs are similar to therapeutic communities, with the crucial difference being that outpatient clients spend much of their time in an unsupervised environment. Otherwise, outpatient nonmethadone treatment programs make extensive use of individual and group counseling, provide a program that may last six months or more, and typically have strengths and weaknesses that parallel those of therapeutic community programs.

Much less is known about the efficacy of chemical dependency programs for drug dependence.[36] Generally, CD programs are modeled after Alcoholics Anonymous-type programs, which address substance abuse as a lifetime affliction to be controlled. Containment of the problem in a CD setting is typically promoted through appealing to belief in a higher power and by requiring the users to effect major lifestyle and personal changes. CD programs are often associated with, or located in, hospitals. Individuals who are hospitalized for acute intoxication, or complications thereof, will be referred to these programs. Because of this happenstance, CD regimes integrate treatment with access to primary health care, a feature often lacking from other programs.

Detoxification programs are intended to redress acute episodes of intoxication. Thus, while detoxification programs are associated with hospitals and primary care facilities like chemical dependency programs, the emphasis is on stabilizing patients who have endangered their health as a direct result of substance abuse. In most cases, detoxification services do not extend beyond medical treatment of intoxication-related maladies. For this reason many do not consider detoxification programs to be true treatment settings.

Treatment of prisoners, and others under the jurisdiction of the criminal justice system, deserves special mention. The penal system has been harshly criticized for not providing sufficient treatment slots despite the fact that many of those incarcerated in the prison system have substance abuse problems.[37] The argument is made that drug rehabilitation should be made available for this type of captive audience. Supporters claim that greater availability of treatment services will lead to reduced drug use and perhaps reduced recidivism. Critics, however, charge compulsory treatment will not work, and that for criminal justice system treatment programs to be effective the inmate population must want treatment services.

There are a number of other acknowledged deficiencies within the existing treatment system that are not connected to the comparison of coerced and voluntary treatment. Perhaps most importantly, treatment programs tend to be isolated from other segments of the health care industry. Treatment services are separated from primary health care services for many reasons, including contrasting regulatory schemes, differing personnel and occupational needs, and separate funding formulas.[38] Since many drug-dependent users have other health care concerns that are aggravated or caused by drug use, the segregation of treatment services from mainstream health care limits the utility of treatment programs to a smaller group and potentially forces a choice between substance abuse treatment and primary health care.

Treatment programs are easy targets for criticism on other grounds as well. One reason treatment programs are considered with suspicion by some is their relatively low "cure" rate. The primary goal of treatment is lifetime abstinence, but many drug users undergo relapses after the initial experience with treatment is completed. A given individual might need to be treated five or more times in a therapeutic community before quitting drugs for good. Similarly, chemical dependency program clients may, for the remainder of their lives, require chemical dependency services. These characteristics not only appear to give treatment a high failure rate, but also entail a long-term approach to drug abuse that may not satisfy short-term political demands.

Finally, few effective treatment mechanisms other than the modalities already described, exist for cocaine. Unlike heroin addiction, whose effects can be mitigated with methadone, and unlike nicotine addiction, whose complications can be ameliorated with prescription patches, there are no known chemical treatments for cocaine dependence. Because of these limitations, treatment alone does not offer a solution to national cocaine consumption problems.

Prevention

In contrast to treatment programs, which attempt to halt drug use after it has started, prevention programs seek to preclude drug use from ever starting, and to prevent relapse by people who have undergone treatment. At its core, drug prevention seeks to modify drug-taking behavior. There are many avenues through which behavior can be affected. Perhaps the most basic method of affecting behavior is the dissemination of knowledge. Behavior modification is also sought by bringing about changes in attitudes, or core beliefs, of individuals. Still, much of drug prevention is communicated through knowledge-based tools, including health monitoring and consultation, structured drug education programs, and media campaigns. Changing attitudes is a more complicated task, but a number of techniques have been developed in this area of drug prevention. Many attitudinal-based programs focus on an approach known as *enhancing social competencies,* through which an individual's ability to resist peer pressure, build self-esteem, and augment other pertinent skills are addressed.

Drug prevention programs, which are based on increasing an individual's knowledge about drug abuse consequences, however, have not proven effective at modifying drug using behavior.[39] Knowledge, it turns out, is relatively easy to change, but the link between knowledge and desired drug-taking behavior is more complicated than can be addressed by passive presentation of information. Similarly attitudes, like knowledge, are not strongly predictive of behavior, and thus changes in attitudinal factors (such as those measured in the NHSDA) do not necessarily mean that the desired changes in behavior will result. Regardless, numerous studies indicate that drug education programs in schools that incorporate both knowledge and attitudes can substantially reduce teenagers' drug use, but that this impact typically persists only for as long as the curriculum is continued.[40] Even though education programs clearly raise students' knowledge and change students' attitudes about drug use, affecting behavior requires continuous reinforcement.

In budget terms, the Department of Education (DOE) operates the largest set of prevention programs, with over $650 million of fiscal authority. Much of DOE's drug prevention effort, and indeed, of all drug prevention efforts, is aimed at the young because they are thought to be particularly vulnerable to the threat of drug abuse, and because their attitudes and behaviors are most malleable. More than twenty other federal organizations operate drug prevention programs, although only two others have budgets of more than $100 million. SAMHSA is the second-largest federal provider of prevention programs; it had a prevention budget of $435.6 million in 1994. HUD, the Department of Housing and Urban Development, spent approximately $290 million on prevention programs in 1994. HUD directs its drug elimination grants to public and Indian housing projects for purposes ranging from security to counseling, referral, and outreach programs.

Because the effects of prevention may erode over time, prevention, like treatment, may be perceived to have a high failure rate. In any event, it is clear that prevention programs alone are incapable of controlling the nation's cocaine problem: even if prevention were 100 percent effective and initiation virtually ceased tomorrow, the size of the heavy user population would fall only about 50 percent over fifteen years.[41]

Alternatives to Enforcement-Based Regimes

Recent changes in the nature of the drug problem, in particular the decline in the initiation rates and the increase in the number of heavy users, have intensified calls from some segments of the drug policy community to redress the imbalance between law enforcement-based and medical-based and harm minimization drug control strategies. That such a large portion of the drug budget is dedicated to international and domestic supply control programs has been criticized frequently. In particular, it is argued that the focus on enforcement has led to an erosion of civil rights, made criminals out of thousands of people because of an arbitrary distinction between licit and illicit drugs, and artificially inflated the profits and, hence, criminal motives behind drug trafficking.[42] As noted before, the ability to move budget resource from the supply side of the ledger to the demand side is limited. Changing the distribution between supply and demand control programs will be difficult, not only because budget resources are not easily reoriented, but because a fundamental change in philosophy regarding drug policy is required. Still, alternatives to supply and demand control do exist, and they will be briefly discussed here. At the opposite end of the spectrum from the existing regime is legalization, or less radically, decriminalization. Legalization and decriminalization are regimes that reject the criminalization of drug-using behavior. In the case of legalization, drug consumption would be subjected to few, if any, criminal sanctions and drug sales by licensed and regulated dealers would not be considered crimes.[43] In contrast, decriminalization is usually thought to refer to reducing sanctions against drug use, but maintaining sanctions against drug trafficking and marketing.[44] Under decriminalization, use of drugs would be tolerated, but sales would still be subject to law enforcement pressure.

Proponents of legalization and decriminalization anticipate numerous benefits from the advent of a less restrictive regime. Many, for example, think that legalization would lead to a large decline in the amount of drug-related crime. Implicit in this expectation is the idea that the existing drug-control regime causes much of the current drug-related crime by provoking conflicts between authorities and dealers or among dealers, and by keeping drug prices artificially high, which leads to an increase in the amount of economic-compulsive drug crime. Opponents argue that legalization and decriminalization will lead to large increases in drug use and that the costs associated with more widespread drug use would swamp the benefits associated with fewer restrictions.

Midway between legalization and enforcement-based regimes is a concept known as harm minimization. Harm minimization may be the approach most consistent with the call for evening out the supply-demand imbalance. Though variations on this approach exist, the basic elements are to minimize the aggregate harms to individuals from drug abuse and, thus, in the process, to minimize the harms to society that result from drug consumption. One prominent feature of a harm minimization approach is to recognize drug use and, in particular, drug abuse, as a medical, rather than a criminal or moral, problem. Thus, elements of harm minimization might include making sterile needles available for intravenous drug users to reduce the transmission of HIV, and to make "illicit" drugs available to addicts through prescription to reduce the medical and criminal consequences of drug use.

In reality, all of these diverse forms of drug-control policy have potential roles in the national strategy. The appropriateness of a given tool will depend on a number of factors, including the type of drug under consideration, where the nation is in the epidemic cycle, and the populations at risk from the epidemic.[45] A consensus appears to be emerging in the academic and analytic communities that future growth in drug-control budgets will be limited, and that future progress on drug control will depend primarily on refining goals, tools, and the allocation of resources. Chapter 3 presents a framework for how one set of tools, source country control policies, might be evaluated and revised.

Notes

1. CBS/*New York Times* telephone surveys of national adult population.
2. MacCoun and Reuter (1992) report on urban and inner-city drug dealing. See also Inciardi (1992), and Reuter and Haaga (1989).
3. *National Drug Control Strategy: Budget Summary* (1992).
4. Reuter (1993).
5. Murphy (1995)
6. ONDCP (1993): 4. *ONDCP Executive Budget* (1992). Figure includes source country control programs, as well as intelligence and other programs designed to improve interdiction programs.
7. Formerly the Bureau of International Narcotics Matters (INM).
8. Reuter (1985): 83–90.
9. Musto (1987).
10. Indeed, President Reagan defined the drug problem in these terms in 1986.
11. For a range of alternatives on drug control regimes, see Nadelmann (1992a), Skolnick (1992), and Szasz (1992). Kleiman (1992) develops the thesis of grudging toleration.
12. See *INCSR* (1989, 1990, 1991) for supply estimates and NIDA (1990, 1991, 1992) for consumption data.
13. Among the analyses developing the parallel explicitly is Andreas, et. al. (1992).
14. McCormick (1991 and 1992) and Palmer (1992).
15. Reuter (1991): 149; Falco (1989) reviews these strategies.
16. Inciardi (1992).
17. Cowan (1986); Thornton (1991).
18. See Kennedy, Reuter, and Riley (1993) and (1994); Riley (1993); and Greenfield (1990) for more detail.
19. Exactly what cocaine consumers would turn to if cocaine became more expensive is an interesting question, and one that deserves some thought. DiNardo and Lemieux (1992) consider some consequences from another chapter in scarcity economics, teenage consumption of alcohol and marijuana.
20. INCSR (1994).
21. *The Drug War: Counternarcotics Programs in Colombia and Peru* (1992); *Drug War: Observations on Counternarcotics Aid to Colombia* (1991).
22. Lee (1989).
23. See *Cocaine Production, Eradication, and the Environment* (1990): especially pages 20–23.
24. Glyphosate sells under the trade name Roundup. Tebuthiuron sells under the brand name Spike, and is manufactured by Dow Elanco. Hexazinone is known as both Velpar and Pronone and is made by E. I. Du Pont de Nemours and Company. Both herbicides are already in commercial use worldwide.
25. *Coca Cultivation and Cocaine Processing: An Overview* (1991). See also, *JPRS Narcotics Report* (5 January 1993): 8–9, for transcription of a report from a Peruvian newspaper.
26. *USAID/Bolivia Alternative Development Strategy* (1991): 9–10.

27. *USAID/Bolivia Program Objectives and Action Plan* (1993-1997), (1992).
28. Reuter (1992); Reuter (1991).
29. Ibid.
30. Ibid.
31. ONDCP (1992).
32. Reuter (1992) discusses the difficulty in estimating local and state enforcement expenditures.
33. Schlesinger and Dorwart (1992).
34. *National Drug Control Strategy: Budget Summary* (1992); Schlesinger and Dorwart (1992).
35. Gerstein and Harwood (1990). Additionally, another major treatment modality, methadone maintenance, exists. Methadone maintenance, however, is not an appropriate treatment program for the cocaine dependent.
36. Ibid.
37. Leukefeld and Tims (1988) takes a detailed look at compulsory treatment.
38. Reuter (1993).
39. Montagne and Scott (1993).
40. Ellickson, Bell, and McGuigan (1993).
41. Everingham and Rydell (1993).
42. See Nadelmann (1992); Szasz (1992); and Kleiman and Saiger (1992) for a range of opinions and regimes.
43. See Kleiman (1992), particularly pages 268-76 for more on decriminalization and legalization.
44. Nadelmann (1992a), (1992b), and (1991) provides perspectives on these issues.
45. See Kleiman (1992) for more on strategy considerations.

References

Andreas, Peter R., Eva C. Bertram, Morris J. Blachman, and Kenneth E. Sharpe, "Dead End Drug Wars," *Foreign Policy* 85 (Winter 1991-92): 105-128.

Coca Cultivation and Cocaine Processing: An Overview (Washington, D.C.: Drug Enforcement Administration, 1991).

Cocaine Production, Eradication, and the Environment: Policy, Impact and Options, Committee on Governmental Affairs, United States Senate (Washington, D.C.: USGPO, August, 1990).

Cowan, Richard, "How the Narcs Created Crack," *National Review* (5 December 1986): 30-31.

DiNardo, John, "Law Enforcement, The Price of Cocaine, and Cocaine Use," *Mathematical and Computer Modelling* 17, 2 (1993): 53-64.

DiNardo, John, and Thomas Lemieux, "Alcohol, Marijuana and American Youth: The Unintended Effects of Government Regulation," NBER Working Paper #4212 (November 1992).

The Drug War: Counternarcotics Programs in Colombia and Peru (GAO: Washington, D.C., 20 February 1992).

Drug War: Observations on Counternarcotics Aid to Colombia, Government Accounting Office (Washington, D.C.: September, 1991).

Ellickson, Phyllis L., Robert M. Bell, and Kimberly McGuigan, "Preventing Adolescent Drug Use: Long-Term Results of a Junior High Program," *American Journal of Public Health* 83, 6 (June 1993): 856-61.

Everingham, Susan S., and Rydell, Peter C., "Modeling the Demand for Cocaine," DRR-390-ONDCP/A/DPRC (Santa Monica, Calif.: RAND, 1993).

Falco, Mathea, *Winning the Drug War: A National Strategy* (New York: Priority Press Publications, 1989).

Gerstein, Dean R., and Henrick J. Harwood, eds., *Treating Drug Problems* (Washington, D.C.: National Academy Press, 1990).

Greenfield, Victoria, "Bolivian Coca: A Perennial Leaf Crop Subject to Supply Reduction Policies" (Berkeley: University of California, Berkeley, 1991).

Inciardi, James A., *The War on Drugs II* (Mountain View, Calif.: Mayfield Publishing Company, 1992).

Kennedy, Michael, Peter Reuter, and Kevin Jack Riley, "A Simple Economic Model of Cocaine Production," *Mathematical and Computer Modelling* 17, 2 (1993): 19–36.

Kleiman, Mark A. R., *Against Excess: Drug Policy for Results* (New York: Basic Books, 1992).

Lee, Rensselaer W., *White Labyrinth* (New Brunswick, N.J.: Transaction Publishers, 1989).

Leukefeld, C. G., and F. M. Tims, "Compulsory Treatment: A Review of Findings," in Leukfeld and Tims, eds., *Compulsory Treatment of Drug Abuse: Research and Clinical Practice*, National Institute on Drug Abuse Research Monograph no. 86 (U.S. Department of Health and Human Services, Rockville, Md.: 1988).

MacCoun, Robert, and Peter Reuter, "Are the Wages of Sin $30 an Hour: Economic Aspects of Street-Level Drug Dealing," *Crime and Delinquency* 38, 4 (October 1992): 477–91.

McCormick, Gordon H., *From the Sierra to the Cities: The Urban Campaign of the Shining Path*, R-4150-U.S.DP, (Santa Monica, Calif.: RAND, 1992).

_____, *The Shining Path and the Future of Peru*, R-3781-DOS/OSD (Santa Monica, Calif.: RAND, 1990).

Montagne, Michael, and David M. Scott, "Prevention of Substance Abuse Problems: Models, Factors, and Processes," *International Journal of the Addictions* 28, 12 (1993): 1177–1208.

Murphy, Patrick, "Keeping Score: The Frailties of the Federal Drug Budget," RAND Drug Policy Research Center Issue Paper (January 1994).

Musto, David F., *The American Disease: Origins of Narcotic Control* (New York: Oxford University Press, 1987).

Nadelmann, Ethan A., "Thinking Seriously About Alternatives to Drug Prohibition," *Daedalus* 121, 3 [Summer 1992(a)]: 85–132.

_____, "Legalization or Harm Reduction: The Debate Continues," *International Journal on Drug Policy* 3, 2 [1992(b)]: 76–82.

_____, "Drug Prohibition in the United States: Costs, Consequences, and Alternatives," *Science* 245 (September 1991): 939–47.

_____, "Drug Prohibition in the United States: Costs, Consequences, and Alternatives," *Science* 245 (1989): 939–47.

National Drug Control Strategy: Budget Summary, The White House, January 1992.

ONDCP Executive Budget (1992).

Palmer, David Scott, "Peru the Drug Business and the Shining Path: Between Scylla and Charybdis," *Journal of Interamerican Studies and World Affairs* 34, 3 (Fall 1992): 65–88.

Reuter, Peter, "Drug Policy: Recent Lessons," Congressional Testimony CT-109 (Santa Monica, Calif.: RAND, 1993).

_____, *On the Consequences of Toughness*, N-3447-DPRC (Santa Monica, Calif.: RAND, 1991).

_____, "Eternal Hope: America's Quest for Narcotics Control," *The Public Interest* 79, 2 (1985), 79–95.

Reuter, Peter, and John Haaga, *The Organization of High-Level Drug Markets: An Exploratory Study*, N-2830-NIJ (Santa Monica, Calif.: RAND, 1989).

Riley, Kevin Jack, *Snow Job? The Efficacy of Source Country Cocaine Control Policies*, RGSD-102 [Santa Monica, Calif.: RAND, 1993(a)].

_____, *The Implications of Colombian Drug Industry and Death Squad Political Violence for U.S. Counternarcotics Policy*, N-3605-U.S.DP [Santa Monica, Calif.: RAND, 1993(b)].

Schlesinger, Mark, and Robert A. Dorwart, "Falling Between the Cracks: Failing National Strategies for the Treatment of Substance Abuse," *Daedalus* 121, 3 (Summer 1992): 195–238.

Skolnik, Jerome H., "Rethinking the Drug Problem," *Daedalus* 121, 3 (Summer 1992): 133–60.

Sollars, David L., "Assumptions and Consequences of the War on Drugs," *Policy Studies Review* 11, 1 (1992): 26–39.

Szasz, Thomas, "The Fatal Temptation: Drug Prohibition and the Fear of Autonomy," Daedalus 121, 3 (Summer 1992): 1361–164.

Thornton, Mark, *Alcohol Prohibition was a Failure*, Policy Analysis Series no. 157 (Washington, D.C.: Cato Institute, 1991).

USAID Bolivia: Program Objectives and Action Plan (1993–1997), United States Agency for International Development (La Paz, Bolivia: 1992).

USAID Bolivia: Alternative Development Strategy, United States Agence for International Development (La Paz, Bolivia: 1991).

3

The Price of War:
An Economic Framework for Analysis

In chapter 1, we examined cocaine as a drug. We looked at who uses cocaine, why they use it, and what some of the consequences of chronic and episodic cocaine use can be. In general, the purpose of chapter 1 was to lay out the dimensions of cocaine consumption, and to give the reader a sense for how rich and diverse the nature of cocaine consumption is in the United States. Chapter 2 described drug policy. Again, the purpose was primarily descriptive. The chapter was intended to give the reader an idea of the tools that are available to combat drug use, and generally, how the tools are expected to influence drug consumption. In contrast, this chapter is analytic. More specifically, this chapter proposes to analyze what happens when the subjects of chapter 1, cocaine users, meet the subject of chapter 2, counterdrug cocaine policies. As usual, the focus will be on the role of source country drug control policies.

Ultimately, most of what this chapter involves is figuring out how drug policies influence drug prices, and how drug prices in turn influence drug use, or, perhaps more precisely, drug-taking behavior. With this framework in mind, the rest of this chapter proceeds in an orderly fashion. The first section addresses cocaine prices along three dimensions. The section begins with a comparison of cocaine prices relative to other licit and illicit intoxicants. The comparison of cocaine to other psychoactive products introduces the notion of what happens when cocaine becomes more expensive than it is supposed to be when source country control policies are implemented. Next, a brief overview of cocaine prices anchors the theoretical discussion of prices' influence on demand to the historical record, and illustrates how difficult it is to isolate prices' impact from other trends in cocaine markets. The second section shifts from the users' perspective to the producers' by detailing how cocaine is made, what the vulnerable points in the production chain are, and how traffickers determine their prices. The implications of this structure for source country cocaine control programs are spelled out in detail, including how the pricing structure limits the impact source country policies can have on retail prices and the rapidity with which most segments of the production chain can recover from policy measures. Examples from existing source country control policies are interwoven throughout these sections. The chapter concludes with a summary of the major issues relating to source country control policies, and with an overview of the case studies that will be presented in part II of the book.

Cocaine Prices

As with so many other aspects of the cocaine trade, it is difficult to summarize cocaine prices in any meaningful sense. For one thing, cocaine prices are volatile. They jump around in response to various influences, including law enforcement pressure, competition in the marketplace, changes in tastes and preferences, and technological advances in manufacturing. Second, of course, buying and selling cocaine are illegal acts, and so the participants in these transactions have an interest in keeping the transactions hidden. Purity also presents a problem, since diluting or cutting cocaine is simply another way of increasing the price of a given size package. The people reporting prices, whether they are law enforcement officials or users, may have no more than a crude idea of the cocaine's purity, and thus, of the effective price of pure cocaine. Finally, prices of cocaine tend to vary substantially from region to region. Prices expressed in the aggregate may therefore mask important market variations occurring at regional levels.

Despite the inability to quote *the* price of cocaine, prices are a central feature of the national drug control debate. Moreover, prices are a key element to developing an understanding of how cocaine markets, and thus antidrug policies, work. In particular, there are three components of cocaine prices to be explored: what cocaine costs relative to other intoxicants; how use patterns may shift as prices change; and how prices have in fact changed over time. Together these three elements of prices relate a complex story. In pure monetary terms, consumers of cocaine pay prices that are roughly equal to the prices of other intoxicants. But measured market prices do not take into account all of the costs cocaine users can face when they purchase cocaine. Nonmonetary costs, such as the risks of legal sanctions and the physical threats that users can confront by participating in drug markets, are crucial elements of cocaine markets. Combined, market prices and nonmonetary costs help explain the apparently illogical result that cocaine initiation rates have been declining, even though prices have dropped considerably over the past decade.

Relative Cocaine Prices

Exact comparisons of the prices between euphoregenic substances are impossible because a standard unit of measure, "euphoria," does not exist. Cocaine, marijuana, and alcohol deliver different types of highs of varying duration. Thus, the ability to say that one dollar spent on cocaine delivers more or less euphoria than a dollar spent on marijuana or alcohol is limited.

Despite the limitations, a comparison is instructive. For purposes of this crude comparison, an amount called "sessional use" will be considered. This is the minimum amount of a drug that people consume in a given session, or use period, to intoxicate themselves. In the case of cocaine, a typical session might be one line of powder or one rock of crack containing 40 milligrams of pure cocaine. The cost of such an amount of cocaine and crack, adjusting for purity, can vary widely. Those who buy in large volumes, and those who have an established relationship with their dealer, can typically obtain cocaine at a lower price; those who buy small quantities, or from a stranger, can expect to pay a higher price. Marijuana, in contrast, is typically smoked in a cigarette known as a joint, in a pipe (by the "bowl"), or in a bong. An ounce of marijuana might yield forty to sixty cigarettes, with each cigarette providing sufficient tetrahydrocannabinol, or THC, to intoxicate the user for several hours. Again, the price will vary in proportion with the variety of marijuana and its THC content, the size of the purchase, and the relationship with the dealer. Finally, alcohol can be consumed in low-concentration forms (beer, wine, mixed drinks) or high-concentration forms (undiluted spirits), and other doses in between. Typically, 3 ounces of pure alcohol or the equivalent amount in beer, wine, and mixed drinks is enough to make a person drunk if consumed in a short period of time.

The cost of a typical intoxication session can vary substantially, even within the same drug. Alcohol, for example, can be obtained relatively economically if purchased at retail outlets. But an alcohol user who buys drinks in a bar or restaurant might pay the equivalent of two or three times the retail price per drink. Similar pricing phenomena exist in the illicit drug markets. A dealer who knows his clients well might offer them a price break because he perceives a low threat of law enforcement risk, but a dealer who sells from a street corner venue to one-time customers might command a high price to compensate himself for engaging in frequent, risky transactions. Figure 3.1 presents illustrative price ranges for cocaine, marijuana, and alcohol based on the notion of per-session intoxication.

The low end of the cocaine price range was derived from the assumption that a gram would yield twenty-five doses, or lines, of cocaine, and could be obtained for around $40. The latter figure appears to the be the lowest gram price available in large American cities over the past few years, and also reflects the type of discount that a gram-level buyer is likely to enjoy. The high end of the cocaine price spectrum was developed from anecdotal reports about retail prices and might be regarded as a "rip-off" price. The mid-range figure represents a common street price for a dose of crack adjusted for purity. A similar methodology was used to estimate the prices for marijuana and alcohol, taking into account the range of circumstances under which the substances can be bought. These ranges are illustrative, and should be read with the caveats about the difficulties of making comparisons across substances in mind.

Figure 3.1 omits some information that might alter the picture substantially. Cocaine and marijuana are illegal substances that are subject to legal sanctions that alcohol is not. For example, cocaine and marijuana users can be arrested and jailed for possession, depending on the jurisdiction where they are caught and the amount of the drug with which they are caught. Similarly, a number of municipalities will seize assets such as automobiles used in conjunction with drug purchases. Also, illicit drug users may have to spend more time and resources locating supplies than users of alcohol, thus raising the search costs associated with illicit drug use. Combined, factors such as these raise the *full use* cost of illicit drug consumption. That is, drug users face risks and nonmonetary transaction costs that are similar in nature to those that traffickers face.

FIGURE 3.1
Relative Cost of Cocaine, Marijuana, and Alcohol

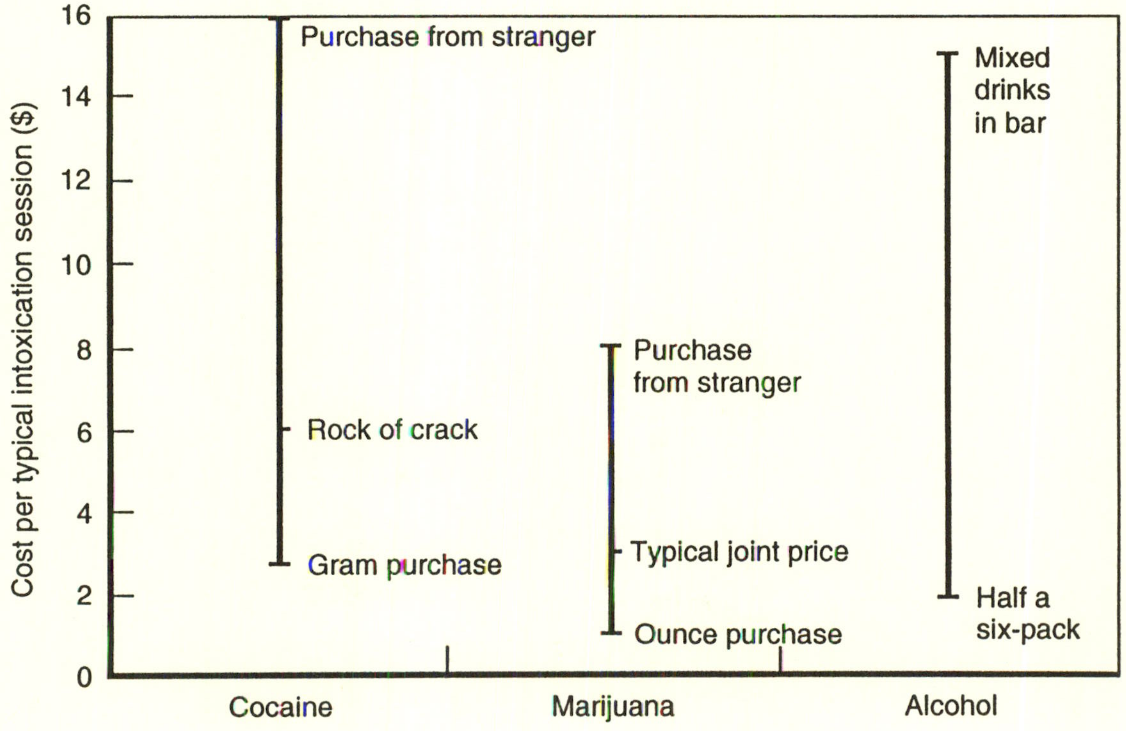

The nonmonetary components of full use costs are subject to manipulation by policy intervention just as direct prices are. Thus, drug control policy is premised on the notion that changes in the nonmonetary components of full use prices will affect consumption as well. To provide a counter example, recent research indicates that marijuana use increased in the 1970s in response to decriminalization measures, which drastically lowered the law enforcement sanctions imposed against marijuana users.[1] Whether the increase in marijuana use resulted from an absolute increase in the number of intoxicant users, or whether it resulted from an increase in substitution of marijuana for other substances among the existing user population is not clear. In either case, the change in marijuana's legal status altered perceptions of the full use price of marijuana.

Thus, despite the reputation of being a relatively high-priced product, cocaine prices are not out of line with those of other intoxicants. Reports that cocaine sells for $150,000 a kilogram, and that leading traffickers and cartel leaders earn millions of dollars a year, might make cocaine seem expensive, but cocaine is not consumed in kilogram units and traffickers earn their vast sums at least in part because of the volume of business they do. Individuals can attain intoxication with as little as 25 milligrams of cocaine in their bloodstream, and such small quantities of cocaine can be bought at comparatively inexpensive prices. Even if legal sanctions and other nonmonetary price considerations effectively double or triple cocaine prices, the cost is still not dramatically greater than that of other intoxicants.

The comparison raises an important point, however. To the extent that much of drug policy is concerned with increasing drug prices as a mechanism for decreasing drug use, prices alone are at best a crude mechanism measuring progress. As subsequent sections will reveal, there have been changes in cocaine use patterns that cannot be explained by simple changes in monetary prices. Moreover, as the next section will reveal, price changes do not necessarily directly control drug-using behavior.

Consumption and Price Changes

One of the objectives of drug policy is to make use of illicit substances more expensive. What is not clear from the price comparison, and where the data are sorely lacking, is how cocaine users would respond to a large increase in cocaine prices. Assuming for the moment that policy intervention succeeds in raising *only* cocaine prices, as cocaine becomes more expensive other substances such as marijuana and alcohol become *relatively* less expensive. The comparatively small range in which intoxicant prices are concentrated suggests that as cocaine prices increase, other intoxicants should become increasingly popular. Recall that when the full use cost of marijuana declined, an increase in marijuana use was recorded. Similarly, an increase in marijuana use was recorded when the full use costs of alcohol increased for the young adult population.[2] Alcohol became more expensive for teenagers, in terms of search costs, potential penalties, and so forth, when the drinking age was raised to twenty-one nationwide. The logic thus extends to cocaine: Why pay exorbitant prices for a cocaine high if more reasonably priced alternatives exist?

There are at least two reasons why cocaine users may prefer to pay a high price over switching to another, drug made relatively less expensive by policy intervention. The first reason is that cocaine users may have an innate preference for the high that cocaine delivers. If such a preference existed, it would not be sufficient simply to be intoxicated; the intoxication of cocaine would be preferred. A variety of factors can drive the formation of such a preference. For example, some substance users may avoid alcohol because it can cause hangovers, while others may avoid marijuana because they cannot tolerate the act of smoking. Still others may prefer the stimulation of cocaine to the effects of marijuana and alcohol. In such cases, alcohol and marijuana, and other substances for that matter, would not be adequate substitutes for cocaine because they would not satisfy the user in one manner or another. Very little research has been done on the preference for cocaine, let alone how preferences vary with price. What is known is that many cocaine users consume other substances as well. Cocaine users frequently use alcohol and heroin to soften cocaine's effects or to augment some aspects of the cocaine high. Poly drug use, as such a habit is known, tremendously complicates the issue of discerning sensitivity to price changes. For example, when cocaine prices increase, will consumption of heroin and alcohol among cocaine users increase or decrease? The answer will depend on the proportion of the population that views heroin and alcohol as substitutes for cocaine, and the proportion that prefers to consume them together as complements.

The second reason cocaine users may prefer to remain with cocaine despite an increase is prices is that a cocaine user may become addicted to cocaine, and thus may be virtually unable to refrain from using cocaine even if it becomes very expensive.[3] In economic terms, addiction is the combination of reinforcement and tolerance, both of which may leave the user unable to cease use and thus willing to pay higher prices. Reinforcement arises when positive experiences from past cocaine consumption lead to the belief that even greater positive results can be attained by increasing current consumption. In contrast, tolerance refers to the diminishing rewards from consumption of a given dose, and the resultant need to increase dose in order to maintain a given reward level.[4] Either of these factors, or both in combination, may lead to a dependence that will cause a user to maintain consumption in the face of price increases.

In either case, whether a person is unwilling or unable to give up cocaine, the person is said to exhibit *low price elasticity of demand*. Another way of stating the same point is to say that cocaine users may be *insensitive to price changes*. These phrases are from economics, and they mean that the quantity of cocaine a person consumes does not vary in proportion with changes in price. Large changes in price do suppress demand for cocaine, but by relatively small amounts. People who prefer cocaine's high are insensitive to price increases because they enjoy cocaine intoxication. To them, an increase in price is simply an unfortunate aspect of using cocaine. Addicts are relatively insensitive to price increases because they cannot abandon use. Some research indicates that addicts' price sensitivity is low at first because key factors associated with the addiction, including environment, personality characteristics, and socioeconomic considerations, are relatively fixed in any given short period of time.[5] But over time, these factors are variable and, thus, individuals can become more responsive to price increases as they are able to change previously fixed aspects of their lives. In either case, users can adjust to higher cocaine prices they adjust by spending less on other goods such as food and clothing, or by increasing income through tactics such as selling assets and theft.

It is not clear exactly how insensitive to price changes cocaine users are. Other intoxicants, such as alcohol, and other addictive substances, such as tobacco, tend to have low price elasticities of demand, although there is not universal agreement on this point.[6] As a consequence of both the disagreement about price responsiveness of other substances, and because cocaine markets and consumption are largely clandestine and, thus, not amenable to easy observation, the price elasticity of cocaine is not known with any certainty. A reasonable guess would be that cocaine's price elasticity is similar to that of other substances such as alcohol and tobacco. Numerous studies have produced a wide range of estimates for alcohol and tobacco, but the consensus seems to be that both are moderately responsive to changes in price. In practical terms, this assumption means something like a 10 percent increase in the price of cocaine might lead to around a 5 percent decline in the quantity consumed.

Novice and Experienced Users

In reality, prices' impact on cocaine consumption is much more complicated than elasticity. Perhaps the most important complication is that by itself, elasticity fails to distinguish between categories, or types, of users. In particular, a single measure of elasticity does not incorporate the differences likely to be found between inexperienced and heavy users. People who are relatively inexperienced with cocaine, or who are trying it for the first time, are likely to be more sensitive to price changes than people who are heavy users. Those with little cocaine experience are unlikely to develop an affinity for cocaine's high, and are less likely to become dependent on cocaine after only a few uses. Thus, when cocaine prices rise, inexperienced cocaine users are likely to seek out other forms of pharmacological stimulation or abandon the use of intoxicants. In contrast, heavy users have developed a preference for, or a dependence, on cocaine, and thus will be more resistant to price changes.

The practical consequences of this distinction can only be seen over time. If high prices deter nonusers from ever trying cocaine and novices from increasing use, then over time the size of the cocaine using population will get smaller.[7] This is one reason the price increase must be sustained; fleeting price rises may not alter the initiation stream. There is reason to believe that price increases and price declines do not have symmetric effects. In other words, downward movement in cocaine prices might induce or recruit new users, while upward movement would fail to reduce their use. Such a phenomenon, known as hysteresis or the ratchet effect, indicates that cocaine use may be elastic (sensitive) to price declines, but inelastic (insensitive) to price increases.[8] As discussed in chapter 1, the United States has experienced a decline in casual and

experimental cocaine use and a corresponding increase in heavy cocaine use, even while prices were falling. There are now fewer initiates
into cocaine use, and, as a result, the rate of growth in lifetime prevalence has slowed considerably. However, as will be discussed in subsequent sections, cocaine prices have been declining, so that the broader
measure of cocaine prices, or the full use price, must be invoked to
explain this pattern.[9]

The significance of price elasticity for source country cocaine control policies will not be clear until the next several sections have been
read. For now, however, it is sufficient to remember that source country
cocaine control policies, as well as most other drug control policies, are
intended to have their effects mostly by raising the cost of drug use to
users. If the assumptions about cocaine's price sensitivity hold true, drug
control policies will have to force substantial increases in cocaine prices
before cocaine use among heavy users is appreciably affected. Among
other factors that will be explored later, this implies that large-scale policy
interventions will be required to reduce cocaine use.

Trends in Cocaine Prices

Broadly, cocaine prices reflect scarcity. The more expensive cocaine
is, the less of it there is to be had, all other factors held constant. That all
other factors are not held constant clouds the analysis and complicates
the link between trends in cocaine prices and evaluating the effectiveness of counternarcotics policies. Ideally, prices would be available for
all phases of production. Then, movements in leaf, paste, base, cocaine,
export cocaine, and retail cocaine prices could be monitored separately
so that the effects of policy on a particular phase of production could be
distinguished more easily. Except for leaf production, reliable price data
are generally not available for the source country production stages.

Several sources for domestic wholesale and retail prices exist, but
the most widely known and widely used source is the System to Retrieve Information from Drug Evidence, or STRIDE.[10] The Drug Enforcement Administration (DEA) collects and disseminates STRIDE
data. Most of the information found in the STRIDE dataset are obtained
from federal investigations conducted by DEA, the FBI, and the Customs Department.[11] The balance of the STRIDE price information, about
25 percent, originates from state and local law enforcement organiza-

tions. STRIDE data are acquired from seizures, undercover purchases, gifts, free samples, and a variety of other mechanisms. Undercover purchases represent about 36 percent of all STRIDE cocaine data, seizures about 57 percent, gifts about 4 percent, and all other categories less than 2 percent.

STRIDE data are primarily collected on what might be called wholesale, rather than retail transactions. In 1991, a small number of STRIDE transactions, approximately 14 percent, involved small buys of a gram or so. Kilogram transactions accounted for about 22 percent of the buys. The balance of the buys, about three-quarters, were at the ounce level (approximately 28 grams). All three transaction amounts (grams, ounces, and kilograms) involve quantities that are larger than the typical street retail transaction. In the case of kilograms and ounces, the individuals involved would likely be high-level or mid-level traffickers.

The quantities involved in the transaction are important because they tend to be a central determinant of price.[12] Generally, the closer the transaction takes place to street retail markets, the smaller the quantity of the transaction and the higher the per unit price. For example, in 1991 kilograms of cocaine were selling for approximately $31,000 in Washington, D.C., and grams for around $216. One thousand transactions of one gram, the equivalent of a kilogram, would be worth $216,000 at prevailing 1991 prices, or nearly seven times the kilogram rate. Figure 3.2 shows STRIDE data collected over the past decade. The data are from gram transactions but scaled to kilogram price levels. That is, these are not the same as the STRIDE kilogram prices that were recorded during the same period.

It is clear from figure 3.2 that cocaine prices have declined substantially over the last decade. In the early part of the 1980s, prices equivalent to $300,000 per kilogram were not uncommon, and prices equivalent to $250,000 per kilogram were the norm. By the end of the 1980s, however, prices were down to less than the equivalent of $150,000 per kilogram, a fall of more than 40 percent from the price of just a decade earlier. There are several reasons why cocaine prices have fallen so precipitously over the last decade. Part of the explanation can be found in expanded production and improved smuggling techniques. Cultivation of coca leaf, the primary input into the production of cocaine, has expanded virtually without interruption since the early 1980s. In conjunction with expanded coca—and, thus, cocaine—output, traffickers have

FIGURE 3.2
Purity-Adjusted Cocaine Prices, 1981–1992

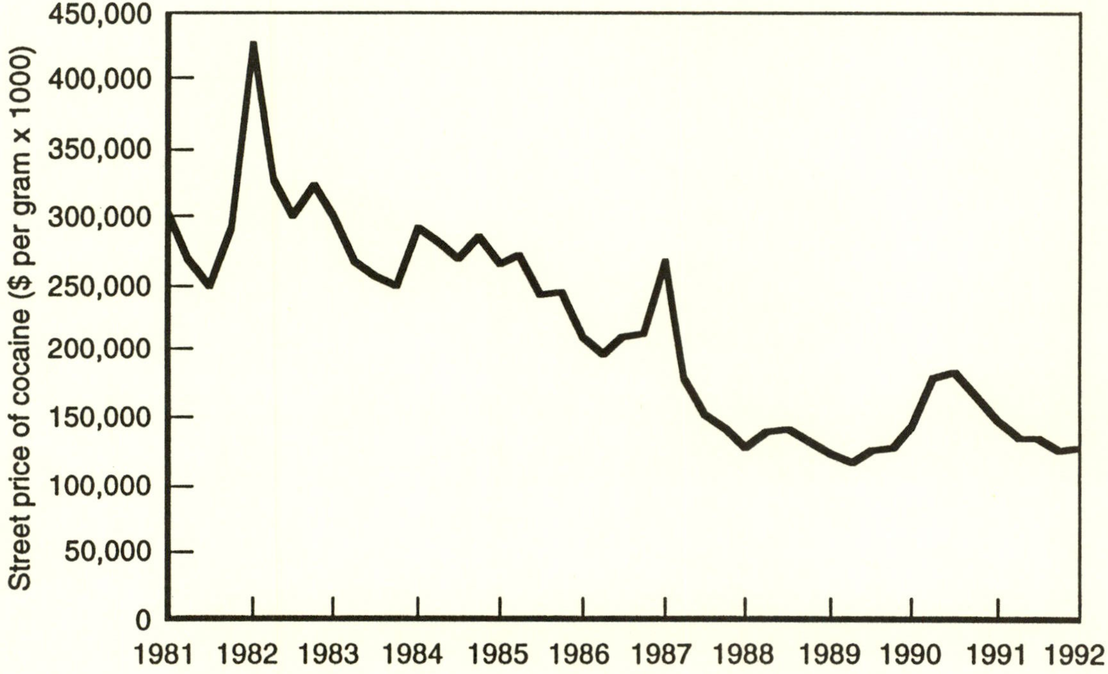

developed sophisticated mechanisms for getting the drugs over the border.[13] Part of the explanation can also be found in increased demand: not only do more people use cocaine now than a decade ago, but individual consumption rates are higher.

What may not be clear from figure 3.2 is that this decline in street retail prices occurred despite *a pronounced increase in law enforcement and other counterdrug efforts against cocaine.* If law enforcement efforts have been stepped up, why have prices declined so much? And if prices have been declining, then why have prevalence and initiation rates also fallen? Economic theory would seem to dictate that a decrease in prices would lead to increased rates of use, which appears to have occurred, and increased rates of initiation, which appears not to have occurred in recent years. Several explanations for this seeming paradox exist. The first is that nonprice factors such as attitudes, peer pressure, and other social conventions may have shifted sufficiently to discourage casual use, but not sufficiently to dissuade heavy use. A second possibility is that risks from increased law enforcement have added to the price of cocaine. As enforcement activities add to the cost of being a participant in cocaine markets, those that are sensitive to price changes will choose to abandon their participation.

There is some evidence that such changes in attitudes and nonmonetary costs have led to increases in the full use cost of cocaine. Recall from chapter 1 that peer attitudes about cocaine use have hardened in recent years. Increasingly large proportions of high-school-age students are inclined to view cocaine use negatively, and this social opprobrium is thought to have led to some reductions in initiation rates among high-school-age students.[14]

Similarly, strenuous law enforcement efforts against cocaine have probably increased the costs of obtaining cocaine, particularly for those who are inexperienced at cocaine use.[15] Experienced cocaine users, for example, have better access to drug supplies and thus can obtain cocaine through transactions that are more easily hidden from law enforcement officials. In contrast, novice and inexperienced users may conduct a higher proportion of their drug transactions with strangers in open-air—or public—drug markets where the risk of observation and arrest are substantially higher. Evidence from criminal justice sources indicates arrests for cocaine buying increased more than tenfold between 1979 and 1988, and sanctions measured in terms of cell years (for both buying and selling offenses) increased more than fifteenfold in the same period. During that same period, cocaine went from being responsible for about 7 percent of cocaine and marijuana arrests and 25 percent of cocaine and marijuana cell years to 48 percent and 72 percent of those categories respectively.[16] In other words, the law enforcement effort against cocaine buying appears to have increased significantly during a period when the cash price for cocaine was declining.

Structure of the Cocaine Economy

The obvious downward trend in cocaine prices conceals two fundamental elements of the cocaine market's structure that are critical to the success and failure of drug control policies in general and source country control policies in particular. First, because of the way the drug trade is organized, and because of the mechanisms through which prices at each stage of production are formed, it is very difficult to use source country policy intervention as a way of increasing retail cocaine prices substantially. Without a substantial increase in cocaine prices it may be difficult to effect even a modest reduction in use. Second, even in instances where policy intervention succeeds in causing an increase in prices, the structure of the drug trade ensures that the impact is fleeting. If higher prices are only a temporary phenomenon, an individual's cocaine consumption may be disrupted for as long as the price increase holds, but will likely return to normal once the price increase fades. In order to understand these principles—and they are crucial to understanding the rest of the book—it is necessary to understand the organization and operation of the cocaine trade.

Making Cocaine

Making cocaine is a relatively simple process, particularly in comparison to other drugs, such as heroin. Cocaine production requires four basic steps: the cultivation of coca plants, followed by successive refinements of the harvested leaves into paste, base, and finally, cocaine. The coca plant, shown in figure 3.3, is a woody, treelike shrub indigenous to much of Andean Latin America. Coca plants tolerate a wide variety of climate conditions, and require relatively little care and cultivation in comparison to other commercial agricultural crops.[17]

The fact that little in the way of agricultural knowledge is required to successfully farm coca plants has made it extremely popular throughout the regions where it thrives. The cocaine alkaloids from which cocaine is produced are found in the leaves, and so the cocaine production process begins with stripping the leaves from the shrub. A typical farmer would sell his coca leaves at a market or directly to a paste refiner in 100-pound bundles. For his efforts, the farmer might be paid around $200.

Once the leaves have been gathered, the cocaine alkaloids are extracted by soaking the leaves in a chemical solution. This stage is commonly referred to as paste production because the cocaine residue left after chemical processing is a gray-white paste. In some varieties of coca leaf, the alkaloids are more easily obtained than in others, so the amount of time and processing required to make paste will vary.[18] Depending on the type and variety of coca leaf used, the 100 pounds of leaf would yield perhaps a pound of coca paste. That is, the weight reduction between the leaf and paste stages of production is approximately a factor of 100. A variety of chemicals, including sulfuric acid, kerosene, lime, and bicarbonate of soda, are used to extract the alkaloids. In addition, the paste-making process requires large amounts of water and maceration pits made of cement or plastic. A typical paste processor will produce several kilograms of coca paste in very short order and then sell it to a base refiner. Each kilogram the paste processor sells to a base refiner fetches a price of around $350.

In the next stage of production, the chemical impurities introduced into coca paste are removed, and the cocaine alkaloids are increasingly concentrated to make a product known as cocaine base, or *pasta basica de coca*.[19] Base laboratories are more elaborate than paste-processing facilities, and thus tend to be located in remote regions, far from the scrutiny that surrounds coca-growing regions.[20] The location of base labs far from coca farms in turn helps explain why bulky coca leaves are first made into smaller, more easily transported bundles of paste before they are transported to base labs. After refining, a kilogram of paste yields 400 to 500 grams of coca base. Base can be produced using any number of recipes or chemical treatment processes, including formulas using combinations of sulfuric acid, potassium permanganate, ammonia, acetic acid, ammonium hydroxide, and acetone.[21] Refined cocaine base commands a price of roughly $1600.

Figure 3.3—Coca Plants

The majority of base is shipped to Colombia for the final step, processing into cocaine. Generalities about cocaine refining are difficult to make. Since base is one of the most expensive inputs into cocaine, many traffickers integrate vertically prior to this stage, and produce both base and cocaine. Production may take place in relatively small facilities or large, sophisticated laboratories. In the conversion from base to cocaine, very little weight reduction takes place. Instead, the most important change that occurs is structural: base is converted from a heat labile, cracklike substance into a water-soluble powder that can be absorbed through nasal inhalation. At this point, the cocaine processing is complete. Once base has been made into cocaine, the cocaine is ready for export to a transhipper at a price of around $4000 per kilogram.

Most refined cocaine, called export cocaine, is shipped north to the United States, although small amounts are shipped to other markets, such as Europe. In the process of being shipped, the drug may change hands several times. A typical arrangement would find a cocaine processor or cartel consigning the cocaine to a shipper. The shipper will smuggle the cargo out of Colombia to a stopover point in Central America or the Carribbean. From there, the cargo may be given to another shipper that specializes in smuggling cocaine into the United States using techniques ranging from paying individuals to carry the cocaine over the border and transporting it through tunnels under the border between Mexico and the United States, to concealing the cocaine into commercial shipments of vegetables, coffee, seafood, and construction materials. The risks involved in getting the cocaine to the border, combined with the distances traveled and the cargo and equipment lost to law enforcement organizations, cause a sharp increase in prices at this stage. By the time a kilogram of cocaine reaches the U.S. border, it may have a price tag of $40,000.

Once the cocaine has been taken over the border, it is sold to domestic distributors. Typically, in the first stage of domestic distribution wholesale distributors dispense the cocaine to regional distributors. Regional distributors may consist of another layer or more of wholesale distributors. The number of wholesale layers before retail distribution will depend on a variety of factors, including the size of the market, the distance from the point of importation, and the form—crack or powder—in which the cocaine will be sold. Typically, cocaine is diluted (or "stepped on") just prior to retail distribution, or as it is processed into crack. At the retail level, the market may exist in a variety of different forms. Perhaps the two most well-known market types are "export" markets, in which a network native to the neighborhood sells to customers who live outside the neighborhood, and the "public market," in which both the retailers and the customers live outside the area.[22] Such markets require a variety of factors to exist, but tend to thrive in areas that are sufficiently run down so that few residents have the energy or interest in repelling the trade, that offer legitimate cover for street activity, that present a steady supply of juvenile labor, which is more likely to receive lenient court treatment, and that provide a steady flow of customer traffic in conjunction with easy escape routes.[23] Retail prices can vary substantially in such markets.

The Producers' Price Chain

The alert reader will have noticed a startling pattern. It takes approximately 350 kilograms of coca leaf, worth about $700, to make one kilogram of cocaine that, diluted in preparation for retail marketing in small bundles, may command upwards of $150,000. Table 3.1, which summarizes the increase in prices and the decrease in weight as cocaine is successively refined and nears retail markets, raises two important questions. First, what accounts for the massive price increases between stages of production? Second, what significance does this structure have for source country control policies?

The price consumers pay for cocaine is simply the sum of the costs at each stage of production, less the value of the intermediate goods used at each stage to avoid double counting. At each stage, the nature of production costs is similar. Producers incur costs for processing materials and services (such as transportation and security), capital investment in production facilities, and wages and salaries. Additionally, producers at every stage buy intermediate products, or goods that go into producing the final good—retail cocaine. Thus, base producers use paste as an intermediate good, paste producers use leaf as an intermediate good, and so forth. A review of these costs for each stage of production reveals some powerful insights.

Materials and services in cocaine production essentially consist of the chemicals needed to process the intermediate good, and the transportation and security arrangements needed to move the shipment to the next stage of production. The chemicals used to extract cocaine from the coca leaves and make paste, base, and cocaine are readily available. Many of the chemicals used to make cocaine and cocaine-related products are in widespread use in other legal industrial and commercial sectors. Some materials, such as the water used for rinsing and dilution, may be essentially free, while others, such as acids and kerosene, are easily obtained from industrial markets. In the latter stages of refining, particularly base to cocaine conversion, the chemicals are more expensive and often must be imported from other countries. Still, processing chemicals, even during the late stages of production, account for only a few pennies of each dollar of production costs.[24] In the early stages of production, transportation and security are probably not important cost factors because the products are not shipped very far (paste processing,

TABLE 3.1
Prices in the Cocaine Production Chain

	Quantity needed to make 1 kg pure cocaine (kg)[a]	Value of amount needed to make 1 kg pure cocaine[a]
Leaf	350	700
Paste	3	1050
Base	1.1	1760
Export cocaine	1	4000
Street cocaine	1	150,000

Note: [a]Composite across coca types and refining techniques [see Kennedy, Reuter, and Riley (1993)].

for example is frequently done near coca markets) and are less valuable compared to the latter stages of production. Even when products have to be shipped greater distances and become more valuable, transportation and security add costs that are probably comparable to those of physical materials.[25]

It turns out that the capital equipment used in the production process cannot explain the tremendous markups between stages of production. For example, the laboratories used to refine cocaine do not add significantly to the costs of production. All that is required for paste production is an open pit, lined with plastic or concrete, a few sticks for stirring, and some cups and measuring implements.[26] Figure 3.4 shows a typical paste pit, and also illustrates the simplicity that allows a pit destroyed by authorities to be replaced in a matter of a few hours. Even the elaborate facilities used to refine base and cocaine do not represent prohibitive amounts of capital investment. Base and cocaine laboratories can be sophisticated facilities, and can include communications centers, filtering and drying equipment, generators, chemical recycling capabilities, dormitories and cafeterias for workers, and storage areas in addition to the processing laboratory itself. Authorities have reported that traffickers build redundant laboratories so that if one is destroyed or rendered inoperable during a raid it can immediately be replaced by another.

The last major cost component to the production of cocaine is the labor needed to produce it, and here the story gets more complicated and more interesting. In order to attract and maintain employees, traf-

Figure 3.4—Paste Processing Pit

fickers must offer a wage that provides at least as much income as the best alternative employment options. But cocaine industry workers face legal sanctions and other threats that employees in legal occupations do not face. These risks translate, on average, into shorter careers for drug sector employees. This would also mean that, over an earnings lifetime, the average trafficker might earn substantially less than the average legal economy worker. If that were the case, there would be little incentive to engage in cocaine trafficking, and labor would be difficult to attract to cocaine production. Instead, cocaine traffickers' wages are supplemented with a *risk premium* that rewards them for engaging in risky occupations and works to equalize average lifetime wages in the legal and cocaine sectors of the economy. Risk compensation, in a sense, is like labor costs, but it represents an additional financial increment that must be offered to the market's participants to secure their participation.

It is easy to see why the risk premiums increase with proximity to retail markets. Coca farmers, for example, do not make large sums of money. Research shows that coca farmers make anywhere from $700 to $1200 per year on average, and that in fact, coca farming may not pay all that much more than other types of agricultural activity.[27] While this finding would seem to fly in the face of reports that cocaine market participants are rewarded with fabulous salaries, it also makes sense. In Bolivia and Peru, coca farming and coca marketing are, in some cases, not illegal. Even in the cases where coca farming and marketing are illegal, the laws against coca farmers are selectively and haphazardly enforced, in part because law enforcement authorities are interested in capturing those who operate higher up in the production chain. Thus, the effective risk of coca farming is very low.

In contrast, the risks associated with participating in cocaine production increase at virtually every stage of production. Paste, base, and export cocaine are much more valuable than coca leaf and much more likely to be targeted for legal sanctions by authorities. Traffickers do not know with any precision what risks they are undertaking on any given trafficking mission. In some cases, drug kingpins face some risk of extradition to the United States, where the threat of conviction is higher. Traffickers also face the prospect that competitors will try to kill them. A trafficker who is arrested loses potential income as does, of course, a trafficker who is killed.

At the retail level in the United States the risks to participants are substantial. In some jurisdictions, convictions for dealing can result in a mandatory life prison sentence for the first offense. The severity of the risks dealers face in the United States is reflected in studies which have found that many dealers sell drugs only part-time, supplement their drug earnings with substantial amounts of legitimate income, and have fairly short drug dealing careers before legal sanctions, death, and addiction claim them.[28] While these dealers were not getting rich, their average hourly earnings from drug dealing appear to vastly exceed their legal hourly wage prospects. Since risks rise with the time spent selling, some dealers chose to confine their selling in an effort to limit risk exposure. More generally, the probability and certainty of arrest and conviction for drug offenses may be much higher in the United States than in Colombia, Bolivia, and Peru where the criminal justice systems are more easily intimidated and corrupted.

Significance of Price Structure

The price structure that prevails in cocaine trafficking has an important implication for counterdrug policies in general, and source country policies in particular. The source country cost components of the price chain, such as leaf, paste, and base, are but a small fraction of retail prices. Even huge price increases in these components, such as a ten-fold rise in leaf prices, will barely effect retail prices. Thus, while the limited available data suggest that source country policies are very effective at raising the costs at various stages of production, particularly in local markets, there is much less evidence to indicate that these source country programs affect U.S. demand through retail prices. Operation Blast Furnace, for example, is credited with temporarily depressing leaf prices in 1986 by destroying the region's paste processing capacity, and thus the market for coca leaves. Lasting about four months, the effort succeeded in destroying dozens of laboratories and airstrips, and resulted in the confiscation of copious amounts of processing chemicals, laboratory equipment, and airplanes. The coca farmers of the Chapare, who previously had sold their leaves to the traffickers whose labs were destroyed in the raids, saw the market for their leaves evaporate. Reportedly, coca prices plummeted from $125 per hundredweight (or carga) to less than $20.[29] No data are available for paste and base prices during Operation Blast Furnace, but the resulting shortages of coca leaf and refining capacity must also have created a shortage of paste and base and sent these prices correspondingly higher.

Operation Blast Furnace came as a relative surprise as it was implemented on a much wider—and more aggressive—scale than previous law enforcement based programs in Bolivia.[30] The purpose of relating the incident is to point out that source country control programs can substantially affect local drug markets and drug prices. Although the data are, in many cases, lacking, it seems clear that Operation Blast Furnace and other programs like it can substantially influence the prices at the various stages of cocaine production. The problem is, however, that the source country stages of production are so far removed from retail markets and represent such a small portion of retail prices that even massive movements in source country prices barely effect retail tariffs. Using source country price increases to create domestic scarcities is similar to attempting to raise glass prices by pushing sand back into the sea.

To more concretely illustrate the difficulty of using source country programs to increase retail cocaine prices, consider an example from coca cultivation. Authorities have collected data on Bolivia coca leaf prices since 1987. The DEA has published STRIDE data on cocaine prices since the 1970s. Figure 3.5 combines these data sources and compares changes in leaf prices with changes in retail cocaine prices for 1987 through 1992. During the 1987–92 period, Bolivian coca farms were subject to small voluntary eradication efforts. As a result, leaf prices have fluctuated widely, although as much as from factors such as oversupply and climactic considerations as from eradication. Regardless of the source of the variance, the point is that the fluctuations have been substantial. Yet despite these swings in leaf prices, the correlation between leaf and retail cocaine prices is very weak. In fact, throughout much of the period in question cocaine prices were increasing as coca leaf prices were declining, or vice versa.

Take the 1988–89 period as an example. During this period leaf prices increased sharply, marking one of the strongest upturns in leaf prices on record. However, cocaine prices generally held steady, albeit with substantial fluctuations. Even if the higher leaf prices got passed along to retail consumers, as they very easily could be, they just as easily could have been mitigated by changes at other stages of production. There is sufficient slack in the production process such that a 5 percent loss can be replaced through techniques such as more thorough leaf harvests, longer processing of coca leaves to obtain more cocaine alkaloids, and other processing compensation measures. While the lack of strong correlation between leaf prices and retail cocaine prices is not conclusive proof that cocaine's retail price structure is impervious to input price changes, it is interesting that the price of cocaine's essential input—coca leaf—does not track more closely with cocaine's price.

Dynamics, Scale of Intervention, and Lagged Response

The preceding section noted that cocaine producers can easily absorb small variations in input availability and prices by adjusting pro-

FIGURE 3.5
Coca Prices in Bolivia and Peru

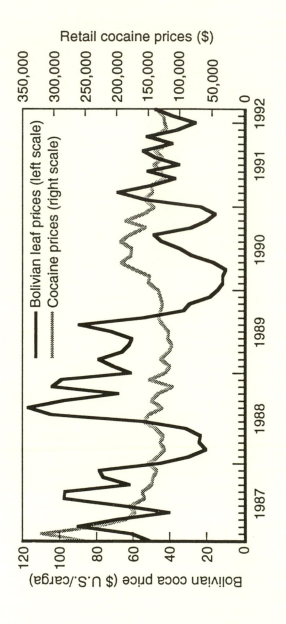

duction techniques. These cases described above involve what might be termed marginal, or small-scale, policy interventions. That is, the results described are premised on relatively small policy efforts, on the order of, say, 5 percent eradication or interdiction. While policy interventions of this magnitude can be devastating for individual traffickers and farmers, and perhaps entire communities or regions (as with Operation Blast Furnace), they are easily absorbed by the cocaine producers as a whole. In part, small policy interventions were considered to illustrate the real limits, both operational and political, to the scales of policies that can be implemented. It would be extremely difficult to identify and intercept a very large fraction, say half, of cocaine shipments before they left the source countries. A policy of such scale would require massive disruption of commerce, a huge intelligence and reconnaissance effort, and unprecedented cooperation. Current source country efforts are limited to a much smaller scale.

Still, massive policy interventions are possible if numerous potential complications (which will be enumerated in subsequent chapters) are ignored. Disregarding political and environmental considerations, for example, it is probably possible to use herbicides to eradicate 50 percent or more of the coca crop. A similar success rate can probably be achieved with the chemicals used in the latter stages of cocaine refining, again ignoring numerous potential complications. Intuition probably suggests that seizing 50 percent of a component important to production is somehow different from seizing 5 or 10 percent. That intuition would be correct because that level of seizures and eradication would generate real shortages, more than could possibly be made up for by cutting corners in the production process, by applying more of the other factors of production to compensate for the loss, or by making other adjustments. In the face of a massive shortage, the only short-run adjustment that could equilibrate the market would be a massive increase in prices.

Imagine for the moment that authorities managed to seize half of the cocaine produced before it left South America for an unspecified, but prolonged, period and that the loss of the shipments came as a surprise. The wholesalers and retailers further down the line would be unable to satisfy the market. Genuine shortages of cocaine would result, and the only way of allocating it to customers would be through large retail price increases. To date, no intervention of this magnitude has occurred, but evidence from smaller interdiction programs and from past research suggests that cocaine prices would rise dramatically.[31] Recall from figure 3.2 that as recently as ten years ago, cocaine prices were substantially higher than current prices. Similarly, Colombian law enforcement authorities initiated a strong crackdown on drug trafficking in 1989 that, in conjunction with other factors, led to perhaps a 25 percent interdiction rate (chapter 5 will address this case in detail). Consequently, retail cocaine prices climbed more than 40 percent. In any event, it seems probable that in the event of a severe shortage of cocaine the market may react more wildly than would be suggested by abstract economic theory about supply and demand and price elasticities.

Unfortunately, the same large price precipitated by a massive eradication or interdiction program also serves to ultimately undo the policy's effects. High retail prices (which also imply high intermediate product prices) signal that there are profits to be made in drug production and drug trafficking. Those traffickers that can successfully get a shipment to the United States might now make three, five, or even ten times as much as they might have made previously. Thus, the higher prices that result from interdiction and eradication also serve to encourage traffickers to expand production.

The notion that a given policy, such as eradication, will provoke a response from the drug traffickers has been clear for some time.[32] This concept of dynamic response also helps explain why a kilogram of cocaine seized in Colombia does not necessarily mean a kilogram less cocaine on the streets of the United States. As noted previously, the producers are able to adapt their production techniques to low levels of interdiction and eradication. What has not been clear until quite recently is how long it would take the drug producers to respond to a policy that severely crippled their production ability. Most critics of international drug control programs implicitly assumed that the response would more or less occur instantaneously, and thus came to the conclusion that international control programs were virtually incapable of curbing drug production. Recent work in this area indicates that while the drug producers cannot respond to all policy measures equally rapidly, they are nevertheless very adept at circumventing source country policies' effects.

How long it takes traffickers to expand production in response to the price signals depends on a number of factors. For example, if the traffickers carry inventory as a hedge against surprise interdiction, then they may be able to get the cocaine to retail markets in very short order and force market prices back down. In contrast, if traffickers hold inventory in the form of coca farms, then there may be a delay of several weeks or months as the leaves are harvested, processed into cocaine, and shipped to the United States. Even longer delays would result if the drug lords did not hold any production in reserve and were forced to respond to the interdiction by expanding their physical capacity to produce. If, for example, they opted to increase production capacity through planting new coca fields, it would take several years for production to return to normal because of the delay in obtaining leaf harvests from freshly planted acreage.

The type of response the traffickers make to a large market disruption will depend, in part, on the form of the policy. A 50 percent interdiction policy, for example, while tremendously disruptive, would be difficult to sustain. Thus, it would likely only be continued for a discrete period of time, much like Operation Blast Furnace. In this case, there might not be any need to expand production capacity. Rather, the appropriate strategy might simply be to wait until the interdiction is discontinued, or to manage the shortages out of inventories if they exist. In contrast, if authorities undertake to eradicate half of the coca crop every year, the drug dealers will need to increase the amount of acreage they put under cultivation in order to ensure that enough coca leaf exists to satisfy the demand for cocaine.

The longer it takes the traffickers to respond to the market signals, the longer production will be disrupted. One of the key objectives of source country control programs should therefore be to implement policies that generate the longest possible lag between implementation and the traffickers' response and recovery. For reasons that will be elaborated upon later in this book, *one-time* forced eradication and *sustained* interdiction work best at delaying the traffickers' ability to increase output. But unlike a small-scale eradication program, which will be easily absorbed by the drug traffickers, a large-scale program that eliminated perhaps half of the coca crop would severely curtail output for as long as it took farmers to find new plots of land, put new coca plants into the ground, and harvest and market the leaves. Similarly, if authorities seized half of the cocaine output on a continuous basis, the traffickers would respond by doubling the amount of coca cultivated to double the amount of cocaine produced, thereby resulting in the original amount of cocaine reaching retail markets. But the doubling of production would be delayed by how long it took to get harvests from the new coca fields.

This insight about lags and delays is a powerful concept, and helps explain why certain policies may be effective at temporarily curbing production, while others will not. Destruction of paste processing pits and labs does relatively little to dent production because the facilities are so easily replaced. Paste processing pits are little more than holes in the ground, and cocaine processing laboratories, while more sophisticated, can be built in a matter of weeks or months. Intense interdiction programs that operate for finite periods of time suffer from a similar limitation. If they are not sustained long enough, they do not force the expansion of productive capacity and thus, their effects evaporate as soon as the interdiction halts.

By far the longest lag in the cocaine production chain is found with the coca leaf. According to available estimates, it takes about eighteen months from the date of planting to get full output from a coca field. Harvests may be possible in as few as six months after planting, but the immature leaves would provide only a fraction of the cocaine that a mature plant would yield. In addition, it takes farmers several months to locate new land and prepare land for farming. In the case of widespread eradication, for example, a large portion of the labor supply might have to relocate to a new planting area in order to evade the eradication threat. Combined, then, it takes the coca farmers approximately two years to recover completely from the shock of a policy.

War Taxes: The Impact of Policies on Cocaine Production

If you skipped the intervening sections of this chapter in order to get to the punchline, let me suggest that you missed the critical elements that underpin the rest of this book. But, since they are so important, let me also repeat them here:

- Price increases have complicated effects on cocaine consumption, but generally demand for cocaine will fall as full use prices rise;
- In general, the price structure of the cocaine industry makes source country control policies a weak way of forcing up retail prices. To seriously disrupt production and raise retail prices with source country policies, massive interventions will be required;

- The same rise in prices that tends to discourage cocaine use also signals that there are profits to be made by increasing production. Thus, source country control programs sow the seeds of their own eventual undoing;
- Nevertheless, if a large market disruption occurs, it may take the cocaine producers up to two years to recover from the impact of certain source country control policies. Hence, to the extent that large-scale policies are realistic options, the selection of policies becomes important.

With these basic concepts in mind, it is now possible to turn to the rest of this book. Proceeding from the premise that the two-year lag is generally the best source country control policies can hope to accomplish, the balance of the book is devoted to exploring the implications of this finding for source country cocaine control policies.[33] Part II of the book will examine in greater detail the conditions necessary to bring about this disruption, and the potential costs and consequences of doing so in a series of case studies. Chapter 4, "White Lies in Bolivia and Peru," is used to examine the effects and utility of eradication and crop substitution policies. Although Colombia produces a small amount of coca leaf, Bolivia and Peru are by far the world's largest producers. Hence, the focus will be on how eradication has fared in those two countries, and what the potential complications, as well as benefits, of expanding source country eradication programs are. In particular, the chapter will examine the political, economic, social, and environmental ramifications of eradication options. Examples from poppy and marijuana eradication in Turkey, Colombia, and Mexico will be considered as well.

Peru and Bolivia are also used as case studies about the utility of development assistance. They are employed as examples for a number of reasons, not the least of which is that several important development projects have been attempted there in recent years. Colombia, too, has benefitted from programs that might be termed *development assistance,* but generally the Colombian programs are not aimed at providing economic alternatives that will induce cocaine trafficking participants to abandon the trade. Such programs tend not to be implemented in Colombia because its role in the cocaine business is one of refining and shipping cocaine and the participants in these aspects of the trade are seen as less worthy of, and perhaps less amenable to, development assistance.

In contrast, chapter 5 ("Blood of a Nation") focuses almost exclusively on Colombia and the role of interdiction and law-enforcement-based source country control policies. Colombia, because of its role in refining and exporting cocaine, emerges as the primary center of interdiction, law enforcement, and asset destruction activity. Again, the chapter will devote considerable space to examining the political and other effects of interdiction and law enforcement source country policies, with particular attention paid to the policies' interaction with the extremely violent and volatile political environment in Colombia.

Chapter 6 ("The Border's the Limit") examines source country control policies' effects on smuggling in the Transit Zone. In particular, the chapter will illustrate the adaptive techniques that smugglers utilize in an effort to stay ahead of advances in interdiction techniques.

The discussion in part II about source country control policies and their attendant strengths and weaknesses paves the way for the concluding section, part III. Chapter 7 ("Losing the Battle, Winning the War") addresses the question, Are source country policies worth it? Evaluating source country control policies is a difficult task in light of the sparse data. Nevertheless, as the cocaine problem matures and evolves, and as our understanding of source country policies' strengths and limitations evolves, it becomes important to reexamine the role these policies play in national drug control. Chapter 7 accomplishes this, from the perspective of how the cocaine problem might evolve with significant changes to source country policies. This chapter will also attempt to discern whether there is something particular about cocaine markets that limit the efficacy of source country control policies, or whether the limits extent to other illicit drugs as well. Part III concludes with an examination of what elements of current source country policies should be retained, and what policies might logically be substituted in their place.

Notes

1. Model (1993).
2. DiNardo and Lemieux (1992).
3. The reaction of dependent users to price increases has been debated in the economic literature. Barthold and Hochman (1988), Chaloupka (1993), Warner (1991), Pollak (1976 and 1970), and Winston (1980).
4. Becker, Grossman, and Murphy (1991) and Becker and Murphy (1988).
5. Becker, Grossman, and Murphy (1991), Becker and Murphy (1988), and Chaloupka (1993).
6. See Manning, et al. (1991) and Schelling (1992).
7. Everingham and Rydell (1993).
8. Boyum (1992) reviews this possibility.

9. That this pattern has emerged in the context of *declining* cocaine prices is not necessarily contradictory. More stringent law-enforcement efforts against cocaine users may have sufficiently raised the nonmonetary cost of cocaine use sufficiently to deter casual and novice users.

10. Other price information sources include the Western States Information Network's *Illicit Drugs Price List*, and monthly price reports available from drug news groups on Internet.

11. Ebener, Feldman, and Fitzgerald (1993).

12. Caulkins (1993) covers this in more detail. The other important determinant is purity, or, according to Caulkins, expected purity.

13. Cave and Reuter (1988) offer a classic analysis of the ability of traffickers to adapt to law-enforcement intervention.

14. Bachman, Johnston, and O'Malley (1990).

15. Cave and Reuter (1988); Reuter, Crawford, and Cave (1988); Reuter (1991).

16. Ibid.

17. Antognini (1990); Plowman (1985).

18. Ibid., 18. The leaf cultivated in the Chapare is apparently not acceptable for traditional use because it does not readily release the alkaloids during chewing.

19. As mentioned in chapter 1, base cocaine is very similar to crack cocaine.

20. *Coca Cultivation and Cocaine Processing: An Overview* (1991).

21. The recipes for processing coca leaf into cocaine vary slightly, depending on the region where the processing is occurring and the type of leaf being processed. The above-mentioned general formulas were found in "Recipe Book: Cocaine Processing Techniques" (DEA: Lima Country Office), undated.

22. Reuter and MacCoun (1992).

23. Conner and Burns (1992).

24. Kennedy, Reuter, and Riley (1993).

25. Lee (1989); Kennedy, Reuter, and Riley (1993); Riley (1993); Morales (1989).

26. Morales (1989) and *Coca Cultivation and Cocaine Processing: An Overview* (1991) provide more details.

27. Kennedy, Reuter, and Riley (1993).

28. Reuter, MacCoun, and Murphy (1990); MacCoun and Reuter (1992).

29. Hargreaves (1992).

30. Hargreaves (1992) disputes the surprise element of the effort; see especially 152–57.

31. Riley (1993) and Caulkins (1990) cover the probable nature of the price increases in more detail.

32. The pioneers in this area of drug policy analysis are Cave and Reuter (1988); and Reuter, Crawford, and Cave (1988). See also Kennedy, Reuter, and Riley (1993).

33. Readers interested in a more detailed and technical exposition of the two-year lag should review Riley (1993).

References

Antognini, Joseph, "The Agronomics of Coca (Erythroxylum Species)," in *Cocaine Production, Eradication, and the Environment: Policy, Impact, and Options* (Washington, D.C.: Committee on Governmental Affairs, United States Senate, August 1990).

Jerald G. Bachman, Lloyd D. Johnston, and Patrick M. O'Malley, "Explaining the Recent Decline in Cocaine Use among Young Adults: Further Evidence that Perceived Risks and Disapproval Lead to Reduced Drug Use," *Journal of Health and Social Behavior* 31 (June 1990): 173—84.

Barthold, Thomas A., and Harold M. Hochman, "Addiction as Extreme-Seeking," *Economic Inquiry* 26 (1988): 89-106.

Becker, Gary S., Michael Grossman, and Kevin M. Murphy, "Rational Addiction and the Effect of Price on Consumption," *AEA Papers and Proceedings* 81, 2 (1991): 237-41.

Becker, Gary S., and Kevin M. Murphy, "A Theory of Rational Addiction," *Journal of Political Economy* 96, 4 (1988): 675-700.

Boyum, David Anders, *Reflections on Economic Theory and Drug Enforcement* (dissertation, Harvard University, 1992).

Caulkins, Jonathan P., *Developing a Price Series for Cocaine*, DRU-339-DPRC (Santa Monica, Calif.: RAND, 1993).

_____, *The Distribution and Consumption of Illicit Drugs: Some Mathematical Models and Their Policy Implications* (doctoral dissertation, Massachusetts Institute of Technology, 1990).

Cave, Jonathan, and Peter Reuter, *The Interdictor's Lot: A Dynamic Model of the Market for Drug Smuggling Services*, N-2632-USDP (Santa Monica, Calif.: RAND, 1988).

Chaloupka, Frank, "Rational Addictive Behavior and Cigarette Smoking," *Journal of Political Economy* 99, 4 (1993): 723-42.

Coca Cultivation and Cocaine Processing: An Overview (Washington, D.C.: Drug Enforcement Administration, 1991).

Conner, Roger L., and Patrick C. Burns, "The Winnable War," *The Brookings Review* (Summer 1992).

DiNardo, John, and Thomas Lemieux, *Alcohol, Marijuana and American Youth: The Unintended Effects of Government Regulation*, NBER Working Paper #4212 (November 1992).

Ebener, Patricia A., Eva Feldman, and Nora Fitzgerald, *Federal Databases for Use in Drug Policy Research: A Catalogue for Data Users*, N-3562-DPRC (Santa Monica, Calif.: RAND, 1993).

Everingham, Susan S., and C. Peter Rydell, "Modeling the Demand for Cocaine," DRR-390-ONDCP/A/DPRC (Santa Monica, Calif.: RAND, 1993).

Hargreaves, Clare, *Snowfields: The War on Cocaine in the Andes* (London: Holmes & Meier, 1992).

Kennedy, Michael, Peter Reuter, and Kevin Jack Riley, "A Simple Economic Model of Cocaine Production," *Mathematical and Computer Modelling* 17, 2 (1993): 19-36.

Lee, Rensselaer W., *White Labyrinth* (New Brunswick, N.J.: Transaction Publishers, 1989).

MacCoun, Robert, and Peter Reuter, "Are the Wages of Sin $30 an Hour: Economic Aspects of Street-Level Drug Dealing," *Crime and Delinquency* 38, 4 (October 1992): 477-91.

Manning, Willard G., Emmett B. Keeler, Joseph P. Newhouse, Elizabeth M. Sloss, and Jeffrey Wasserman, *The Costs of Poor Health Habits* (Cambridge, Mass.: Harvard University Press, 1991).

Model, Karyn, "The Effect of Marijuana Decriminalization on Hospital Emergency Room Drug Episodes: 1975-1978," *Journal of the American Statistical Association* 88, 423 (September 1993): 737-47.

Morales, Edmundo, *White Gold Rush in Peru* (Tucson, Ariz.: The University of Arizona Press, 1989).

Plowman, Timothy, "Coca Chewing and the Botanical Origins of Coca (*Erythroxylum spp.*) in South America," in *Cultural Survival Report #23: Coca and Cocaine,* Deborah Pacini and Christine Franquemont, eds. (Ithaca, N.Y.: Latin American Studies Program, 1985).

Pollak, Robert A., "Habit Formation and Long-Run Utility Functions," *Journal of Economic Theory* 13 (1976): 272–97.

_____, "Habit Formation and Dynamic Demand Functions," *Journal of Political Economy* 78, 4 (July/August 1970): 745–63.

Reuter, Peter, *On the Consequences of Toughness,* N-3447-DPRC (Santa Monica, Calif.: RAND, 1991).

Reuter, Peter and Robert. J. MacCoun, "Street Drug Markets in Inner-City Neighborhoods: Matching Policy to Reality," in *Urban America: Policy Choices for Los Angeles and the Nation,* James B. Steinberg, David W. Lyon, and Mary E. Viana, eds., MR-100-RC (Santa Monica, Calif.: RAND, 1992).

Reuter, Peter, Robert MacCoun, and Patrick Murphy, *Money from Crime: A Study of the Economics of Drug Dealing in Washington, D.C.,* R-3894-RF (Santa Monica, Calif.: RAND, 1990).

Reuter, Peter, Gordon Crawford, and Jonathan Cave, *Sealing the Borders: The Effects of Increased Military Participation in Drug Interdiction,* R-3594-USDP (Santa Monica, Calif.: RAND, 1988a).

_____, *Sealing the Borders: The Effects of Increased Military Participation in Drug Interdiction,* R-3594-USDP (Santa Monica, Calif.: RAND, 1988b).

Riley, Kevin Jack, *Snow Job? The Efficacy of Source Country Cocaine Control Policies,* RGSD-102 (Santa Monica, Calif.: RAND, 1993).

Schelling, Thomas C., "Addictive Drugs: The Cigarette Experience," *Science* 225 (24 January 1992): 430–33.

Warner, Kenneth E., "Legalizing Drugs: Lessons from (and about) Economics," *The Milbank Quarterly* 69, 4 (1991): 641–61.

Winston, Gordon C., "Addiction and Backsliding," *Journal of Economic Behavior and Organization* 1 (1980): 295–324.

Part II

War Stories

4

White Lies in Bolivia and Peru

Cocaine production begins in the mountain valleys and jungles of Bolivia, Peru, and increasingly, Columbia. Despite Colombia's growing role, Bolivia and Peru still grow most of the world's coca, the woody bush from which cocaine is derived.[1] Coca has deep roots in Bolivian and Peruvian society, stretching back many centuries into Andean history. Coca has assumed religious and cultural significance in Andean society, and has been employed in a variety of capacities, including that of a spiritual link between man and God, and as a form of currency.[2] In addition to being ascribed mystical qualities, coca has been, and still is, used to relieve fatigue, hunger, and *sorochi*, the altitude sickness common throughout the region.[3]

Striking at the Source

From the United States' perspective, it is easy to see why there is an interest in controlling the coca trade. Coca is the essential ingredient in cocaine, and without it the traffickers would be driven out of business. Coca plants themselves represent the most visible—and, thus, vulnerable—point in the production chain.[4] Certainly, coca fields are much easier to detect than small bundles of cocaine. The coca plants are fixed assets that are not easily moved in the very short run; they can be destroyed hours or days after detection with no risk that the fields will have disappeared. The interest in controlling foreign sources of drug production represents a consistent pattern in the history of U.S. drug policy.[5]

Perhaps less obvious is why Bolivia and Peru would want to control coca production. Coca, as the linchpin of the cocaine economy, has helped transform vast swaths of the Andean countryside from sleepy, impoverished hamlets to booming centers of commerce. Where subsistence ag-

riculture once marked the extent of economic development, cash economies now thrive. For years, Peruvian and Bolivian leaders resisted U.S.
pressure to mount a more vigorous attack on coca farming. In effect,
they argued that the coca trade should be left alone. The rationale for
this argument, which carried very little weight in Washington, was that
the farmers are essentially innocent victims. Coca and coca farming are
centuries-old traditions, and there is nothing dangerous or addictive about
coca leaves themselves. Farmers produce coca, not cocaine, and are therefore not responsible for the destruction and harms of cocaine trafficking. And while coca farmers hardly get rich from coca farming ($2,000
was probably an average income from farming during the 1980's boom,
but it also probably declined some since), such earnings are vitally important in impoverished regions where few alternatives exist. Instead,
the argument went, policy efforts should be focused on those responsible for the social harms of cocaine, the drug traffickers. Implicit in this
argument is the notion that the consuming countries should take greater
responsibility by controlling demand for illicit drugs.

The costs of hosting the coca trade have steadily risen, however,
prompting the source country governments to be more receptive to control measures. The costs borne by the source countries include drug-
related violence;[6] development of synergism between drug trafficking
and guerrilla groups;[7] economic dependence on coca production;[8] displacement of other agricultural production;[9] ecological destruction;[10] and
drug-related corruption.[11] Two Bolivian presidential administrations,
those of Hugo Banzer and Garcia Meza, have been marked by drug-
related corruption. Recently, the movement of cocaine processing laboratories from Colombia into Bolivia and Peru has been confirmed, an
unsettling reminder of the violence and consequences of higher-level
trafficking that Colombia has endured for more than a decade. Farmers,
eager to expand their coca farming, have destroyed untold thousands of
acres of pristine forest land. Rivers run polluted from the chemicals used
to extract cocaine alkaloids from the harvested coca leaves. More recently, substance abuse has begun to emerge in some sectors of Andean
society as a concern. Coca has also brought bloodshed: Shining Path
guerrillas in Peru have embarked on a campaign for the loyalty of Peruvian farmers, and Bolivian farmers threaten unrest if mandatory eradication programs are implemented. Additionally, it became increasingly
less possible for Bolivian and Peruvian farmers to hide under the fig

leaf of innocence as more and more farmers became directly connected to the cocaine trade through paste processing. In short, coca has left virtually no corner of Andean society untouched.

It would be incorrect to say that there is complete agreement about how to approach source country control policies. However, to the extent that there is agreement that something must be done about coca farming, two options have emerged. The first is to destroy the coca trade by treating it as a law enforcement matter, and the second is to buy the trade out by treating it as a matter of economic development. In recent years, both approaches have been tried, and indeed they can be mutually reinforcing. Peru has been more aggressive in attacking coca farming directly, at least in part because its peasantry was already restful. In contrast, Bolivia resisted efforts to "militarize" counternarcotic efforts, particularly those relating to coca farmers, by deliberately pursuing less aggressive, more development-oriented policies.[12]

Such approaches have worked, at least temporarily, with other illicit substances in other regions of the world. Why eradication and development assistance have not worked in Bolivia and Peru, and why they will never work to permanently control cocaine production, is simultaneously a complicated and a simple parable. The complications are found in the geography, profitability, mobility, and structure of the drug trade that make it impossible to effectively regulate coca—and therefore cocaine—production and in the political, economic, and social tensions that have constrained use of these policy tools. The simplicity is found in basic economic and market dynamics: as long as there is a demand for cocaine, there will be production of it.

It is worth reiterating that people often misinterpret the point of this analysis to be, "nothing can be done that will drive up the cost of producing cocaine." That is not true. In fact, most of the policies discussed here do raise the costs of production for the industry, some slightly, others substantially, but always for short periods of time. For individual producers and traffickers, a given policy such as eradication may well have devastating effects in the short-run. Rather, the point of this message is as follows. First, we have failed to find, and indeed probably cannot find, policies that will drive up production costs permanently. Second, the costs, both monetary and nonmonetary, of imposing temporary production surcharges appear to exceed the benefits derived from their imposition.

Coca is King

Despite the seemingly daunting barriers to farming in the Andes, including poor soil, torrential rains, limited market facilities, and lack of infrastructure, it does not take much effort to be a successful coca farmer. The jungle soil, for example, is very acidic and will not support many types of commercial crops. Coca, however, thrives in such soil. In parts of the region the terrain is steeply sloped, limiting the farmers' ability to plant some crops. Coca plants grow well on steeply sloped plots. Coca tolerates substantial rainfall, growing in regions receiving 1000–4200 mm of annual precipitation.[13] Coca will survive without the use of pesticides to control insect infestations, although occasional weeding is required and farmers occasionally use pesticides and fertilizers to increase yields.[14] Another advantage is that coca can grow in poor and depleted soils as a replacement for crops that have exhausted existing farmland or it can be used to expand the agricultural frontier to otherwise unusable property. The plant grows best between 500 and 1500 meters, but is adaptable to lower altitudes, albeit with lower cocaine concentrations.[15] In fact, coca plants can tolerate just about every condition and extreme imaginable, except frigid weather.[16]

In terms of commercial attributes, it is difficult to imagine a better plant. Coca provides up to six harvests a year in a region where most other crops come into season once a year. Coca's multiple harvests provide year-round income and reduce the risk that an entire season's income will be lost to freak weather or other such catastrophe. Seasonal crops, particularly if cultivated exclusively (or "monocropped"), cannot offer such insurance. Coca reaches production maturity much faster than other permanent crops, such as coffee and tea, can provide initial harvests six months after planting, and mature harvests in as few as eighteen months. Coffee bushes and citrus groves may require a half a decade or more to reach maturity. Coca plants live as long as thirty years, although fifteen years appears to be a reasonable upper limit for useable harvests. Coca maintains its advantages even after harvest. Harvested leaves spoil relatively slowly, and do not damage during transport.[17] Both factors are significant advantages because transportation is difficult throughout the Andes. Transportation over rough roads can damage delicate crops such as bananas and can cause shipping delays that result in spoilage. The lack of train routes and expense of shipping by air make it difficult to profitably grow and market many other crops.

Coca has become so valuable that many farmers grow it exclusively. Traditionally, farmers of the Andean highlands[18] minimized economic risk by diversifying cropping practices.[19] Diversification methods evolved over time in response to the highly varying climatological conditions in the Andes, and to the high cost and slow dissemination of agricultural technologies such as insecticides, high-yield seeds, and disease-resistant crop strains that would help farmers evade commercial crop disasters. A typical highland farmer plants a number of different crops at a variety of altitudes facing several different exposures. This practice ensures that if rain, frost, insects, or some other factor wiped out one crop, that crops located elsewhere would probably survive. When farmers originally settled the lowlands, where most of the coca is now grown, in the 1950s they continued the diversification strategy at first. The continuation of traditional practices had less to do with insurance against climate and other risks, and more to do with the need to be self-sufficient in food production because of the coca regions' isolation and lack of markets. Gradually, however, both highland and lowland farmers saw coca's potential as a cash crop, and many began to cultivate it exclusively.[20]

Coca production, and thus efforts to control it, is primarily confined to several subtropical (or lowland) and highland regions in Bolivia and Peru. In Peru, the Upper Huallaga Valley, along with the Central and Lower Huallaga Valleys, comprise the main growing areas. Cuzco, Apurimac, and other regions in Peru are of lesser, but growing, importance. Bolivia's primary coca farming area, known as the Chapare, is located at the eastern edge of the *Cordillera Oriental* range of the Andes. Additionally, Bolivia's Yungas highland valleys are important production centers. Coca farming in the Yungas not only supplies the cocaine industry, but is also the center of traditional and cultural uses that stretch back many centuries.[21] Figure 4.1 shows the main cultivation and trafficking centers in Peru and Bolivia and their proximity to regional and national population centers.

The Upper Huallaga Valley, Peru

Until recently, Peru's coca production was concentrated in the Upper Huallaga Valley, a Massachusetts-sized area located in central Peru. From

FIGURE 4.1

Coca Cultivation in Bolivia and Peru

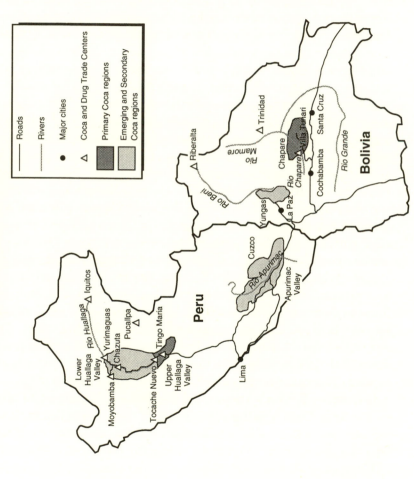

the headwaters in Pasco Department, the Huallaga River flows more than 500 miles northward, through Tingo Maria, Santa Lucia, and Yurimaguas. North of Yurimaguas, the Huallaga river joins with other rivers and tributaries that eventually form the western end of the Amazon river. The Upper Huallaga Valley is located near the river's southern end, and consists of the portions of Huanuco and southern San Martin Departments, which drain into the Huallaga river basin. At its peak in the late 1980s the Upper Huallaga Valley produced 30–40 percent of the world's coca supply.

Of late, however, Peru's coca production has begun to disperse in response to both counternarcotics efforts and the emergence of a natural fungus that kills coca plants. In late 1992, the Peruvian Air Force (FAP) initiated efforts to control the airspace and airports around major Upper, Central, and Lower Huallaga valley coca and paste consolidation and shipment centers, including Santa Lucia, Tocache, Uchiza, and Juanjui. Prior to the crackdown, the traffickers consolidated coca paste shipments in these cities and towns, and then used the local airports to ship the paste north to Colombian refining facilities. FAP's control over airports forced the traffickers to move their consolidation centers to other regions of the Upper Huallaga Valley, such as Pucallpa and Tarapoto to the north and east. Subsequently, in 1993 FAP extended its air control efforts to include airports in and around Saposoa, Bellavista, Tarapoto, Yurimaguas, Sion, Palmapampa, Izcosazin, Caballococha, Puerto Bermudez, and Pucallpa. FAP's airport control efforts have been aided by the installation of radar facilities in Yurimaguas, Iquitos, and Andoas.[22] The Yurimaguas radar has a maximum range of 180 nautical miles, although the region's terrain limits its effectiveness to perhaps half that distance. Nevertheless, FAP's efforts have been very effective in the Upper Huallaga Valley. Formerly bustling shipment centers, including Tocache, Uchiza, and Juanjui, have turned into ghost towns.

The movement of consolidation centers has largely been paralleled by displacement of coca farming from a natural form of eradication that appears to be occurring in the Upper Huallaga Valley.[23] A fungus, *fusarium oxysporum*, has killed off thousands of hectares of coca plants in the Upper Huallaga Valley. This fungus, which apparently has both pernicious and benign forms, has spread throughout the Valley and resulted in extensive damage to coca crops. By some estimates, the coca fungus may have destroyed 30 percent or more of the Upper Huallaga

Valley's coca crop, with the greatest damage occurring around Uchiza and Tocache.[24] The fungus' impact has been amplified by soil depletion, inadequate crop rotation, and monocropping. Over time, these factors weaken coca crops and leave them vulnerable to fungal intrusion. The damage to coca in the Upper Huallaga Valley is evident in the resurgence of crops other than coca. As late as 1991 through 1992, many Upper Huallaga Valley farmers still monocropped coca. Throughout the 1980s as coca became increasingly important, farming of other commercial crops declined to very low levels. The Upper Huallaga Valley was no longer self-sufficient in production of some crops, and was forced to import food. However, the coca fungus, in conjunction with the crackdown on air shipments out of the Upper Huallaga Valley, led to a weakening of coca prices. As a result, some farmers are shifting away from monocropping of coca, and increasing the cultivation of other commercial and subsistence crops. But, as coca farming in the former main production centers of the Upper Huallaga Valley has weakened, it has risen substantially in other areas. Growing centers have emerged in the lower and central Huallaga Valley, including such towns as Yarina, Pelejo, Shapaja, Leticia, Chazuta, Alto Mayo, Rioja, and Moyobamba (figure 4.1 shows some of these locations).

The primary coca growing regions, and indeed most of rural Peru, consists of extremely rugged terrain with limited links to urban manufacturing and commerce centers. Despite the inhospitability of the area, the Peruvian government encouraged colonization of the region beginning in the 1950s. Overcrowding and migration were particular problems in Lima, and thus the government used colonization and homesteading programs to encourage migration away from the city. In addition, authorities for a time considered many of the river valleys, including the Upper Huallaga Valley, to be prime candidates for development of commercial agriculture. The Marginal Highway, which connects Lima to the Valley, eased access to the interior portion of the country. Settlements and towns such as Tingo Maria grew rapidly in the ensuing decades. The Upper Huallaga Valley's population increased at an average annual rate of 6 percent between 1965 and 1988.[25]

The prospects for commercial agriculture in the valley regions turned out to be overstated. Although the upper jungle regions experienced a number of agricultural booms prior to the 1970s, they were always followed by equally precipitous busts. Coffee and bananas, for example, were expected to lead the development of the Upper Huallaga Valley in the 1950s and 1960s. But while the Valleys's lands were adequate for limited farming, the desired transformation to commercial agriculture required large investments in agriculture and development projects that were not forthcoming. Most assistance was given to coastal plantations, and the limited resources transferred to the valleys were often dedicated to irrigation programs that did not meet regional development needs. The government reneged on many agreements to buy produce at specified (profitable) prices because volatile economic conditions constrained its ability to honor purchase agreements. Food imports from foreign producers were subsidized as part of a commitment to maintaining affordable food prices,[26] but this practice made it difficult for farmers to profitably supply agricultural products.[27] Much of the soil in the Upper Huallaga Valley would not support commercial tropical crops, a factor not foreseen at the time settlement was being encouraged.[28] The promising banana trade, for example, was cut short by a disease that limited its geographic range, and the Peruvian coffee trade fell victim to world competition, soft prices, and inefficient production.[29] By 1970, with the collapse of the Peruvian coffee trade, the Upper Huallaga Valley was without a steady cash crop.[30]

These factors–steady migration to the valleys, a weak agricultural base, and key crop failures—combined to exceed the region's development capacity. The region's inability to carry and sustain its population in turn augmented the expansion of coca farming. The lack of good-quality land encouraged settlement of so-called marginal lands, which were unsuitable for most crops other than coca.[31] Concomitantly, land use patterns in the valleys shifted away from seasonal agriculture, which required intensive tending, applications of fertilizers to maintain soil quality, and a steady supply of scarce labor, toward the cultivation of permanent crops, of which coca is a primary example. Unlike seasonal crops, permanent crops do not provide a fallow period in which land can replenish nutrients. As perennial cultivation expanded, the stock of land suitable for commercial agriculture was further eroded.[32] Finally, as commercial crops (other than coca) became inviable, increasing amounts of prime cropland were turned over to coca farming. Cultivation of most noncoca crops in the valleys, particularly the Upper Huallaga Valley, plummeted during the coca boom, although they have since resurged slightly.

The Chapare, Bolivia

The Chapare is the primary coca growing region in Bolivia, producing over 60 percent of Bolivia's coca crop, and 15 percent of the world total (see figure 4.1 for a map of the region). The Chapare is an area approximately the size of New Jersey, bounded by the Andes mountains and the traditional highland coca cultivation areas to the west and south and lowland jungle to the north and east. North of the Chapare lies El Beni Department, home of most of the drug refining and processing that occurs in Bolivia. Situated midway between the major regional cities of Cochabamba and Santa Cruz, the latter having assumed the role as the nerve center of the Bolivian drug trade, the Chapare continues to be Bolivia's most important coca production center. The Yungas, a highland valley region north and west of the Chapare, is also a major coca production center, although much of the Yungas coca is, at least ostensibly, grown for legal uses.

Coca farming in Bolivia has strong historical roots, but the commercialization of it parallels the process that occurred in Peru. As in Peru, the completion of highway, in this case between Cochabamba and Santa Cruz, opened the interior for settlement. Settlers were encouraged not only by the easier access that the road offered, but by land reform, which released much of the native population from the *latifundia* land tenure system.[33] Once released from this system, the Bolivian Indians were free to migrate in search of other employment, and many chose to settle in the newly opened lands.[34]

During the next several decades, the Chapare grew rapidly in population. In 1967 the population stood at around 27,000,[35] but by 1987 had climbed to over 200,000.[36] Many settlers arrived from the Yungas region, where coca was traditionally farmed for personal and legal use and other food crops were grown for subsistence.[37] This settlement wave, which lasted through the 1970s, helped form the foundation of the region's nascent agricultural industry, but also helped introduce commercial coca cultivation to the Chapare.[38]

Commercial agriculture, however, proved to be a tenuous base on which to build regional development. From the opening of the highway through the late 1970s, Bolivia's economy was organized around the exports of primary products and attempts to develop agricultural markets.[39] The world agricultural markets for primary products, particularly tin, proved volatile, and ultimately failed as stable sources of employment. A similar story emerged in the agricultural sector as well. Sugar cane was one of the first crops to be commercially exploited in the Bolivian interior, but Bolivia's place in world markets proved fleeting. Segments of the commercial farming industry in and around Santa Cruz, particularly cotton farmers, were devastated over the years by weak international prices.

But the economy was worse elsewhere in Bolivia, particularly in urban areas and mining communities. Weakness in natural resource markets, combined with government settlement programs, ensured that settlers kept arriving even as agricultural prospects in the interior weakened. Many who migrated in the 1970s and early 1980s, such as unemployed tin miners, did not possess the skills to farm in the tropics, but found few nonagricultural opportunities were available in the interior.[40] As a result, many were drawn to coca farming because it required little in the way of agricultural expertise, and because it was one of the only options available. This group formed the core of the original coca-cocaine economy that developed in the late 1970s and early 1980s, and they became some of the first to monocrop coca in the Chapare. Their influence is seen in land use surveys, which report a sharp increase in coca farming at the expense of other crops in the region. According to surveys, commercial crops such as bananas, rice, yucca, and oranges constituted approximately 75 percent of agricultural activity and coca about 25 percent in 1971, but by 1985 the percentage of coca had risen to 66 percent and legal cultivation had declined to 34 percent.[41] A later wave of migration, which began approximately in 1986, marked the final phase of the Chapare's development as a drug center. Unlike the other settlement waves, in which the colonists moved to the Chapare primarily in expectation of legal employment but ultimately found coca to be the most lucrative choice, this wave of migrants arrived in the Chapare primarily to participate in the drug industry. Many arrived intending to farm only coca from the outset.

Eradication: Striking at the Source

Without coca, the drug traffickers could not make cocaine. Throughout the last decade, the United States has supported numerous eradication programs in an effort to deprive traffickers of this vital input, as well as to curtail trafficking in other drugs. The ability of eradication to stop production at its source, as well as its perceived technical and logistical simplicity, makes it an intuitively appealing policy option. In order to be effective the eradication has to be complete and involve the removal or death of the entire plant. Chopping the plants down, for example, is not sufficient, since, if the extensive root system is not removed or destroyed, the plant will grow back, perhaps even providing higher yields.[42] Likewise, merely stripping the leaves off does not constitute eradication, but rather is what happens when coca leaves are harvested.

Eradication can take one of two forms: manual and herbicidal. Manual eradication offers greater political acceptability with the producing nations and has been experimented with in the past. The difficulty with manual eradication lies in the fact that men and equipment must be moved in large numbers to remote growing areas. Once there, the coca plant itself proves resilient to eradication efforts. It takes perhaps twenty man days of effort to pull up an entire hectare of coca plants by their roots.[43] Once pulled up, the plants themselves must be destroyed or burned so that processors and traffickers do not retrieve the plants once the eradication teams leave the area. While the numbers of people required to eradicate the entire coca crop in Bolivia might not be prohibitive, other costs of the operation might be. For example, 10,000 people working full-time could eradicate perhaps 100,000 hectares in a year. However, it would prove extremely difficult to transport and defend 10,000 eradication team members in the relatively friendly confines of Bolivia, let alone in the hostile and forbidding coca regions of Peru.

In fact, it is the security threat that poses the most difficult challenge to manual eradication, particularly in Peru. Large portions of Peruvian territory remain under effective control of the Shining Path, a guerrilla organization that has plagued the countryside for over a decade.[44] The Shining Path's control over rural territory, including many of the primary coca-producing regions, means that an effective eradication policy would need to surmount this formidable obstacle. In fact, the opposite has occurred, and eradication workers have endured armed attacks at the hands of insurgents and coca producers in the Upper Huallaga Valley. As a result, Peruvian eradication operations have been scaled back and are now concentrated in more remote areas of the Valley and are directed at seed beds. Bolivia confronts a different problem with respect to eradication. In Bolivia, an organized union represents the interests of coca farmers at the national level, which presents the government with an entrenched, vocal opponent, albeit one that does not possess the violent, revolutionary nature of the Shining Path in Peru. Nevertheless, Bolivian farmers have repeatedly expressed opposition to eradication,[45] and the threat of escalation to violent confrontation is always present. Opposition also appears to be growing in Colombia, which is now estimated to produce approximately 20 percent of the world's coca crop. Press reports, for example, indicate that Colombian-operated U.S. helicopters flying eradication missions in southwestern Colombia have been fired upon by restive locals.[46]

In contrast, herbicidal eradication promises greater ease of implementation but conjures up visions of chemical contamination, environmental destruction, and other ecological, political, and social problems. Recent studies point to potentially effective herbicidal treatments for coca plants.[47] At least three herbicides—glyphosate, tebuthiuron, and hexazinone[48]— demonstrate the ability to kill coca plants. Only glyphosate has been widely applied to drug crops. Colombia, in particular, has made extensive use of glyphosate against poppies, marijuana, and, more recently, coca. Dow Elanco officials have stated that they will not sell tebuthiuron for drug eradication purposes. Questions persist, however, as to whether these chemicals are appropriate for use in the tropical environment in terms of soil persistence, damage to other crops, and the health hazard posed to humans in the area. In addition, the use of herbicides to eradicate coca raises the larger issue of whether eradication, herbicidal or otherwise, poses a larger threat to the environment than coca farming.[49]

Nevertheless, herbicides can be aerially applied, reducing the transportation needs and risks of armed conflict to personnel. Glyphosate is applied in an aerosol form, and tebuthiuron and hexazinone are applied in a pellet form. The latter application substantially reduces the possibility of drift contamination and increases the accuracy with which they can be delivered. As a practical matter, however, herbicidal eradication remains politically unpalatable, and thus much less likely to be employed than manual eradication.

Eradication in Peru

In the early 1980s, the Peruvian government, encouraged and supported by the United States, attempted to curtail illicit coca farming in the Upper Huallaga Valley through a forced eradication program. The results of the program were discouraging. At its peak in 1984, the program destroyed less than 4000 hectares per year, a number that is probably smaller than the acreage annually retired and replaced because it has ceased to be productive. Still, supporters of the policy point out that significant bureaucratic and logistic problems hampered the effort and prevented further progress from taking place.[50]

By far the most important obstacle encountered in the course of eradication was violent opposition from the peasants. While to be expected, and sometimes even interpreted as a sign of policy success, the violence that erupted in the Upper Huallaga Valley assumed a much darker dimension in 1983 when the Shining Path, or *Sendero Luminoso*, began to assert its authority throughout the Valley. The Shining Path succeeded in depicting the program as an imperialistic attack on local interests and began coordinating violent counterattacks against the government eradication teams. In August, 1984, the Peruvian government placed the region under a state of emergency and ordered in army troops to stabilize conditions. Attempts to quell the violence, however, met with little success. Shortly after the army's arrival, narcotics traffickers murdered nineteen eradication workers.[51]

Despite stepped-up Peruvian efforts to contain the Shining Path, the area has since remained under effective guerrilla control. Because of the danger to personnel, the United States withdrew its support for forced eradication efforts in 1987, confining its support to seed-bed eradication programs at the edge of the Upper Huallaga Valley. Since then it has wrestled with the increasingly difficult issue of how to pursue counternarcotics objectives in Peru. The issue is complicated by frequent complaints of human rights abuses by the army in the region, by the ineffective control that the government maintains over army and police units, and by corruption among the participants in Peruvian counternarcotics efforts.[52] Military aid has been suspended since Peruvian President Alberto Fujimori's 1992 coup and the April, 1992 shootdown of a U.S. cargo plane.

Eradication in Bolivia

The Bolivian government committed itself to modest eradication objectives in 1983 as well. The United States conditioned continued receipt of over $80 million in development assistance and narcotics control aid on Bolivian eradication of 4000 hectares of coca by 1985 and establishment of effective narcotics police control over the region.[53] Despite these commitments, however, the Bolivian government took little action, and the U.S. government responded by implementing procedures under which aid was to be withheld in the absence of a firm commitment to counternarcotics efforts. In May, 1985, the Bolivians moved to defuse the crisis by drafting legislation that restricted coca farming to the highland regions, and which would have subjected all coca farming in the Chapare to eradication. The decree, however, was never implemented by the legislature and, thus, did not have the force of law. The Bolivian government relented to U.S. pressure in 1988 and enacted *Ley 1008*, a law that made most coca farming outside traditional high-altitude coca zones[54] illegal.[55] The nontraditional areas, such as the Chapare, were designated transitional zones, were given a ten-year period in which to voluntarily eradicate all coca, and were targeted with development assistance to encourage voluntary eradication. At the end of the transitional decade, all coca cultivation in nontraditional areas is to become illegal as well. Subsequently, the United States began to compensate peasants in the Chapare $2,000 per hectare removed from production in the transitional zones.[56] Production taking place outside of the traditional and transitional zones was considered illegal and subject to forced eradication. In addition, all acreage in the transitional zone placed under cultivation after enactment of *Ley 1008* was also considered illegal and subject to eradication.

Since implementation of the agreement, Bolivia has found it difficult to meet the voluntary eradication targets in the transitional zones. The justifications regarding the failure of the voluntary eradication program have ranged widely. There have been complaints about the slow speed with which farmers were compensated for eradication, and also about how slowly alternative development programs designed to reward villages for eradication came on line. In addition, Bolivian authorities have noted that interdiction operations have failed to keep leaf prices low on a sustained basis. It is believed that consistently low leaf prices would force farmers to consider the option of voluntary eradication. Bolivian authorities blamed wet weather in 1991 for limiting regional activities, including farming and development, and consequently for reducing the incentives to voluntarily eradicate. Additionally, authorities point out that those who have yet to participate in voluntary eradication are unlikely to do so because they settled in the region primarily to participate in the cocaine trade and lack basic farming skills needed for other crops. On the U.S. side, officials point to lackadaisical enforcement of *Ley 1008*, particularly the prohibition against new cultivation in the transition zones as a contributing factor to the slow pace of voluntary eradication.

The lax enforcement of the prohibition against new cultivation is a particularly sore point in U.S.-Bolivian counternarcotics relations. The U.S. side sees it as the key to ensuring the success of voluntary eradication since the law permits destruction of legal coca plants if the farmer is found in violation of laws governing transitional coca. Bolivian officials, for their part, are very reluctant to conduct forced eradication. They fear that forced eradication will radicalize the peasants and result in an armed conflict between the eradication teams and the farmers. This fear is grounded not only in the experience of Peru in the early 1980s, but because of the strength that the coca unions maintain throughout the Chapare.[57] Several times already the coca unions, or *sindicatos*,[58] have blocked commerce in the region by shutting down the main highway to show their distaste for coca policies and have mobilized members to participate in hunger strikes, "chew-ins," sit-ins at government offices, and public protests. The local *sindicatos* have also succeeded in keeping the issue of coca cultivation on the national farming agenda through their affiliation with the national peasant labor organization. A number of armed confrontations have already occurred in the region over the issue.[59] The fact that DINACO, the Bolivian authority created in conjunction with *Ley 1008* to regulate coca markets, must negotiate with farmers in several of the regional coca markets for the right to regulate markets that it is authorized, and required, by law to monitor, is a measure of the farmers' strength. Similarly, farmers have continued to evade sanctions against farming illicit coca because DIRECO, the state coca reduction agency, has yet to conduct a census of new and old coca that would allow authorities to distinguish between legal and illegal coca.

Compensation for voluntary eradication may also, perversely, act as insurance for those who decide to undertake coca farming. Compensation establishes a floor price. When coca prices are above the compensation price, farmers have no economic incentive to eradicate. When prices are below the floor, the compensation provides the farmers an income and thus helps underwrite the downside risk associated with coca farming. In other words, the only way a farmer will not benefit is if he grows no coca at all.

The future of eradication in the Chapare is not promising. For the reason discussed previously, forced eradication will remain problematic. At the same time, however, voluntary eradication is likely to become increasingly impractical over the next few years. At the age of three to four years, coca plants acquire a moss at the base of the plant. Once this moss is present it is virtually impossible to tell the age of the plant. This has a dramatic impact on voluntary eradication programs because, under the program's rules, the United States cannot offer compensation for coca planted in the transitional zone after the enactment of the 1988 law. However, because authorities failed to complete a land-use census in 1988, and have not done so since, they have lost their ability to distinguish between "legal" coca in the transitional zone (that planted before 1988) and "illegal" coca in the zone (that planted after enactment of *Ley 1008*). Without the ability to distinguish between crops, the program acts as insurance for farmers who planted illegally. These factors, in conjunction with the Bolivian government's reluctance to forcibly eradicate coca, make it unlikely that the program will endure in its present form.

Alternative Development: Aid and Comfort to the Enemy?

Alternative development and economic assistance are designed to provide coca farmers with the means and incentives to quit coca production permanently.[60] In some cases, development assistance is provided concomitantly with eradication on the premise that eradication will drive farmers away from coca and development assistance will provide ready, viable alternatives. Such instances are typically of the crop substitution variety, meaning that the alternatives created by the development assistance are agricultural, and intended to allow for an easy transition from coca to other crops. Similarly, the United States has granted debt relief to the Bolivian government, but has conditioned continuation of the aid on steady progress toward eradication targets. In other cases, development assistance is quite divorced from the coca regions and eradication. For example, development projects have been implemented in regions adjacent to coca zones in an effort to lure labor away from coca production. In any event, the policies work on essentially the same principles either by subsidizing other economic opportunities so that they are as profitable as coca, or by interfering with coca farming to the extent that its rewards are reduced to the level of other opportunities in the region.

Alternative Development in Bolivia

Migrant labor from other parts of Bolivia, particularly the highland valleys, supplies the Chapare with the work force it needs to produce coca. Thus, in addition to attempting to reduce coca farming directly in the Chapare through eradication, the United States has also supported projects designed to stem the flow of labor to the Chapare in an effort to limit the labor pool available for coca farming. In Bolivia, the largest attempt to control migration is the Associated High Valleys (AHV) project. The AHV is an area adjacent to the Chapare that not only supplies the coca zone with some of the migrant and seasonal labor needed for coca production, but is also the origin of many of the homesteaders who have settled in the Chapare. The AHV projects entail a series of development projects designed to increase opportunities in the AHV in hopes of both stemming the flow of seasonal and migrant labor to the Chapare, and attracting back some of the migrants who have moved to the Chapare.

The AHV programs have received modest levels of funding, on the order of less than $5 million for each of fiscal years 1989 through 1992. Agriculture in the AHV is constrained by the availability of arable land, and yet agriculture is the primary activity of most of the population. The projects therefore tended to focus on expanding the arable land stock through the augmentation of irrigation and soil management techniques.[61] Combined, funding for irrigation and soil management projects accounts for about 65 percent of the short-term projects implemented and 50 percent of the long-term projects put in place.

Recent reports indicate that the population of the Chapare is declining. It is not clear that those who have left are settling in the AHV, nor is it clear that coca production is declining. Rather, it appears that the migrants out of the Chapare are the traditional farmers who settled in the area in the pre-1970 phase.[62] On balance, those remaining in the Chapare appear to be more committed to illicit coca farming and impervious to exhortations to voluntarily curb their cultivation activities. In some sense, these are a professional cadre of coca farmers who have worked at increasing yields and developing strategies (such as paste production) for combatting the wide swings in coca prices and profitability.

For those remaining in the Chapare, there are a number of programs intended to pull them away from coca farming. USAID/Bolivia, for example, provides marketing and export assistance, agricultural extension and research services, credit, and infrastructure development programs.[63] Under these programs, Chapare farmers are provided technical expertise, loans, and services in an effort to increase the agricultural diversity of the region. Through these programs more than 1000 Chapare farmers have received $5.6 million in loans; 4000 farmers have received training; and exports of local crops to Argentina, Chile, and Venezuela have been established.[64]

The AHV and Chapare development programs are premised on effective law enforcement pressure causing interest in voluntary eradication and alternative crops. To compensate the Bolivian government partially for lost revenues, particularly lost foreign exchange, the U.S. government provides up to $66 million in balance of payments support. This funding is designed to transform the Bolivian economy through increased employment, income, investment, and productivity gains in noncoca activities.[65] Continuation of this development support is predicated on development and implementation of sound macroeconomic policies and maintenance of counternarcotics goals, including voluntary eradication targets.

Alternative Development in Peru

Two factors continue to hamper prospects for alternative development in Peru. First, the generally unstable nature of the Peruvian economy prevents implementation of national programs such as balance of payment support. Factors such as hyperinflation and exchange rate overvaluation lower profitability and discourage investment in programs that would otherwise be used to lure farmers away from coca. Second, widespread political violence, primarily perpetrated by the Shining Path or *Sendero Luminoso,* has complicated the picture. Much of the countryside is effectively in control of the guerrillas, and thus the government cannot ensure the protection of development workers. In the past, those found to have cooperated with the government on development projects have been subject to retribution from the guerrillas.

Despite these two obstacles, a number of development programs have been implemented over the past decade, most aimed at controlling the coca trade in the Upper Huallaga Valley. This area was targeted for assistance as early as 1981 with the commencement of the Upper Huallaga Area Development Program (UHADP). UHADP consists of three parts: eradication, development and commercialization, and control of coca commerce. CORAH, Peru's national coca eradication authority, was given responsibility for the eradication programs; PEAH (Special Project for the development of the Alto Huallaga) was directed to establish and implement a regional development program; UMOPAR (Mobile Rural Police Unit) agents became responsible for regulating coca commerce in the Upper Huallaga Valley. In November, 1991, the Peruvian government created IDEA, the Instituto de Desarrollo Alternativo (Alternative Development Institute). This organization will be in charge of proposing, negotiating, and signing agreements to replace coca plantations.

Evaluations conducted of the project in 1986 showed disappointing results.[66] The primary shortcoming was the fact that coca maintained a tremendous economic advantage over all other forms of commerce in the valley, and no amount of interdiction and development was adequate to overcome this leverage. Many of the farmers whose plots were eradicated simply relocated elsewhere in the valley and replanted their coca.[67]

By 1986 several menacing factors combined to create an extremely violent atmosphere in the Upper Huallaga Valley. Coca farmers reacted negatively to the eradication programs and often resorted to violent methods of protests. The unpopularity of the eradication in turn provided an opening that the Shining Path exploited by encouraging the peasants to use violence. Finally, the drug dealers themselves increasingly resorted to violent tactics in an effort to not only protect themselves from law enforcement operations, but from the Shining Path guerrillas as well.

Poor relations between the various authoritative agencies operating in the valley complicated issues. In particular, the Peruvian Army, charged with suppressing the *Sendero,* and the police, tasked with counternarcotics operations, demonstrated an inability to cooperate.[68] In part because of the poor cooperation between authorities, violence in the area continued to grow and many development programs were discontinued. As a result, the Upper Huallaga Valley's development needs remain massive. Studies have shown that the Upper Huallaga Valley needs development assistance on the order of $500 million to improve the road system alone in the coca zones.[69]

All-Out War

Predictably, in light of the intensive efforts over the past decade to control coca production in Bolivia and Peru, the question of how these policies have affected coca production arises. Unfortunately, the answer appears to be "not much," though not without some caveats. A complete census of the area cultivated is not possible. Instead, cultivation statistics are derived from estimation techniques. The four primary estimation methods are land use potential, labor availability, precursor chemical use, and aerial photography. Naturally, these techniques do not provide consistent results. The problem is further complicated by the need to consider acreage yields, a factor that can vary substantially depending on the coca type considered, the age and maturity of the stock, and weather conditions over the harvest cycles.[70] The result has been cultivation estimates that vary by as much as a factor of two, depending on the source and the method used.[71]

The consensus is that despite eradication efforts, coca cultivation has increased relatively steadily since 1974, although the rate of growth appears to have slowed in recent years, and substantial reallocations of production share between countries are occurring.[72] Figure 4.2 shows *INCSR* estimates of the amount of land devoted to coca cultivation in Bolivia, Colombia, and Peru.[73] The notable drop in Peruvian cultivation in 1993 is thought to be due primarily to the effects of the fungus in the region, and not to eradication programs or to any underlying shift in the profitability and economics of coca farming. The cultivation data tend to correlate with available data and observable trends regarding cocaine use. That is, the measures of cocaine availability and cocaine prices indicate that supply has not been seriously interrupted in recent years.[74] The estimated 220,000 hectares under cultivation is equivalent to less than 900 square miles of territory. To provide some indication of how compact coca farming is at this point, Bolivia, Colombia, and Peru combined have over 1.3 million square miles of territory.

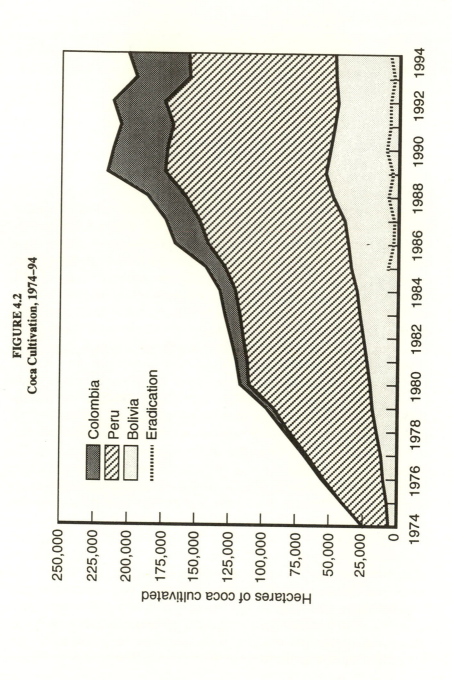

FIGURE 4.2
Coca Cultivation, 1974–94

Impact of Eradication

The upward trend in coca cultivation has continued despite the tremendous fluctuations in coca prices. Figure 4.3 shows Bolivian and Peruvian leaf prices over the 1987-92 period, as well as eradication occurring in Bolivian during the same period.[75] Coca prices have fluctuated widely for many years, and no authoritative explanation for these fluctuations exists. The marketing of coca typically takes place in towns and villages proximate to the coca fields. Some markets, such as the six that serve Bolivia's Chapare, are municipally sponsored and, at least ostensibly, federally regulated. At these formal markets, prices are posted for three qualities of leaves. First quality leaves, as measured in terms of color, spotting (such as from mold), and suppleness, command the highest price and are typically desired by cocaine traffickers because of the quantities of cocaine the leaves yield. Second and third quality leaves, which are subject to a 15-35 percent discount, require more processing for lower yields. Much of the commerce, however, takes place at night after the markets have closed, or along the sides of the roads leading into and out of the villages. It is not clear how prices for these transactions differ from those of the village markets.

The periodic oversupply of leaf—and, thus, low prices—and the periodic shortages of leaf, with corresponding high prices, may arise from a variety of factors. The extraordinary profits coca offered in the late 1970s and early 1980s probably encouraged an oversupply of leaf in the early and mid-1980s. However, coca is an agricultural commodity, and so it is subject to most of the variations inherent in farming. For example, heavy rains have reduced harvests and prevented farmers from drying their leaves during several growing cycles. Structural matters, such as poor market signals and erratic buying patterns by processors, may also contribute to price instability. One of the largest declines in prices (pictured in figure 4.3), that of the September through December 1989, can be attributed to the Colombian government's destruction of refinery capacity and the consequent decline in demand for coca. Without refiners and refineries, there was no market for coca. Alternatively, price variations may mark global changes in cocaine markets. For example, in 1987 the traffickers ceased buying coca leaf from farmers, and announced that they would only buy processed paste instead.[76] This move transferred risks to coca farmers who engaged in paste refining,

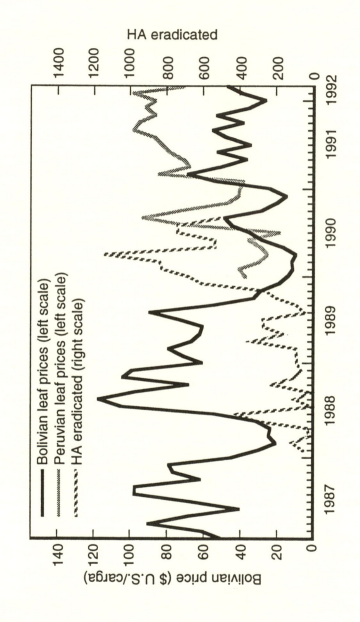

FIGURE 4.3
Coca Prices and Coca Eradication in Bolivia and Peru

and increased their sensitivity to local law enforcement operations that targeted paste processing.

Figure 4.3 also shows eradication data. These data are national level, and mask what are probably important effects of eradication on local or isolated markets. But the data do point to the problem that, at least to date, eradication programs have not been large enough to have a pronounced, visible effect on coca markets. In Bolivia, eradication has been voluntary, while in Peru it has been, at times, compulsory. Voluntary eradication can be expected to be correlated with sustained low prices. That is, farmers would willingly turn over their acreage in exchange for compensation only where the long-term prospects for coca farming are weak, or where they have old stock that has neared the end of its productive life, and which therefore was likely to be removed from production anyway.[77] High leaf prices would yield lower *voluntary* eradication rates because the compensation floor is lower than the prevailing price, and low prices would result in higher voluntary eradication rates since the floor compensation would exceed earnings from coca farming. Compulsory eradication, in contrast, raises farmers' risks and should work to increase prices.

However, tables 4.1 and 4.2 illustrate that, even when coca prices are low, coca farming still typically provides more profits than most other forms of farming. One reason that coca can remain profitable is that the farmers can adapt their production techniques. When the market is good, the farmers can afford to use more sophisticated means, including chemicals and fertilizers, to increase yields and profits. However, when the market is weak, the farmers can use less-intensive production methods, and take advantage of inexpensive family labor.[78] These shifting production methods appear to be an integral part of the coca industry.

The tables, which show the 1987 Chapare coca profits and 1990 Peruvian profits, illustrate why coca became the crop of choice. When coca prices were $100 per carga (100 pound bale), as they were in 1987, no crop could match coca's profitability. The relative profit rankings appear to change substantially when coca prices drop below $40 per carga, as they have several times since 1987. However, the profits reported for the legal crops assumes continued subsidies from the government, without which the profits on many of the legal crops would decline or disappear.[79] Table 4.2, which does not include any subsidies, confirms that many crops may not be profitable in the absence of continued

TABLE 4.1
Profits for Crops in Subtropical Bolivia

	Profit per hectare[a]	Years to first commercial harvest	Profit per metric ton
Coca ($100/Carga)	17,714	1.5	$5,368
Coca ($40/carga)	2,530	1.5	767
Pineapple	10,022	2–3	NA
Macadamia Nuts	5,436	5–7	NA
Oranges	4,280	4–5	271
Coffee	4,110	3–8	NA
Cacao	3,087	2–3	NA
Corn	2,761	<1	NA
Bananas	2,622	<1	93

Note: Compiled from Drug Policy and Agriculture (1991); Kumar, Carter, and Samuelson (1986); Final Report on the Evaluation of AID Project No. 527-0244, Development of the Alto Huallaga Area (1987); and conversations with United States Department of Agriculture officials. [a]Net present value of ten years' revenue. NA: not available.

TABLE 4.2
Profits for Crops in Upper Huallaga Valley, Peru, in 1990

	Profit per hectare[a]	Cost of Production ($/hectare)	Yield (kg/hectare)
Coca	1,680	720	1,200
Tea	−820	1,100	4,000
Coffee	−170	440	500
Cacao	−160	440	400
Red Beans	−140	390	700
Corn	10	430	1,700
Rice	−90	690	4,000

Note: Compiled from "Analysis of Coca Industry Generated from Chapare Leaf Production" (1990). [a]Net present value of one year's revenue.

support. The profit projections in table 4.1, for example, include the $2000 offered for voluntary eradication, and assume that the crops can be sold in markets that do not yet exist.

Clearly, efforts to control coca production have been tested in a complicated, hostile environment, and equally clearly they have been implemented on a small scale relative to the size of cocaine production and coca farming. Before reaching conclusions about these policies' effectiveness and appropriateness for the region, it might be instructive to consider some other cases from the annals of eradication and development assistance history. And indeed, there are other cases. The United States has supported a variety of source country intervention programs over the years.[80] Two of the most successful, and two of the most analyzed, programs were implemented in Turkey and Mexico in the early and mid 1970s.

Poppy Production

Heroin is produced, through a multistage refining process, by extracting gum from opium poppies. In many regions of the world, poppies have legitimate uses. The seeds, for example, are used to flavor foods, or pressed to produce oil for cooking, and the stems (called *straw*) can be used as animal feed. During the last three decades, the United States has supported two poppy control programs that met with temporary, but significant, success, and a third, which has achieved more enduring results. The first, operated in Turkey during the early 1970s, led to a substantial reduction in Turkey's share of heroin exports to the United States. Prior to the intervention, Turkey supplied perhaps 80 percent of the United States' heroin; after the intervention, its share dwindled to less than 2 percent.[81] The second important poppy control program was erected in Mexico, approximately a year after the Turkish program. The third program, in Thailand, was implemented over a much longer period stretching back to the 1960s.

In 1971 and 1972, the Turkish government moved to prohibit poppy cultivation in exchange for compensation from the United States. The compensation, which amounted to more than $35 million, offset Turkey's foreign exchange and revenue losses from the decline in poppy cultivation. Restrictions against cultivation for illicit purposes were backed up with regulations under which authorities could destroy the crops of an entire village if even one resident was caught supplying the illegal market.[82] The earnings from legal production combined with the potential penalties associated with illegal production proved sufficient to largely bring illegal Turkish production under control. The October, 1973 elections, however, returned the country to representative government, and also brought about changes in poppy control programs. The new government moved to appease the populace by ending the ban, and by 1975 poppy cultivation had resumed in Turkey's seven major producing provinces. Turkish officials maintained some control policies after 1975, including efforts to direct poppy output to straw processing plants, and efforts to introduce nonopium-bearing poppies into the main cultivation centers.[83]

The duration of the heroin market interregnum created by the Turkish efforts was short-lived, however, because Mexico rapidly replaced Turkey as the leading supplier of heroin to the United States. At approximately the same time that Mexico was emerging as the leading supplier of heroin to the United States, Mexico embarked on its own ambitious eradication program. The eradication program, which began gearing up in 1973, utilized aircraft to locate cultivation regions and ferry eradication crews. Eventually, beginning in 1975 and 1976, the aircraft were used to spray herbicides over poppy production centers. Additionally, the campaign sought to integrate the diverse elements of the program, including Justice Department and Army operations, into a single, coordinated effort. According to reports, Mexican heroin production declined substantially between 1976 and 1980. In the same period, heroin markets saw purity levels decrease, prices increase, and consumption levels decline as a result of the scarcities created by the control program.[84] Other measures, including estimates of heroin-related deaths and emergency room admissions, indicate that heroin was in relatively short supply for this period.[85]

The Thai program, which has met with more enduring success, is an interesting case.[86] In the 1960s, Thailand's poppy farming and heroin production was concentrated in the country's northern regions among the hill tribes. For reasons that had very little to do with heroin production, the hill tribes were vital to the Thai government's efforts to extend political legitimacy over the entire Thai territory. Gaining the loyalty of the hill tribes was important not only because other ethnic tribes had fostered violent separatist movements in adjacent countries, but because Thailand faced a potent Communist insurgency that sought alliances among the disaffected people. National integration, then, was a key component of the Thai program.

Thai drug control programs themselves emphasized both development and poppy control. The development commitment spanned more than twenty years and totaled more than $100 million in the hill tribe regions. Integration efforts resulted in significant achievements, including a regional road network that rival the national Thai network (and that far surpasses Bolivian and Peruvian networks), and establishment of government and nongovernment development organizations in more than half of the northern Thai villages. In addition, the Thai economy experienced sustained, rapid economic growth that provided alternatives to drug production. The growth, which has *averaged* more than 7 percent for thirty years, was not just confined to Thai urban areas; the northern provinces grew at comparable, albeit slightly slower, rates.

Although poppy cultivation declined by 60 to 70 percent between 1965 and 1981, by 1984 Thai poppy cultivation had risen substantially from the post-war low recorded in 1981. The growth in cultivation necessitated implementation of an eradication program. However reluctant the Thai government had been to eradicate, the national integration campaign made the practice possible. In particular, development programs had helped raise incomes in the northern regions to the point where poppies could be eradicated without significantly endangering the populace's livelihood, and thus endangering the government's legitimacy.[87] In recent years Thai poppy cultivation has continued to decline, and it now stands at perhaps one-tenth the level of 1965 and one-quarter the level of 1985.

On the surface, the Thai heroin control program thus appears to be a successful model. Caution should be used when attempting to generalize the results to other situations. Perhaps most importantly, Thailand's success in reducing heroin production must be compared to much larger increases in global heroin production over the past twenty years. The progress made in Thailand has been more than offset by worsening conditions elsewhere. Global poppy cultivation increased from almost 221,000 hectares in 1990 to more than 246,000 in 1994. The increase is more than the total amount cultivated in Thailand during the peaks of the 1960s. Also, while Thailand has succeeded in reducing drug production within its borders, it remains an important trafficking nation. Given Thailand's phenomenal economic growth over the past forty years, and the consequent increases land and labor prices, it is not surprising that Thailand now participates primarily in the higher value-added portions of the heroin trade. In other words, Thai economic growth has given low-wage nations like Burma cost advantages, but the rewards at the latter stages are sufficient to ensure Thai participation. The role of economic growth in displacing the Thai drug trade should not be underestimated. It is also worth noting that Thailand's strategy was implemented over multiple decades, and that it embraced principles such as national integration and political legitimacy that transcended simple counternarcotics objectives. These factors will figure prominently in the final chapter of this book.

Marijuana Control

In the 1970s, Mexico was the leading supplier of marijuana to the United States. Mexican authorities, however, duplicated many of the efforts used against heroin production to attack marijuana production. Authorities created a special counternarcotics force, which reported to the Attorney General, and which also worked in conjunction with the Mexican armed forces. Since the special forces reported directly to the national government and often deliberately had no family ties in the regions where they operated, they could bypass local authorities to significantly reduce the chances that operations would be corrupted or co-opted. Mexican authorities, using U.S.-supplied equipment, sprayed thousands of acres of marijuana with herbicide. Mexican counternarcotics operations significantly reduced Mexican marijuana production between 1976 and 1983, but also, by virtue of the herbicides used, generated precipitous drop in the *demand* for Mexican marijuana. U.S. users rejected marijuana from Mexican sources out of fear that the herbicide's residues posed a heath risk. Colombia replaced Mexico as the primary marijuana supplier to the United States until the early 1980s when memories of the spraying scare faded and a tough maritime interdiction program forced up Colombian marijuana prices.

The success against Mexican marijuana also forced other innovations in the industry. Interestingly, the United States began to supply a sizable portion of its own demand through domestic production. U.S. suppliers, concentrated in Hawaii, California, and Kentucky, now satisfy approximately 30 percent of the U.S. market.[88] Some of the cultivation has moved indoors to greenhouses and other facilities in an effort to evade detection by authorities and provide year-round production. And since marijuana is a bulky product, the producers have devoted efforts to increasing the potency of their product in an attempt to both condense the volume and increase the value relative to weight. By all accounts, this effort has paid off, as marijuana potency has increased substantially over the past decade.

Waging a Successful Campaign

Poppies and marijuana provide interesting, and at times contrasting, lessons about the utility of eradication and development for controlling drug production. At first glance, the success of the 1970's poppy and marijuana programs would appear to validate the notion coca production and exports can be successfully controlled. In the aftermath of the 1970's programs, Turkey ceased to be a major supplier of heroin to the United States. Moreover, despite the fact that Mexican traffickers stepped in to replace Turkish suppliers, the eradication program generated a substantial disruption of U.S. heroin markets, albeit assisted by timely droughts in both the Asian and Mexican producing regions. At the same time, however, there was no comparable disruption of marijuana production. True, the Mexican eradication campaign temporarily shut down Mexican traffickers' ability to supply the U.S. market, but that capacity was almost immediately absorbed by Colombia. Thus, the program was effective at reducing Mexican marijuana production, but not at reducing the supply reaching the United States.

Waging a Successful Campaign

From these divergent experiences, a list of components essential to successful source country control emerges. One critical element is the presence of a strong central government with the authority, and willingness, to act vigorously against drug production in the source countries. Effective execution of an eradication strategy requires control over material and resources and that local leaders respond to national political directives (or at least not work counter to them). Thailand succeeded only after it worked to integrate alienated segments of its population into the political and economic processes. That is, the Thai government found it necessary to cultivate its political legitimacy before it pursued aggressive crop reduction strategies.[89] In contrast, Turkey's poppy reduction program succeeded because the Turkish government applied stringent sanctions against illicit production that were unhindered by "American notions of due process and individual justice."[90] Similarly, the Mexican regime provided a stable political authority and the *Partido Revolucionario Institucional* (PRI), then Mexico's unrivalled and dominant national political party, exerted strong and controlling influence throughout Mexico at that time. No region of Mexico, and no element of the government, including the Army and the Judiciary, was beyond PRI's influence.[91] When Mexican officials decided to strengthen government counternarcotics operations, the Mexican government, through its strong party structure, was able to mobilize the requisite forces. To some extent, these elements can be cultivated, and indeed the United States made the strengthening of source countries' national will to combat drug trafficking an explicit part of the national drug strategy.[92] But cultivating the capacity and willingness to combat drug production is a process which can take years, if not decades, to establish, with no guarantees of long-term success.

Turkish, Mexican, and Thai control policies also succeeded because drug production was a localized problem, contained within small, readily identifiable regions. Mexican and Turkish growers made very little effort to conceal their activities, beyond perhaps choosing relatively remote locations, because farming attracted little law enforcement attention until the early 1970s. The relatively compact nature of Thai production not only allowed government officials to provide alternatives to poppy cultivation, but to provide the infrastructure, such as roads, that integrated the alternative crops with urban markets. In Mexico, both poppies and marijuana were cultivated in unconcealed, albeit relatively inaccessible, fields prior to the implementation of the eradication program. U.S. counternarcotics aid, which included aircraft and helicopters, proved extremely useful because it allowed the Mexican government to abandon slow and inefficient manual eradication programs in favor of aerial spraying. Additionally, aircraft put even the most remote farms within the eradication teams' reach. Shortly after eradication began in earnest, however, poppy farmers began to shift their production to more remote locations, and to use smaller, less easily detected plots of land.[93] By the mid 1970s, Mexican farmers were using plots of land that were a tenth the size of the plots at the decade's beginning. Where once the Mexican drug industry was geographically contained, production now extends throughout much of the country.[94] More recently, poppy cultivation has been detected across the border from Mexico in Guatemala, and has been detected in large quantities in Colombia.

If drugs are a major portion of the local economy or an important part of the social structure, source country control policies may be rendered less potent. Drug production tends to concentrate where all the factors of production—land, labor and capital—are inexpensive. Clearly, in Thailand's case, these factors of production became more expensive by virtue of Thailand's rapid economic growth. In contrast, neighboring countries, such as Burma, offered much lower costs for the factors of production. By developing country standards Mexico and Turkey have relatively high wage structures, and this factor tended to make the two countries less cost-effective at drug production in comparison to other producers. Similarly, Mexico and Turkey have relatively large economies so that when drug production was targeted for control it affected a relatively small portion of the labor pool and national output. Also, at least in the case of Mexico, poppies and marijuana held no special cultural significance. Drug production, as opposed to transshipment, in Mexico did not emerge significantly until the 1940s, when supply routes to the United States from more distant sources were severed by World War II and Mexican traffickers began to capitalize on their proximity to the United States.[95] Thus, marijuana and poppy cultivation in Mexico has hardly attained the cultural and social significance of coca cultivation in the Andes.

Finally, and critically, production can be disrupted only for as long as there is no alternate supplier or source country. Mexico's marijuana control program had little effect on supply because Colombia was able to satisfy the U.S. market within a matter of a few months. In contrast, the Turkish and Mexican poppy control programs together disrupted production in the two nations best suited to supply the United States. A number of other nations produce and supply heroin, and certainly the drug was plentiful throughout the rest of the world at the time it was scarce in the United States. Why, then, did no other producer step in to replace the lost Turkish and Mexican production? One possible explanation is that since the Turkish and Mexican crackdowns were virtually coincident with the U.S. withdrawal from Vietnam, in reality three major heroin markets were more or less simultaneously disrupted during the early and mid 1970s. As thousands of U.S. soldiers returned home and, more generally, U.S. presence is Southeast Asia was reduced, trafficking and distribution networks from Southeast Asia dried up. The lack of a ready substitute for Turkish and Mexican suppliers may reflect the difficulty traffickers had in developing trafficking routes because of the perceived small size of U.S. heroin markets, heightened suspicions and tensions in the U.S. with Southeast Asians, and a population core of Southeast Asians that was insufficient to base familial trafficking networks on until well into the 1980s.[96] Another possibility is that regional droughts in both Asia and Mexico prevented new suppliers from quickly establishing large market shares.

Unfortunately, almost none of the conditions that contributed to success in Turkey and Mexico exist in Bolivia and Peru. The lack of these factors, combined with the inherent limits to source country control policies and the resilient structure of the cocaine trade, severely limit the potential for eradication and development assistance to affect coca production in Bolivia and Peru. At a minimum, the scale of existing source country control policies is too small to compensate for weak government control over coca regions, dispersed production, importance of coca to the local economies and communities, and the plethora of coca farmers and suppliers currently available. However, as the subsequent sections will reveal, increasing the scale of source country intervention can only partially compensate for the missing factors, and will potentially bring about consequences that may, in some ways, be more troublesome than unregulated coca production.

Government Authority in Bolivia and Peru

The Bolivian and Peruvian governments exert very weak control over the drug producing portions of their countries. Their weakness is a function of a myriad of factors, not all of which are common to the two countries. Peru's coca reduction operations are primarily limited by the need to address more pressing national problems, most notably the ongoing guerrilla campaign conducted by the *Shining Path*. Bolivia's inability to exert control over its coca farmers is founded, perhaps, in a more complex set of conditions, but one that includes the Bolivian government's grave reluctance to provoke its currently quiescent coca farmers.

Peru confronts an ongoing guerrilla war that has, at times, threatened the government's existence. For most of the last decade, Peru has been in danger succumbing the radical-terrorist *Shining Path* guerrilla group. The conflict has been particularly deadly in rural portions of the country, as the *Shining Path* and the Peruvian army have waged a battle for control of territory and for the loyalty of peasants. Much of the territory being fought over is in the heart of Peru's drug producing regions. As a result, the *Shining Path* has been able to portray government efforts to control coca farming as a threat to the farmers' livelihoods, and to parlay this characterization into a strong base of farming support in certain segments of the country. *Sendero* fortifies its hold over the peasants by ruthless tactics intended to intimidate the farmers into supporting the rebels, including grisly murders and the subsequent public display of the victims' bodies.[97] There are also frequent reports that *Sendero* guerrillas charge the traffickers landing fees at airstrips controlled and protected by the *Shining Path*, and the guerrillas have worked to stabilize farmers' profits by setting a minimum price for coca.[98] The exact nature of the narco-guerrilla cooperation, and the revenue the *Shining Path* derives from it, is not entirely clear. The reports, however, are persistent, and even if the guerrillas manage to tax only a small portion of Peru's drug trade, their actions may still generate a substantial amount of revenue.[99]

The Peruvian government has given high priority to halting the *Shining Path*'s advance, a cause that was given a strong boost with the September, 1992 capture of the organization's charismatic leader, Abimael Guzman. Nevertheless, Peru's campaign against the *Sendero* continues to consume scarce resources and continues to be the government's main priority. One consequence of this effort is that police and counternarcotics units are often confined to their barracks not only out of fear of *Shining Path* ambushes, but also because coordination with, and the protection offered by, army troops is so poor.[100] Government authority in Peru is also undermined by frequent reports of military and police human rights abuses committed against the rural population, ostensibly in the name of controlling the guerrilla conflict.

Problems of a different sort have emerged in Bolivia. Bolivia's political history has been marked by a revolutionary alliance of miners, peasants, and students poised against military strongmen, all of whom have periodically sought to overthrow or influence the government.[101] Colonel Hugo Banzer, who assumed control after a coup in 1971 and ruled Bolivia until 1978, ushered in Bolivia's cocaine era. His administration turned a blind eye to the military's complicity in drug trafficking and brutally suppressed leftist activity by closing universities, abolishing unions, crushing strikes, and massacring protesting peasants.[102] The backlash to Banzer's rule propelled Bolivia down the path of democracy, a journey that was derailed on a number of occasions, including the July, 1980 coup by General Luis Garcia Meza. The Garcia Meza regime lasted all of a year, but elevated government complicity in drug trafficking to the highest levels.[103] The deposed Meza made another lunge for power in 1982 but, after a tortuous period that brought the country close to civil war, civilian, and ultimately democratic, rule was restored with the installation of Hernan Siles Zuazo as President.

Because of Bolivia's fractured political history, democratic institutions in Bolivia are weak. One consequence of this weakness is that the government remains reluctant to provoke potentially radical social elements. The strength of Bolivian unions, including peasant farmer unions and coca growers' unions, has placed Bolivia's coca farming population squarely in the camp that the government wants to appease. Bolivian farmers play on the government's weakness by cloaking their objections to eradication in arguments about coca's value as a cultural icon, this despite the fact that Bolivian farmers produce many times more coca than for which there is legitimate use or demand. For example, *Ley 1008*, a law passed by the Bolivian government, was supposed to mark the beginning of unprecedented U.S.-Bolivian cooperation and the death knell of farming in the Chapare by providing farmers generous amounts of time to transition out of coca farming, a shift that was encouraged by both compensation for voluntary eradication and sanctions against those caught violating the program's rules.[104] Bolivian officials have struggled to meet the phase out goals, in large part because the farmers have intimidated the government with threats of force and organized violence. Farmers have protested *Ley 1008* vigorously on many occasions, and the tense atmosphere kept Bolivian authorities from regulating and shutting down coca markets and forcibly eradicating coca fields found with paste processing pits until very recently.

Unfortunately, the lack of governmental control, even without the threat of political unrest, diminishes the prospects for successful eradication and development assistance in Bolivia and Peru. Even if eradication and development can be increased to a scale sufficient to disrupt the coca farming, both the Peruvian and Bolivian governments have credibility problems. Neither government, nor the United States for that matter, has earned a reputation for following through on commitments to farmers. In Bolivia, for example, many of the farmers who turned over their coca crops took out loans to begin production of other crops. The promised markets for the alternative crops, however, have failed to materialize, and training and extension services to prepare the farmers for the new crops have been scarce, putting many of the farmers at risk of defaulting on their loans and returning to coca. Other planned improvements, including local development projects tied to the attainment of voluntary eradication goals, have not been forthcoming, leaving many farmers to conclude that they eradicated their acreage in vain. Similar problems exist in Peru, where development projects have been further hampered by the violent climate.

In short, forced eradication will almost certainly provoke violence among the farmers and could serve as the catalyst for increasing the farmers' affinity to nongovernmental organizations such as the Shining Path in Peru and coca unions in Bolivia.[105] Voluntary eradication, because it provides the farmers with compensation, is much less likely to incite violence, but it is also much less likely to be effective than forced eradication.[106] While the eradication program itself may or may not be temporary, there is no guarantee that the political consequences of the intervention would die out. Indeed, it is possible that the policy would set in motion a response that is not easily reversed.

Extent of Cultivation in Bolivia and Peru

The rugged terrain in Peru and Bolivia has worked to limit the government's presence and influence in rural regions, but it has done relatively little to check the spread of coca farming. Although data for the eradication programs of the early 1970s are scarce, it appears that Mexico's and Turkey's cultivation centers were confined to under 10,000 hectares. In contrast, coca cultivation certainly exceeds 200,000 hectares, and may occupy more than 300,000 hectares in the Bolivia, Colombia, and Peru.[107]

Cultivation regions remain relatively concentrated in Bolivia, but coca farming in Peru is widespread, affecting central Peru from the northern to the southern ends of the country. To date, most farmers have not taken many steps to conceal their coca farming because farming in Bolivia and Peru is largely conducted without fear of sanctions. However, the scale of coca farming in Bolivia and Peru makes the prospect of forced eradication a much different prospect than it was in Mexico.

Such an eradication operation would almost certainly require strong U.S. support and presence, and probably could not be accomplished without the use of herbicides. The alternative to a chemical campaign would be to move in large numbers of men and equipment, with correspondingly large risks of physical harm to the eradication teams. Hence, the first hurdle to a large eradication campaign in Bolivia and Peru would be deciding on appropriate levels and avenues of U.S. involvement. Certainly, U.S. military forces would balk at a support role in eradication operations on a number of grounds, including reluctance to cooperate with Peru's military because of its human rights violations, the security threat posed by the *Shining Path*, and the U.S. military's general reluctance to press for direct responsibility in counternarcotics operations. The host nations would probably similarly object to the "militarization" of the drug strategy that a large U.S. presence would indicate. Some evidence for the perils of a visible and large U.S. presence can be seen in *Operation Blast Furnace*, a high-profile 1986 effort to disrupt coca-cocaine trafficker transactions in the Chapare.[108] *Operation Blast Furnace* succeeded in temporarily disrupting cocaine trafficking in the Chapare, but at a cost of steeling the farmers' resolve to oppose such intervention and heightening suspicions about U.S. intervention intentions.

One key aspect of the Mexican program was the creation of an elite counternarcotics unit specifically deployed to conduct surprise, coordinated operations, and operated to minimize the potential for corruption. The chances of maintaining secrecy and preserving operation security in Peru and Bolivia are probably very remote, if for no other reason than the sheer size of the coca farming industry and the number of people employed in it. Certainly, most coca cultivation takes place in a relatively compact area, but by any absolute measure of size, the coca cultivation regions present important logistical obstacles. The Upper Huallaga Valley in Peru is roughly 9,000 square miles, the Chapare in Bolivia is roughly 20,000 square miles and both embrace terrain that can be extreme. These growing regions are isolated from populated portions of the country, so that large eradication and development assistance crews would have to be moved in. This would complicate eradication because the teams would stand out as unwelcome outsiders. Moreover, the task of preventing corruption becomes geometrically more complicated the more personnel that are involved. Counternarcotics patrols, eradication crews, and development teams would have to live in relatively primitive conditions, factors which probably increase their susceptibility to corruption. Finally, cooperation of the type demonstrated between Mexican governmental agencies during its 1970s eradication campaign does not exist in Peru, and probably does not exist in Bolivia. In Peru, the military, the police and eradication teams have often have antagonistic relations because of conflicting objectives and a lack of resources.

The potential effects of a large-scale eradication campaign in Bolivia and Peru are distressing even if the potential health and economic effects of eradication are ignored.[109] By itself, a large eradication program would probably kill the vegetation throughout large areas of jungle territory. Even if the herbicides selectively killed only coca plants, a minimum of several hundred thousand additional hectares of land would be deforested, but if the chemicals in fact affect all forms of vegetation, much larger areas could be denuded. Eradication-induced deforestation would eliminate natural barriers that prevent the region's heavy rains from washing away the topsoil, a problem that is particularly acute in zones where coca is grown on mountainsides, steeply sloped and terraced plots. Peru recorded heavy flooding in 1987 flooding in some of its deforested regions that was at least partially attributable to expanded coca farming.[110]

Additionally, as the Peruvian coca trade's mobility in response to the fungus outbreak has demonstrated, eradication would simply displace much of the existing coca trade to other regions where the law enforcement pressure was less intense. But as this displacement occurred, problems with deforestation would almost certainly intensify. Currently, coca cultivation is estimated to account for 10 percent of the deforestation that occurs in the Andes. Farming-induced deforestation begins when farmers clear their future cultivation sites by burning off the existing vegetation. Not only do these fires occasionally get out of control and deforest more acreage than intended, but they would also subject the new cultivation areas to the same erosion and flooding problems.

Coca's Significance in Bolivia and Peru

Coca has accumulated economic and cultural significance that poppies and marijuana never achieved in Mexico and that, arguably, poppies never achieved in Turkey.[111] Mexico and Turkey are relatively large economies, and thus drug trafficking in the mid-1970s never made more than a marginal contribution to their economic activity. Similarly, marijuana and poppies have had a negligible role in Mexican cultural and social settings. Indeed, very little marijuana and poppy production even took place in Mexico until after World War II. Poppies have a role that stretches back thousands of years into Turkey's history, including use as a fuel source, food flavorant, and animal feed. Additionally, of course, they have been a source of opium and heroin. Unlike the coca plant in the Andes, however, at least some of the poppy's functions can be fulfilled by using nonopium-bearing types of the flower.

In contrast, coca remains a cultural and economic icon in Bolivia and Peru. Coca remedies and coca products are openly sold in Bolivia, and the Andean farming and mining communities continue to use coca in a variety of capacities. Miners, for example, frequently chew coca for the energy boost it delivers and to relieve fatigue and hunger.[112] Coca has also become one of the region's most important agricultural commodities, supplanting most other commercial crops in acreage, income, or both. Incomes are extremely low in Peru and Bolivia, on the order of $800 per year so that coca farming, which can provide income of around $2000, is obviously an attractive alternative.[113] In Bolivia, more than 13 percent of the eligible labor force may be directly employed in the cocaine business; in Peru, more than 4 percent is so employed.[114] The successful destruction of the cocaine trade through a large eradication program would therefore eliminate a significant portion of the coca regions' jobs and incomes.

In theory, coca farmers could be compensated for the loss of their income through development assistance.[115] Indeed, the purpose of development assistance is to provide farmers with alternatives that are as economically rewarding as coca farming itself. Turning to economic theory for a minute, what would happen when the cocaine trade was eliminated, and how would development assistance compensate for the loss? Destroying the cocaine trade would force all of the farmers who formerly worked in coca to find other jobs, or be unemployed. However, as more labor clamored for the remaining available jobs in the region, wages would fall. Unemployed workers, unable to find jobs, would offer to work at a lower wage than the remaining workers. In general, wages would fall by a percentage equal to cocaine's share of regional GDP. Since incomes in the region are already so low, this kind of decline in regional income could be devastating, and would probably provoke a revolt from the affected populations. Policymakers would want to try to provide enough development assistance so that the farmers and the remaining workers would at least be as well off after eradication as they were before it. It turns out that only about $5 billion in development assistance would be required to open enough factories and farms to absorb the cocaine industry's labor supply and keep wages and incomes from falling.[116]

Unfortunately, however, the above scenario is not the end of the story. It is a snapshot, or a static picture, of an adjustment process that would occur after eradication. Once the eradication process was complete, cocaine would presumably be very scarce in the United States.[117] Cocaine prices would rise substantially, providing any trafficker that could supply the market with windfall profits. The lure of the profits would send the traffickers scrambling for ways to get more cocaine to the markets. Of course, they would need the farmers to plant more coca in order to produce and market more cocaine. But if all the farmers who lost their crops to eradication had been hired by newly opened farms and factories, where would the traffickers find farmers to grow their coca? The answer is that the traffickers would lure them away from the enterprises built with development assistance funds by offering them a slightly higher wage than they were earning on their new jobs and therefore at a higher wage than they were earning from coca farming before eradication. In other words, some of the windfall from higher cocaine prices would pass down to the farmers. Authorities could offer to provide more development assistance in order to keep ahead of the wages offered by the traffickers, but the traffickers could always outbid the government because coca farming wages are such a trivial share of retail cocaine prices, and because development assistance can elevate wages only over long periods of time.[118] Even if the traffickers had to offer farmers ten or fifteen times as much to grow coca, street prices would not be drastically affected.

The discussion of development assistance also helps explain why voluntary eradication does not work. As farmers voluntarily turn their acreage over for compensation, a correspondingly smaller amount of coca is produced. But nothing has happened to change the demand for cocaine, so as less coca is farmed, coca prices rise, ensuring that enough is produced to meet cocaine demand. The rise in coca prices increases the income that farmers can get from coca farming. Eventually, the price will rise above the price offered for voluntary eradication, and at that point farmers will stop turning their acreage over for compensation.[119] In fact, a voluntary eradication program may encourage farmers to keep more acreage under cultivation than they otherwise would so that they can turn over a portion of their stock in times of weak prices and still earn an income, but also retain a fraction for when prices rebound.

Alternate Suppliers of Coca

The problem with coca production in Bolivia and Peru is not so much the ready availability of alternate suppliers as it is the inability to control the existing production territory. Combined, Bolivia and Peru cover more than 900,000 square miles of territory, an area roughly one-quarter the size of the entire United States. Of this vast territory, coca farming occupies approximately 200,000 hectares, or less than 900 square miles. As if this statistic were not discouraging enough, ONERN, Peru's National Office of Natural Resource Evaluation, estimates that perhaps 20 million hectares (or 80,000 square miles) of the medium and high forests in Peru alone could support coca production.[120] It seems reasonable to assume that a similar amount of land is suitable for cultivation in Bolivia. If the estimates are correct, and if the assumption holds, coca is currently being cultivated on less than 1 percent of the land where it could be grown in Bolivia and Peru. In order to prevent regrowth in the recently eradicated regions (the Upper Huallaga Valley and the Chapare), authorities would need to develop a strategy for holding the eradicated territory.[121] Such a strategy would undoubtedly require the stationing of troops and equipment. The potential land use estimates, however, highlight the impracticality of preventing coca farming from resurfacing in other portions of the country where operating conditions are more extreme or less amenable to observation and intervention. To prevent the dispersal of coca farming, authorities would literally need to cordon off most of the region's territory, a task that is clearly beyond present means.

Even if coca is somehow almost fully eradicated from Bolivia and Peru, and even if all of the territory suitable for cultivation in Bolivia and Peru can somehow be controlled to prevent coca farming from re-emerging, Colombia, Venezuela, Brazil, and Ecuador stand ready as potential alternate suppliers. Colombia currently produces enough coca to make about 20 percent of the world's cocaine, and Venezuela, Brazil, and Ecuador produce tiny amounts of coca.[122] But there is little to prevent coca farming from expanding in these areas if land becomes unavailable in Bolivia and Peru. Certainly, none of these countries are optimal choices for coca farming. The types of coca that grow in them, for example, are of lesser quality. Additionally, there would be the added expense of establishing and maintaining trafficking routes, factors that would add unknown amounts to the costs of coca farming. However, as we have seen, coca prices can increase by vast amounts and still have relatively minor effects on drug prices and drug use in consuming markets. In effect, nothing short of a comprehensive regional policy will do much to contain the coca trade.

Clearly, the prospects for globally containing the coca trade on a long-term basis are dim. But what of the short-term prospects? Surely, a large eradication program would disrupt production. As mentioned previously, it takes farmers approximately two years to locate a plot of land, clear it, establish their coca fields, and get full harvests from them. This delay between the implementation of a counternarcotics policy, in this case eradication, and the cocaine industry's ability to respond is the key to determining how effective the policy intervention will be. The longer the lag, or delay in response, the more drug production will be curtailed. It turns out that coca farming is subject to the longest lags in drug production precisely because of the time it takes farmers to start cultivation from scratch.

There are, in fact, a number of ways that the farmers and traffickers could reduce the impact of a large eradication program by reducing their response time. Some of the impact, for example, could be mitigated by simply processing the portions of the crop that were not eradicated more efficiently. Basically, this is another way of saying that there is slack in the production process, and that by harvesting the remaining plots more carefully, extracting more of the alkaloids during processing, and other conservation techniques, an unknown, but perhaps not insignificant portion of eradication's impact could be ameliorated.[123] By some estimates, refiners may lose as much as one-third of their output to sloppy refining techniques.

Another easy way for farmers and traffickers to avoid disruption from eradication is to carry inventory. Farmers can put extra plots of land under cultivation prior to eradication, perhaps in areas relatively removed from the current farming areas, but not harvest them unless something drastic (such as eradication) happens to their crop. More likely, however, is that the traffickers would hold inventory of refined cocaine that they could use to meet demand in the event that coca farming were ever disrupted. Of course, carrying inventory entails risks. Inventory may spoil, be stolen, trigger a raid, or entail some other such cost. However, the risks and costs of carrying inventory are likely to be extremely low in the source countries, where there is little risk of prosecution, where the value of the product is low relative to the street price, and where there are vast amounts of territory in which the inventory can be concealed. The limited available evidence suggests that traffickers may in fact hold inventories as a hedge against law enforcement operations. Raids in the Bolivian jungle, for example, turned up numerous drums of cocaine suspended in solution. This liquid cocaine, called *aguarica* ("rich water") apparently allowed the cocaine to be stored indefinitely in the jungle humidity without spoiling. Similarly, raids in the United States have turned up multiple ton caches of cocaine that appear to exceed the retailing network"s dealing capacity, leading to the conclusion that perhaps they were inventory sites. Finally, there are strong rumors in Peru and Bolivia, which have been published in local papers, that the traffickers have stored a twenty-year supply of cocaine. While such an inventory does not make logical sense, it does point to the fact that the traffickers have likely considered, or at least heard about, the concept of holding inventory.

Summary

A paradox of sorts exists with respect to eradication and development assistance. On the one hand, eradication and development assistance are currently not implemented on scales that will meaningfully affect coca farming, but if they are implemented to the extent that farming is significantly disrupted, they may well yield costs in the form of political violence, environmental degradation, and dispersal of the trade that are not acceptable. Moreover, there is virtually no chance that eradication and development assistance will permanently curtail coca production. Eradication would be implemented only at the very great risk of provoking a violent backlash from the coca farming populations. The central governments of the coca-producing nations are very reluctant to provoke this response, and may not be strong enough to control it. Their reluctance to implement large eradication and development assistance programs is complicated by the fact that coca farming covers vast amounts of territory. Eliminating coca production, and preventing its reestablishment in other regions, is a monumental task, one that is clearly larger than any other source country intervention contemplated or implemented in the past. Coca has established a large and important role in the local economies and social structures, so that even if it were somehow successfully eliminated, its importance, combined with the drug industry's price structure, ensures that production would begin again. Finally, there are numerous potential alternate suppliers and mitigating steps that coca farmers and traffickers can take to lessen the impact of eradication and development assistance.

Notes

1. Colombian farmers now grow approximately 20 percent of the coca used to make cocaine. However, Colombia is not a very efficient producer of coca because Colombian coca leaf is of lower quality. Quality considerations are apparently increasingly being offset by the Colombian producers' proximity to end-stage refineries.
2. Klein (1985), 53.
3. Allen (1985), Murra (1985), and Klein (1985).
4. One reason coca fields remain so visible is because the risks of coca farming have typically been very low. Even though some coca fields have been destroyed, law enforcement sanctions have generally not been applied against the farmers. They lose their crops, but are not punished for coca farming. Should that situation ever change, and should coca farmers begin to face legal sanctions for coca farming, it is probable that farmers will begin to make greater efforts to conceal their coca plots.
5. Reuter (1985), 83–90.
6. Healy (1985); Riley (1993).
7. Ehrenfeld (1992); McCormick (1992) and (1993); Palmer (1992); Riley (1993).
8. Alvarez (1992)
9. See "Cultivos de Coca: Produccion, Comercializacion y Desarrollo Alternativo en el Subtropico de Cochabamba," Narcotics Affairs Section (Bolivia: U.S. Embassy, March 1992); Adolfo Figueroa and Farid Matuk, "Fuerza Laboral y Mercade de Trabajo en el Valle del Alto Huallaga," Report prepared for USAID (December 1989); and *Final Report on the Evaluation of AID Project No. 527-0244, Development of the Alto Huallaga Area* (Lima: Econosult, 1987).
10. Garland (1987); Dourojeanni (1990).
11. Hargreaves (1992); and Malamud-Goti (1992).
12. Hargreaves (1992); and Malamud-Goti (1992).

13. Dourojeanni (1990).
14. *Coca Cultivation and Cocaine Processing: An Overview* (1991), 12–13 reports on insects that damage coca plants. All can be controlled through the use of pesticides.
15. Ibid., 65.
16. Antognini (1990), 65.
17. The leaves, however, can be ruined by moisture. According to *Coca Cultivation and Cocaine Processing: An Overview* (1991), 3, if the leaves are left out in the rain after harvest, the accumulation of moisture will lead to the breakdown of the cocaine alkaloids.
18. "Highlands" refers to areas in the lower hills and high valleys of the Andes. "Lowlands" refers to the broad jungle plains and foothills beyond the mountains.
19. For a discussion of risk aversion and diversification see: Browman (1987); *Andean Peasant Economics and Pastoralism* (undated); Michael Chibnik (1988); Rhoades and Bidegaray (1987).
20. To be sure, the rise in coca cultivation also reflects other factors, including land quality that was poorer than anticipated at the time when settlement was being encouraged, the vast migration of unskilled agricultural labor to coca farming from depressed mining, natural resource industries and urban areas, and persistent production problems with other crops. The particulars of coca production in the Chapare and the Upper Huallaga Valley are discussed in subsequent sections.
21. Coca is manufactured into many legal products, such as tea, toothpaste, and altitude-sickness remedies, in Bolivia.
22. The Iquitos and Andoas radar facilities were dismantled in June, 1992. The Yurimaguas facility is still in operation.
23. *Coca Cultivation and Cocaine Processing: An Overview* (1991). See also, *JPRS Narcotics Report* (5 January 1993): 8–9, for transcription of a report from a Peruvian newspaper.
24. Rosenquist (1994).
25. *Peru: Compendio Estadistico, 1988* (1989).
26. Alberts, 233–47.
27. Alvarez (1992), 4.
28. Stocks (1987).
29. Huallaga Valley Agribusiness.
30. Ibid., 697.
31. Garland (1987), 310. Marginal lands are lands that, because of poor soil quality, drainage, and so forth, will not support most commercial crops. There is some disagreement over what portion of the valley lands are marginal. A 1964 ONERN (Nation Office for the Study of Natural Resources) study conducted during Fernando Belaunde's tenure found only 11 percent of the land to be marginal, but a 1983 ONERN study reported a much higher rate of marginality.
32. The poorer the quality of the land, the longer it must remain fallow to regain productive capacity. Fallow periods of seven years and more are suggested for the region.
33. Klein (1985); Healy (1985); Morales (1992).
34. See Heath, et al. (1969) for a complete analysis of the land tenure reform, its objectives, and its impact.
35. Healy (1985), 102

36. DESFIL (1987). Using a variety of estimation techniques, this report gives population estimates ranging from 197,000 to 274,000 people. Other sources, including USAID (1991), point to a figure of slightly over 200,000.
37. Healy (1985), 102.
38. *Cultivos de Coca* (1992), 3.
39. Alvarez (1992), 7.
40. Ibid., 4.
41. Ardila (1990), 7. Study conducted by CIDRE, Center for Research and Regional Development.
42. Plowman (1985).
43. Lee (1989).
44. For a comprehensive look at the Shining Path, its history, strategy, and objectives, see McCormick (1990 and 1992).
45. One of the more famous examples involved the Peasant Coca Farmers Union closing off a main road from La Paz to Santa Cruz for several days. See Bagley (1985).
46. Brooke (1995).
47. See *Cocaine Production, Eradication, and the Environment: Policy, Impact and Options,* Committee on Governmental Affairs, United States Senate, (Washington, D.C.: USGPO, August, 1990), especially pages 20–23.
48. Glyphosate sells under the brand name Round Up. Tebuthiuron sells under the brand name Spike, and is manufactured by Dow Elanco. Hexazinone is known as Pronone and is made by E. I. Du Pont de Nemours and Company. All three herbicides are already in commercial use worldwide.
49. *Cocaine Production, Eradication and the Environment: Policy, Impact and Options* (1990) examines this issue in more detail.
50. Craig (1985), 109.
51. Ibid., 105.
52. *The Drug War: U.S. Programs in Peru Face Serious Obstacles* (1991).
53. *Drug Control: U.S.-Supported Efforts in Colombia and Bolivia* (1988).
54. The Yungas is the major traditional zone.
55. *Ley 1008* (1988), articles 9–11, pages 4–5.
56. Of this, $1650 is in cash, $350 in labor.
57. The unions were created at the time of the 1952 land reform to address local community needs. Healy (1991), 88.
58. Sindicatos function at the community level. They are aggregated into *centrales* above the community level, and into *federaciones* at the national level. Two *federaciones* control approximately 85 percent of the *sindicatos* in the Chapare. Healy (1991), 88–89.
59. Personal communication, DIRECO official in Villa Tunari.
60. See Kennedy, Reuter, and Riley (1993) and (1994) for concise summaries.
61. *A Midterm Review* (1990), 22–24.
62. Clawson (1994).
63. *USAID/Bolivia Alternative Development Strategy* (1991), 9–10.
64. *USAID/Bolivia Program Objectives and Action Plan (1993-1997)* (1992).
65. Ibid.
66. *Final Report on the Evaluation of AID Project No. 527-0244, Development of the Alto Huallaga Area* (1987).
67. Ibid., 3.

68. Palmer (1992).
69. *Huallaga Valley Agribusiness and Marketing Study* (1985).
70. *INCSR* (1994), 15.
71. Estimates vary widely, but other sources report that coca cultivation may cover more than 300,000 hectares. See Clawson (1992) and Laity (undated memorandum by P. Laity, U.S. Embassy, Peru discussing crpp estimation) for other estimates.
72. In some cases, the increases in cultivation may be because of drug-control efforts. See Riley (1993) for an explanation.
73. *INCSR* (various years). Colombian farmers cultivate nearly as much land as Bolivian farmers, but their efforts yield much less cocaine. Figures from years prior to 1988 were drawn from a variety of sources.
74. STRIDE data, for example, show that retail cocaine prices have declined sharply from the levels of the early 1980s. Counterdrug operations in 1989 and 1990 prompted a noticeable increase in retail cocaine prices, but that increase has since evaporated. Similarly, data from the Monitoring the Future interview indicate that in recent years students have found drugs, including cocaine, fairly easy to obtain and have not encountered systematic shortages.
75. *Accuracy and Trends in Bolivian Coca Prices* (1991).
76. Malamud-Goti (1992), 15.
77. Spedding, 5.
78. Clawson (1994).
79. For example, the profit estimates for other crops include the $2000 bonus offered to someone who voluntarily eradicates his coca fields.
80. Falco (1992) provides an overview of U.S. foreign drug-control efforts.
81. *Heroin Situation Assessment* (1992).
82. Reuter (1985), 90.
83. Spain (1975).
84. Reuter (1985), 90.
85. *Heroin Situation Assessment* (1992). Reuter (1984) reports on the problems of determining the number of heroin addicts. See also Reuter (1993).
86. Lee (1994) discusses the Thai case in detail.
87. Ibid.
88. Kleiman (1989), 71–73, reports on the growth in and organization of domestic marijuana production.
89. Lee (1994).
90. Reuter (1985), 90.
91. Lupsha (1981).
92. *National Drug Control Strategy: Progress in the War on Drugs* (1993); *National Drug Control Strategy: A Nation Responds to Drug Use* (1992); *National Drug Control Strategy* (1991).
93. See Nadelmann (1985), Reuter (1992), and Reuter and Ronfeldt (1992) for a discussion of Mexican farmers' adaptive techniques.
94. *Drug Control: U.S.-Mexican Opium Poppy and Marijuana Aerial Eradication Program* (1988).
95. Lupsha (1981).
96. The Asian-American population in the United States more than tripled between 1970 and 1985, with much of the increase coming from immigration [*Report on Asian Organized Crime* (1988)].
97. McCormick (1990) and (1992).

98. Claudio and Stewman (1992); Ehrenfeld (1990).
99. Clawson (1992) reports that the *Shining Path* may receive more than $20 million a year from the drug business.
100. Ehrenfeld (1990).
101. Malloy (1979) offers some insights into Bolivian governmental authority. See also Morales (1992).
102. Hudson and Hanratty (1991).
103. Hargreaves (1992) provides a compelling account of the Meza regime.
104. *Ley 1008* (1987).
105. Healy (1991 and 1988), McCormick (1992 and 1990), Palmer (1992), and Riley (1993).
106. Riley (1993).
107. The chairman of the Peruvian Senate's Special Standing Committee on the Drug Traffic reports more than 350,000 hectares under cultivation in Peru alone (JPRS-TDD-92-014-L, Senator Comments on Crop Substitution Program, March 31, 1992). This appears to be an exaggeration.
108. Hargreaves (1992) provides a summary of this program. See also Mensel (1989).
109. See earlier portions of this chapter for a discussion of chemical eradication's potential effects.
110. Clawson (1992), 13.
111. Spain (1975) summarizes the poppy's role in Turkey. Lupsha (1981) reports on marijuana, poppies, and drug trafficking's significance to Mexico.
112. It is typically chewed with a pinch of lime, or some other reagent, to release the cocaine alkaloids from the leaves.
113. Kennedy, Reuter, and Riley (1994).
114. Ibid.
115. Higher-level traffickers would presumably lose their incomes as well. They also could be provided with development assistance in an effort to keep them from reorganizing the cocaine trade, although it is unlikely that the governments would be inclined to provide them with assistance.
116. Kennedy, Reuter, and Riley (1994).
117. Presumably is used because the traffickers may in fact keep an inventory on hand that would allow them to absorb the impact of eradication by selling off the inventory.
118. Or, the traffickers could simply take another tack and destroy the factories and farms built with development assistance to eliminate the need to offer higher wages.
119. Some devious farmers may turn over stock that they were about to retire anyway, and thereby receive compensation for acreage that was at the end of its productive life. Even experienced botanists have difficulty determining the age of coca plants once they have reached about four years of age and acquired a characteristic moss at the base.
120. JPRS-TDD-92-038-L (15 September, 1992). Effects of coca, poppy cultivation explained.
121. As Ehrenfeld (1992) points out, holding liberated (or eradicated) territory does not appear to be an explicit consideration of eradication programs.
122. For 1994 *INCSR* raised its estimate of Colombia's share from approximately 10 percent to 20 percent.
123. *INCSR* (1994) touches on some of the uncertainties in estimating harvests and yields. *Coca Cultivation and Cocaine Processing: An Overview* (1991) notes where there is some slack in the production process.

References

Accuracy and Trends in Bolivian Coca Prices (La Paz, Bolivia: U.S. Embassy, February 1991).

Alberts, Tom, *Agrarian Reform and Rural Poverty: A Case Study of Peru* (Boulder, Colo.: Westview Press, 1983).

Allen, Catherine J., "Coca and Cultural Identity," *Cultural Survival Report #23: Coca and Cocaine*, Deborah Pacini and Christine Franquemont, eds. (Ithaca, N.Y.: Latin American Studies Program, 1985).

Alvarez, Elena, "Opportunities and Constraints to Reduce Coca Production: The Macroeconomic Context in Bolivia and Peru," paper prepared for the Office of Technology Assessment, Food and Renewable Resources Program, Project: "Agricultural Alternatives to Coca Production," 1992.

"Analysis of Coca Industry Generated from Chapare Leaf Production" (Bolivia: U.S. Embassy, February 1990).

Andean Peasant Economics and Pastoralism, Department of Rural Sociology, University of Missouri, Columbia.

Antognini, Joseph, "The Agronomics of Coca (Erythroxylum Species)," in *Cocaine Production, Eradication, and the Environment: Policy, Impact, and Options* (Washington, D.C.: Committee on Governmental Affairs, United States Senate, August 1990).

Ardila, Patricia, "Beyond Law Enforcement: Narcotics and Development" (The Panos Institute, February 1990).

Bagley, Bruce, "Myths of Militarization: Enlisting Armed Forces in the War on Drugs," in Peter H. Smith, ed., *Drug Policy in the Americas* (Boulder, Colo.: Westview Press, 1992).

Brooke, James, "U.S. Copters are a Target in Colombia," *New York Times* (27 March 1995).

Browman, David L., "Agro-Pastoral Risk Management in the Central Andes," *Research in Economic Anthropology* 8 (1987): 171–200.

Bruun, Kettil, Lynn Pan, and Ingemar Rexed, *The Gentlemen's Club: International Control of Drugs and Alcohol* (Chicago, Ill.: University of Chicago Press, 1975).

Chibnik, Michael, "Double-Edged Risks and Uncertainties: Choices about Rice and Loans in the Peruvian Amazon," in Elizabeth Cashdan, ed., *Risk and Uncertainty in Tribal and Peasant Economies* (Boulder, Colo.: Westview Press, 1988).

Claudio, Arnaldo, and Stephan K. Stewman, "Peru, *Sendero Luminoso*, and the Carcotrafficking Alliance," *Low Intensity Conflict and Law Enforcement* 1, 3 (Winter 1992): 279–92.

Clawson, Patrick, "How Profitable for Farmers is Cultivation of Coca Leaves?" in *Conference Report: Economics of the Narcotics Industry* (Washington, D.C.: Bureau of Intelligence and Research, U.S. Department of State and the Central Intelligence Agency, 1994).

Coca Cultivation and Cocaine Processing: An Overview, (Washington, D.C.: Drug Enforcement Administration, 1991).

Cocaine Production, Eradication, and the Environment: Policy, Impact, and Options, Committee on Governmental Affairs, United States Senate (Washington, D.C.: USGPO, 1990).

Cooper, Donald A., "Clandestine Production Processes for Cocaine and Heroin," in *Clandestinely Produced Drugs, Analogues and Precursors: Problems and Solutions* (Washington, D.C.: DEA, 1989).

Craig, Richard, "Illicit Drug Traffic: Implications for South American Source Countries," *Journal of Interamerican Studies and World Affairs* (Summer 1987).

_____, "Illicit Drug Traffic and U.S. Latin American Relations," *Washington Quarterly* (Fall 1985): 105–24.

Cultivos de Coca: Produccion, Comercializacion y Desarrollo Alternativo en el Subtropico de Cochabamba, NAS-Bolivia (March 1992).

de Soto, Hernando, *The Other Path: The Invisible Revolution in the Third World* (New York: Harper & Row, 1989).

Dickinson, Joshua, Michael Painter, Marko Ehrlich, Edwin C. French, and Johannes Oosterkamp, *The Associated High Valleys Project in Cochabamba, Bolivia* (Washington, D.C.: DESFIL, 1988).

Dourojeanni, Marc J., "The Environmental Impact of Coca Cultivation and Cocaine Production in the Peruvian Amazon Basin," in *Cocaine Production, Eradication, and the Environment: Policy, Impact, and Options,* Committee on Governmental Affairs, United States Senate (Washington, D.C.: USGPO, August 1990).

Drug Control: U.S.-Supported Efforts in Colombia and Bolivia (Washington, D.C.: GAO, November 1988).

The Drug War: U.S. Programs in Peru Face Serious Obstacles (Washington, D.C.: General Accounting Office, 1991).

Drug Policy and Agriculture: U.S. Trade Impacts of Alternative Crops to Andean Coca (Washington, D.C.: GAO, 1991).

Drugs and Latin America: Economic and Political Impact and U.S. Policy Options, Report of the Select Committee on Narcotics Abuse and Control (Washington, D.C.: USGPO, 1989).

Durana, Patricia, J., "Alternative Development as a Coca Reduction Strategy in the Andean Region: Lessons from Past Efforts," in *Conference Report: Economics of the Narcotics Industry* (Washington, D.C.: Bureau of Intelligence and Research, U.S. Department of State and the Central Intelligence Agency, 1994).

Eastwood, D., and H. Pollard, "The Accelerating Growth of Coca and Colonization in Bolivia," *Geography* (1987).

Ehrenfeld, Rachel, *Narco-Terrrorism: How Governments around the World have Used the Drug Trade to Finance and Further Terrorist Activities* (New York: Basic Books, 1990).

Falco, Mathea, "Foreign Drugs, Foreign Wars," *Daedalus,* 121, 3 (Summer 1992): 1–14.

_____, *Winning the Drug War: A National Strategy* (New York: Priority Press Publications, 1989).

Figueroa, Adolfo, "Agrarian Reforms in Latin America: A Framework and an Instrument of Rural Development," *World Development* 5, 1 and 2 (1987): 155–68.

Figueroa, Adolfo and Farid Matuk, "Fuerza Laboral y Mercado de Trabajo en el Valle del Alto Huallaga," Report prepared for USAID (December 1989).

Final Report on the Evaluation of AID Project No. 527-0244, Development of the Alto Huallaga Area (Lima: Econosult, 1987).

Flores, G., and J. Blanes, *¿A donde va el Chapare?* (Cochabamba, Bolivia: CERES, 1984).

Garland, Eduardo Bedoya, "Intensification and Degradation in the Agricultural Systems of the Peruvian Upper Jungle: The Upper Huallaga Case," in *Lands at Risk in the Third World: Local-level Perspectives,* Peter D. Little and Michael Horowitz, eds. (Boulder, Colo.: Westview, 1987).

Greenfield, Victoria, "Bolivian Coca: A Perennial Leaf Crop Subject to Supply Reduction Policies" (Berkeley: University of California, 1991).

Hargreaves, Clare, *Snowfields: The War on Cocaine in the Andes* (London: Holmes & Meier, 1992).

Healy, Kevin, "Political Ascent of Bolivia's Peasant Coca Leaf Farmers," *Journal of Interamerican Studies and World Affairs* 33, 1 (Spring 1991): 87–121.

_____, "Bolivia and Cocaine: A Developing Country's Dilemmas," *British Journal of Addictions* 83 (1988): 19–23.

Heath, Dwight B., "U.S. Drug Control Policy: A Cultural Perspective," *Daedalus* 121, 3 (Summer 1992): 269–92.

Heath, Dwight B., Charles J. Erasmus, and Hans C. Buechler, *Land Reform and Social Revolution in Bolivia* (New York: Praeger, 1969).

Heroin Situation Assessment: A Report Prepared for the Office of National Drug Control Policy (Cambridge, Mass.: BOTEC Analysis Corporation, 1992).

Huallaga Valley Agribusiness and Marketing Study (Stamford, Conn.: IRI Research Institute, 1985).

Hudson, Rex A., and Dennis M. Hanratty, eds., *Bolivia: A Country Study* (Washington, D.C.: Department of the Army, 1991).

Husch, Jerri A., "Culture and U.S. Drug Policy: Toward a New Conceptual Framework," *Daedalus* 121, 3 (Summer 1992): 293–304.

Impacto Economico del Narcotrafico en el Peru (Lima: Macroconsult, February 1990).

International Narcotics Strategy Report (INCSR), United States Department of State, Bureau of International Narcotics Matters, (Washington, D.C.: USGPO, various years).

Kennedy, Michael, Peter Reuter, and Kevin Jack Riley, *A Simple Economic Model of Cocaine Production* (Santa Monica, Calif.: RAND, 1994).

_____, "A Simple Economic Model of Cocaine Production," *Mathematical and Computer Modelling* 17, 2 (1993): 19–36.

Klein, Herbert S., "Coca Production in the Bolivian Yungas in the Colonial and Early National Periods," *Cultural Survival Report #23: Coca and Cocaine*, Deborah Pacini and Christine Franquemont, eds. (Ithaca, N.Y.: Latin American Studies Program, 1985).

Kumar, Krishna, Ernest Carter, and Stan Samuelson, *Review of AID's Narcotics Control Development Assistance Program* (Washington, D.C.: AID, 1986).

Lee, Rensselaer W., "Controlling the Production of Opiates: The Case of Thailand," in *Conference Report: Economics of the Narcotics Industry*, Bureau of Intelligence and Research, U.S. Department of State and the Central Intelligence Agency (1994).

_____, "Making the Most of Colombia's Drug Negotiations," *Orbis* (Spring 1991).

_____, *White Labyrinth* (New Brunswick, N.J.: Transaction Publishers, 1989).

Ley del Regimen de la Coca y Sustancias Controladas (Ley 1008), Gaceta Oficial de Bolivia (1988 ano de los Ferrocarriles de Bolivia, 22 July 1988).

Lupsha, Peter, "The Political Economy of Drug Trafficking," paper presented at *The Role of the Military in the War on Drugs Conference*, San Antonio, Texas (5 January 1993).

Malamud-Goti, Jaime, *Smoke and Mirrors: The Paradox of the Drug War* (Boulder, Colo.: Westview Press, 1992).

McCormick, Gordon H., *From the Sierra to the Cities: The Urban Campaign of the Shining Path*, R-4150-USDP (Santa Monica, Calif.: RAND, 1992).

_____, *The Shining Path and the Future of Peru*, R-3781-DOS/OSD (Santa Monica, Calif.: RAND, 1990.)

Menzel, Sewall H., "Operation Blast Furnace," *Army* (November 1989): 24–32.

A Midterm Review of the Bolivia Associated High Valleys Project (Washington, D.C.: Development Alternatives Incorporated, 1990).

Morales, Edmundo, *Cocaine: White Gold Rush in Peru* (Tucson: The University of Arizona Press, 1989).

Morales, W. Q., *Bolivia: Land of Struggle* (Boulder, Colo.: Westview, 1992).

Murra, John, "Notes on Pre-Colombian Cultivation of Coca Leaf," *Cultural Survival Report #23: Coca and Cocaine*, Deborah Pacini and Christine Franquemont, eds. (Ithaca, N.Y.: Latin American Studies Program, 1985).

Nadelmann, Ethan, "Thinking Seriously about Alternatives to Drug Prohibition," *Daedalus* 121, 3 (Summer 1992).

National Drug Control Strategy: Progress in the War on Drugs, The White House (January 1993).

National Drug Control Strategy: A Nation Responds to Drug Use, The White House (January 1992).

National Drug Control Strategy, The White House (January 1991).

National Strategy for Alternative Development 1990, Presidency of the Republic of Bolivia (La Paz: Government of Bolivia, undated).

Orellana, A. C., and J. C. Zanner, *Bolivia: Coca, Cocaina, Subdesarrollo y Poder Politico* (La Paz: Los Amigos del Libro, 1983).

Painter, M., "Institutional Analysis of the Chapare Regional Development Project (CRDP)," Abridged Report, Institute for Development Anthropology (IDA), Binghamton, N.Y. and Clark University International Development Programs, Worcester, Mass. (April 1990).

Palmer, David Scott, "Peru the Drug Business and the Shining Path: Between Scylla and Charybdis," *Journal of Interamerican Studies and World Affairs* 34, 3 (Fall 1992): 65–88.

Pando, Roberto, Jose Mercado, Erick Roth, Mancilla Mauricio Mamani, and Ivan Guido de Quiroga, "Coca, cocaismo, y Cocainismo en Bolivia," *La Coca...Tradicion, Rito, Indentidad* (Mexico City: Instituto Indigenta Interamericano, 1989).

Peru: Compendio Estadistico, 1988 (Lima: Instituto Nacional de Estadistico, 1989).

Peru: Proyecciones de Poblacion por Anos Calendarios segun Departmentos, Provincias y Distritos (Lima: Instituto Nacional de Estadistico, 1989).

Plowman, Timothy, "Coca Chewing and the Botanical Origins of Coca (*Erythroxylum spp.*) in South America," *Cultural Survival Report #23: Coca and Cocaine*, Deborah Pacini and Christine Franquemont, eds. (Ithaca, N.Y.: Latin American Studies Program, 1985).

Rasnake, R., and M. Painter, "Rural Development and Crop Substitution in Bolivia: USAID and the Chapare Regional Development Project," Abridged Report Institute for Development Anthropology (IDA), Binghamton, N.Y. and Clark University International Development Programs, Worcester, Mass. (April 1990).

"Recipe Book: Cocaine Processing Techniques," (DEA: Lima Country Office, undated).

Report of Audit: Drug Control Activities in Bolivia (Washington, D.C.: United States Department of State, Office of Inspector General, October 1991).

Report on Asian Organized Crime (Washington, D.C.: U.S. Department of Justice, Criminal Division, 1988).

Reuter, Peter, "The Limits and Consequences of U.S. Foreign Drug Control Efforts," *The Annals* 521 (1992), 151–62.

_____, "Eternal Hope: America's Quest for Narcotics Control," *The Public Interest* 79 (2) (1985), 79–95.

Reuter, Peter, and David Ronfeldt, *Quest for Integrity: The Mexican-U.S. Drug Issue in the 1980s,* N-3266-USDP (Santa Monica, Calif.: RAND, 1992).

Rhoades, Robert E., and Pedro Bidegaray, *The Farmers of the Yurimaguas: Land Use and Cropping Strategies in the Peruvian Jungle* (International Potato Center, 1987).

Riley, Kevin Jack, *Snow Job? The Efficacy of Source Country Cocaine Control Policies,* RGSD-102 [Santa Monica, Calif.: RAND, 1993(a)].

_____, *The Implications of Colombian Drug Industry and Death Squad Political Violence for U.S. Counternarcotics Policy,* N-3605-U.S.DP [Santa Monica, Calif.: RAND, 1993(b)].

Rosenquist, Eric, "Narcotics and Agricultural Economics," in *Conference Report: Economics of the Narcotics Industry,* sponsored by Bureau of Intelligence and Research (Washington, D.C.: U.S. Department of State and Central Intelligence Agency, November 21-22 1994).

Rydell, C. Peter, and Susan Everingham, *Controlling Cocaine: Supply Versus Demand Programs,* MR-331-ONDCP/A/DPRC (Santa Monica, Calif.: RAND, 1994).

Spain, James W., "The United States, Turkey and the Poppy," *The Middle East Journal* 29, 3 (1975): 295-309.

Spedding, A. L., "Coca Eradication, A Remedy for Independence?—With a Postscript," *Anthropology Today* 5, 5 (October 1989): 4-9.

USAID/Bolivia: Program Objectives and Action Plan (1993-1997) (La Paz, Bolivia: United States Agency for International Development, February 1992).

USAID/Bolivia: Alternative Development Strategy (La Paz, Bolivia: U.S. Agency for International Development, 1991).

Zonas de Produccion por Cultivos y Subregiones (Cochabamba, Bolivia: Instituto Boliviano de Tegnologia Agropecuaria, 1992).

5

The Blood of a Nation

No nation has paid a higher price for its cooperation with the United States in the war against cocaine than Colombia. Colombian drug lords have ordered the assassinations of countless government officials, including hundreds of policemen, dozens of judges and journalists, an attorney general, two cabinet ministers, three presidential candidates, a governor, and three chiefs of police. Countless other Colombian officials, including DAS chief Maza Marquez, escaped or survived attacks. Similar terrorist attacks against civilians have been recorded. Two of the most repulsive drug-sponsored terrorist acts occurred in 1989, at the height of the Colombian government's counterattack against the drug trade. In November, an *Avianca* airliner en route to Cali exploded just after take-off from Bogota's airport. The blast killed over 100 passengers and crew on board flight HK-1803. Days later, the drug traffickers detonated a bomb in front of DAS headquarters. The blast ripped the facade of the building off and killed more than sixty bystanders. So brazen have been the attacks, so stark the terror, that there is little to which Colombia's violence can be compared except, perhaps, civil war.

The drug traffickers' direct frontal assault against political authority, however, is not the only threat that they pose to the Colombian state. Cocaine trafficking revenue supports violent right-wing militias that terrorize the Colombian countryside and are responsible for a large fraction of Colombia's murders.[1] Militias, also known as death squads, paramilitaries, self-defense groups, and private armies, have as their objective purging Colombian society of leftist and deviant elements, especially the guerrilla organizations that have plagued Colombia for decades. But death squads also victimize petty criminals, homosexuals, prostitutes, intellectuals, the mentally ill, drug addicts, and beggars. This campaign, called *limpieza social* (or social cleansing), has claimed thousands of lives over the past decade.[2] More than a hundred death squads are thought to operate in the Colombian countryside, and they have executed brutal attacks and massacres against unions leaders, leftist political officials, and left-sympathizing towns and villages. Police and military units share a mutual antipathy for the guerrillas with the death squads. Some officers stand accused of forging an unholy alliance with the death squads by ignoring and abetting death squad murders.[3] Since the drug industry supports the death squads, this cooperation has brought some Colombian security officers uncomfortably close to direct cooperation with Colombian drug traffickers.

Directly and indirectly, Colombian drug lords are responsible for much of the violence that has wracked Colombia over the past decade.[4] Violence has reached such proportions in Colombian that males are more likely to die at the hands of another person than they are to succumb to cancer, heart disease, or any other natural cause of death.[5] Even though perhaps as few as 15 percent of the murders recorded in Colombia have been directly carried out or ordered by the cocaine traffickers, and even though many of these murders entailed the settling of intra-drug industry disputes, murder rates in Colombia vastly exceed those in the United States, and indeed, approach the levels of countries at war. Much of the blame for this bloodshed can be put on the leadership of the Medellin cartel. The Medellin cartel leadership, at one time composed of Pablo "The Godfather" Escobar Gaviria, Fabio, Juan David, and Jorge Luis "The Fat One" Ochoa Vasquez, Jose "The Mexican" Gonzalo Rodriguez Gacha, and Carlos Lehder Rivas, consistently chose violence as a mechanism for protecting and expanding the cocaine trade. From earliest recorded cartel history the traffickers were famous for offering government authorities and judges *plata o plomo*, literally "silver or lead," but colloquially a reference to the choice between cooperation through corruption or death via bullet.[6] The traffickers were more than willing to use bribery to secure cooperation, but would not hesitate to use violence where corruption failed.[7]

The Battle Plan

The horrific violence and widespread corruption have been used to protect and defend Colombian drug lords' two primary contributions to the cocaine business: providing a link between wholesale and retail markets and refining cocaine. Together, these two activities have generated billions of dollars in revenue over the last decade, and made some Colombian drug traffickers among the wealthiest people in the world. In the late 1970s and early 1980s, the cocaine trade may have made a net positive contribution to Colombia's national well-being. Then, the cocaine trade was small, and its corrosive influence not firmly set. Colombian cocaine trafficking provided perhaps 50,000 to 75,000 jobs, a relatively small number compared to both the levels of direct cocaine industry employment in Bolivia and Peru and to the size of the Colombian economy. Indirectly, however, the drug industry provided additional thousands of jobs as the traffickers laundered their vast revenues and invested it in businesses and enterprises in Colombia. Moreover, the traffickers were virtually heroes to some segments of the public, not only because they were fabulously wealthy and bestowed largess on some of the poorest segments of the population, but because they served as a virtual surrogate government in some portions of the country.

By the early 1980s, however, signs were clearly emerging that the drug trade also brought tremendous costs to Colombia.[8] Internationally, a stigma was being attached to Colombia. Goods were held up in ports as customs authorities thoroughly checked the cargo for drugs, and Colombian visitors were regarded with suspicion. At home in Colombia, reports surfaced of the apparent interaction between the drug lords and both left-wing guerrilla groups and right-wing death squads.[9] The growth in political violence was matched by an explosion of criminal violence. In the almost lawless atmosphere that prevailed, hired killers roamed the streets and conducted hits for as little as ten dollars. Substance abuse among Colombians grew, particularly the use of dangerous cocaine derivatives such as *basuco*.[10] There were also hidden effects, such as the erosion of political authority in Colombia. Intimidation, corruption, and assassinations took their toll on leading public officials, particularly the judicial branch.

As the costs of hosting the drug trade grew, Colombia, with U.S. support, committed itself to a path of confrontation with the drug industry. Colombian counternarcotics strategy has evolved in four distinct phases, which I have labeled advances, retreats, second fronts, and war. Each of these important stages, and the attendant victories and losses, are discussed separately. The current state of Colombian counterdrug efforts, and its implications for drug control objectives, is discussed at the end of the chapter.

Advances

Colombia awoke to the drug industry's pernicious effects in 1982 when leading Liberal party politicians, including Luis Carlos Galan Sarmiento and Rodrigo Lara Bonilla, decided to challenge the drug industry's evident influence and immunity. It was during this period that the false image of the traffickers as beleaguered citizens began to unravel. Galan and Lara Bonilla sponsored Colombia's first official public investigations of the drug industry, moves that threatened the traffickers' comfortable positions in Colombian society. Several months into office, Lara Bonilla ordered an investigation pertaining to Pablo Escobar's 1976 arrest and release without trial on cocaine smuggling and bribery charges, and the subsequent murder of the arresting officers. Additionally, Lara Bonilla, under pressure from Galan's New Liberalism Movement (MNL, or *Movimiento Nuevo Liberalismo*) colleagues, was investigating drug traffickers' financial ties to leading politicians. Though Escobar avoided arrest and prosecution over the 1976 case, the publicity and exposure relating to the criminal and financial investigations were sufficient to force Escobar to resign his position as an alternate congressman to the House of Representatives.

In late April, 1984, in retaliation for both Escobar's political humiliation and for a raid on *Tranquilandia*, a large cocaine processing laboratory, the Medellin cartel ordered Lara Bonilla's assassination. Lara Bonilla's assassination shocked the country by illustrating how vulnerable the government was to the traffickers' retribution and brought into sharp focus the danger that the cocaine industry presented to Colombian society. True, the cocaine business was violent from its inception. But violence occupies a prominent and peculiar place in Colombian society so that the traffickers' criminal and violent tendencies did not, at least initially, threaten their social standing. From 1948 to 1966, Colombia endured a civil conflict rooted in left-right political divisions that claimed more than 200,000 lives.[11] But Lara Bonilla's assassination changed the calculus with which Colombians accepted violence, if for no other reason than his murder marked one of the first visible attacks against the national political system by the drug industry. Colombian policies and attitudes about drug trafficking have undergone a number of changes over the years, and opinions continue to wax and wane, but Lara Bonilla's assassination signaled one of the first times that both the public and the national leadership simultaneously regarded the drug industry as a threat.

One immediate consequence of the Lara Bonilla assassination was a renewal of the Colombian government's commitment to extradition. Less than a week after Lara Bonilla's murder, President Betancur signed an extradition order for Carlos Lehder under the terms of a 1982 treaty signed with the United States. Escobar and the other leading traffickers feared the extradition treaty because it gave Colombia the power to extradite subjects to the United States for drug crimes that were organized, originated, and committed in Colombia. The traffickers realized that trial in the United States represented a potent weapon. U.S. courts not only worked much more rapidly than the Byzantine Colombian system, but they also appeared to be much more difficult to influence and intimidate. All things considered, the traffickers were safer if they were held for trial in Colombia.

Betancur also stepped up law enforcement operations against the Medellin cartel. Caught by surprise, the pressure forced some drug lords into exile in Panama and Spain. Although some cartel members remained in exile for only a few months, Jorge Luis Ochoa and Gilberto Rodriguez Orejuela were arrested and detained in Spain for almost two years. During the course of their exile, the drug lords exhibited some willingness to negotiate a settlement with the Colombian government.[12] Eventually, they returned and prepared for future confrontations with the government by developing intelligence networks, constructing safe houses, and hiring more security.[13] Former President Alfonso Lopez Michelsen established what was to become a recurring pattern when he met with the drug leaders while they were in Panamanian exile to discuss the issue of their negotiated surrender. Although the government rejected the traffickers' 1984 offer of retirement in exchange for amnesty, it did set a precedent for future negotiations, including those that led to Pablo Escobar's surrender in 1991.

Retreats

Colombia's retreat from confrontation with the drug lords began in 1985 when the drug lords initiated a series of attacks that revealed the weakness of the Colombian judicial system and its vulnerability to manipulation by the traffickers. In November, 1985 M-19 guerrillas, funded by drug lord Carlos Lehder, attacked the Colombian Palace of Justice. The attack, which resulted in more than 100 deaths, came at a time when the constitutional chamber of the Supreme Court was nearing a decision on the legality of Colombia's extradition treaty with the United States. The attack on the Palace of Justice left the judicial system in disarray, and efforts to rule on the treaty were temporarily halted.

Throughout the intervening year, the traffickers placed intense pressure on the beleaguered judicial system. More than 200 court personnel, and more than forty Colombian judges, were killed in the 1980s. Gunmen, again M-19 assassins thought to have been hired by Medellin, shot and killed Attorney General Carlos Mauro Hoyos in January, 1988.[14] A little more than a year after the Palace of Justice attack, however, the Colombian Supreme Court ruled against the treaty's legality by upholding a challenge to Colombia's extradition treaty with the United States. Ruling on narrow technical grounds, the court stated that the enabling legislation, which gave the 1979 treaty force, was invalid because it had been signed by an interim President. Although the enabling legislation was immediately resigned by sitting President Barco, this too was quickly subjected to new legal challenges. The government managed to sustain the treaty's provisions for two months, until the Supreme Court's criminal chamber announced that it could not rule on extradition because the treaty was not in force.

The Supreme Court next ruled, in June, 1987, that the enabling legislation was invalid. The ruling meant that the Barco Administration, which was eager to cooperate with the United States on extradition, would have to shepherd the enabling legislation through the Colombian Congress again in order to continue extraditions under the treaty. Prospects for passage were dim, given the intense pressure on the government to abandon extradition. The Barco government sought to sidestep the impasse by directly, that is, under existing Colombian laws that bypassed the court system, ruling on extradition requests under the force of an 1888 treaty. Barco's Justice Minister opposed the direct extraditions on the grounds that approval of the (voided) 1979 treaty nullified the 1888 treaty. In May, 1988 the point became moot when the Supreme Court again ruled against extradition, this time by rejecting the direct process as unconstitutional. From that point forward, all future extraditions would require participation of the Colombian courts, which in turn meant the enabling legislation would have to be reapproved by the Colombian Congress. Extradition was dead.

Despite the fact that most public institutions in Colombia, including the police and the military, had roles in counternarcotics operations, the traffickers chose to focus on the courts for several reasons. One of the court system's obvious weaknesses was that most judges had little protection and security, and thus were very vulnerable to the traffickers' threats. A second avenue of influence for the traffickers was the court system's structure. At the time, Colombian judges maintained responsibility for investigating their cases, as well as deciding on whether to issue an indictment.[15] This structure rendered them extremely vulnerable to pressure because they, effectively alone, investigated and prosecuted criminal cases. Despite their daunting tasks, however, Colombian judges, at least in the early 1980s, were given few resources for fulfilling their tasks. Consequently, case loads tended to back up as judges were unable to cope with the flood of cases reaching the courts.[16] In the rare cases where a drug case did reach the court, it was a relatively simple matter for the traffickers to intimidate the justice into dropping the case during the course of an investigation. Without the force of court orders and judicial threats, Colombia's government was relatively powerless against the traffickers. With the exception of Carlos Lehder, whose arrest and extradition other leading traffickers probably desired because of his violent, erratic behavior, the judicial system's impotence was sufficient to ensure that the leading traffickers would not be extradited to the United States for trial on drug-related charges.

Second Fronts

The third phase of Colombian counternarcotics policy, which lasted from mid-1988 into 1989, is perhaps best characterized as a period of diversion. Relations between the traffickers and guerrillas began to sour in the early to mid-1980s as the traffickers began to purchase large amounts of land in the Colombian countryside. These purchases, often located in the heart of the Revolutionary Armed Forces of Colombia, or *Fuerzas Armadas Revolucionarias de Colombia* (FARC) and other rebel territory, placed the traffickers and guerrillas directly at odds with each other. As the traffickers moved into the rebel strongholds, they found natural allies in the other landowners, ranchers, and cattlemen who the guerrillas were targeting for kidnapping.[17] The drug lords' relations with the region's landowners eventually led to the strengthening of rural death squads that targeted the guerrillas for elimination.

The drug lords' relations with the guerrilla left began to unravel at an accelerated pace in 1986, when the Colombian government began to conduct peace negotiations with Colombian guerrilla groups and when *Union Patriotica* (UP), FARC's legitimate electoral arm, met with important local and national electoral successes. As one condition of negotiations with the guerrillas, the Barco government demanded that the rebels disarm. At first, FARC rejected disarmament because death squads had murdered hundreds of UP activists, and the FARC leadership felt that they would be even more vulnerable. Eventually, however, FARC began to issue public statements condemning the drug traffickers, Rodriguez Gacha in particular, and their support of the death squads.[18]

In 1988, the Colombian government was embroiled in peace negotiations with Colombia's leftist guerrilla groups, and much of the Colombian countryside was in violent turmoil. Direct mayoral elections occurred for the first time in 1988, and leftist candidates won many of the contests. Their success, however, aggravated right-wing death squads, which had for years been attempting to reduce the radicals' influence through a "cleansing" campaign of terror. The result was an explosion of right-wing violence against the guerrillas and suspected leftists in the late 1980s.[19] Colombia was swept by the revelations of Diego Viafara, a former M-19 guerrilla kidnapped by a death squad, who escaped to provide first-hand accounts of militia operations in 1988.[20] Perhaps the most stunning of Viafara's revelations was that the death squads were receiving training from Israeli and British mercenaries. Viafara also reported that the drug mafia financed these assassin schools, as well as assassination operations, equipment, and housing. Further investigation by DAS revealed that the drug lords were responsible for financing and organizing much of the death squads' training.[21]

The death squads quickly became ruthless persecutors of guerrillas, leftists, labor leaders, and laborers in the Colombian countryside. *Union Patriotica* party members in particular seemed to bear the brunt of the squads' political assassinations, with 1988 being the peak year.[22] More UP members were killed than Liberal and Conservative party members combined. But the citizenry did not escape the violence. Between March and November, 1988, death squads carried out more than ten massacres, or mass murders, three of which had thirty-six or more victims. In a number of cases, local military officials were accused of standing idly by while the massacres occurred.[23] The Colombian National Police have also been accused of such complicity.[24]

In response to the terror, the government implemented, or planned to implement, several measures to address the burgeoning right-wing violence. These measures, including a broad antiterrorist law and creation of Public Order courts, were directly and indirectly aimed against the traffickers because of their financial and organizational support for the death squads. Also in 1988, gunmen, hired by Medellin, shot and killed Attorney General Carlos Mauro Hoyos Jimenez in a botched kidnap attempt.[25] Subsequent to Hoyos's assassination, President Barco directed the military to assume a larger role in narcotics operations. He authorized the Army to take the lead in counternarcotics operations in insurgent zones and in areas where the Colombian National Police (CNP) had no capacity to operate.

War

Phase four of Colombian counternarcotics efforts, which began in August, 1989 after Medellin assassinated probable Liberal party presidential nominee Luis Carlos Galan Sarmiento, can only be described as a war. In 1989, the presidential election cycle began to gear up, and leading politicians began to stake out positions on drug trafficking. Galan rejoined the Liberal party on the condition that the party use a primary election to select its candidate, and by early 1989 he had emerged as the Liberal party's likely presidential candidate. He was murdered seven months before the party's primary, however, because of his stance against drug trafficking and animosity with leading cartel members that stretched back to Galan's dissatisfaction with Liberal party politics, Escobar's removal from office, and the raid on Tranquilandia.

Medellin's assassination of Galan touched off a conflict between the cartel and the government that reached epic proportions. The Colombian government responded to Galan's assassination by implementing several important counternarcotics measures, including permitting extradition through an administrative process, longer detention of suspected drug criminals without presentation of formal charges, and extension of the government's powers to seize suspected traffickers' assets. Colombian authorities also implemented an intense campaign to capture the leading traffickers, a noticeable departure from prior counternarcotics campaigns' focus on interdicting and destroying drugs and drug industry assets. The government's crackdown included a sharp increase in laboratory raids and interdiction activity that contributed to spot shortages and price increases in U.S. markets.[26]

Extradition alone was sufficient to create a credible legal threat against the traffickers, and was exactly opposite the outcome they had hoped to prompt with Galan's assassination. By March, 1990, fifteen traffickers had been extradited to the United States. Moreover, the other emergency decrees and measures, including detention without trial, seizure of drug traffickers' assets, posting rewards for leading traffickers, and the arrival of U.S. military-type aid, put tremendous pressure on the traffickers. Escobar escaped capture, just barely, on several occasions.

In response to the government's new-found courage, the Colombian traffickers, fearing extradition (and calling themselves *Los Extraditables*), embarked upon a vicious, bloody campaign. Perhaps the most notable change in the drug lords' strategy was their willingness to attack civilian targets in an effort to change government policies.[27] In the past, violent tactics had largely been reserved for use against government and security personnel. But, as the bombing of the *Avianca* jetliner underscored, this time around the traffickers used the citizenry as a way of influencing state policy. The traffickers also waged unprecedented war against the state. In April, 1990, Escobar offered more than $4000 for each police force member killed, and more than $8,000 for officers of the Elite Corp that were killed.[28] By the year's end, more than 200 Medellin policemen had been killed.

In scale and intensity, Colombia's efforts against the drug industry during this period were unprecedented. In late 1989 and early 1990, authorities interdicted approximately 10 percent of the cocaine processed and exported from Colombia; destroyed over 100 processing laboratories, twenty-nine of which were described as major refining centers, and arrested thousands of suspected traffickers, several of whom were extradited to the United States.[29] In addition, U.S. border authorities recorded a 30 percent increase in cocaine seizures over 1988 to nearly a quarter of the amount thought to have been produced and exported in 1989.[30] Additionally, 1989 also saw the seizure of 20 mt of cocaine from a warehouse in Los Angeles, along with numerous other domestic seizures.[31] Combined, the elements of the strategy had a significant temporary effect on drug production. Traffickers fled to Bolivia, Panama, and other relatively safe havens, and power in the cocaine industry shifted from the Medellin to the Cali cartel.[32] The traffickers' movement and the government's attacks caused a shortage of refining capacity that significantly reduced Colombia's export capacity for a time.[33]

Figure 5.1 shows that street retail cocaine prices increased significantly after the law enforcement surge. The increase in prices was primarily concentrated in the September, 1989 to March, 1990 period. After March, 1990, prices began to drift downward, although there were substantial fluctuations. The trough-to-trough increase in prices lasted approximately eighteen months, from November, 1989 to April, 1991. After April, 1991 retail cocaine prices continued to move erratically, but they rarely, and then only temporarily, exceeded the prices that prevailed before the crackdown. Prices remained above $150,000 per kilo, or approximately 10 percent above precrackdown prices, consistently for only eight months, from March to November, 1990. A 10 percent increase in costs can probably be passed along by diluting cocaine, rather than by raising the actual retail price, with little risk of losing customers. In other words, it is probably fairly easy to maintain sales volume in the advent of a 10 percent cost increase by cutting cocaine, but it is more problematic to pass along a 50 percent increase in costs without the volume of sales being affected. Nevertheless, the crackdown does demonstrate that law enforcement programs can successfully disrupt supplies.

The costs of the Colombian strategy become apparent when the level of violence in Colombia is examined during that period. Literally hundreds of Colombian elected officials and security officers lost their lives during this period, as Medellin declared open war on the government. Additionally, hundreds of citizens lost their lives as Medellin turned its wrath against civilian targets. Figure 5.2 provides an overview of who the drug lords targeted between 1986 and 1991.[34] Note that retail cocaine prices, shown on the right scale in figure 5.2 below, moved virtually in tandem with the drug-related murders.

Beyond the unspeakable human toll, it is difficult to put dollar value on the violence that Colombia experienced in 1989 and 1990, but many sectors of the economy were disrupted by the conflict. Foreign investment fell, construction plummeted, and tourism suffered.[35] The level of

FIGURE 5.1

Monthly Purity-Adjusted Street Retail Prices, 1989–92

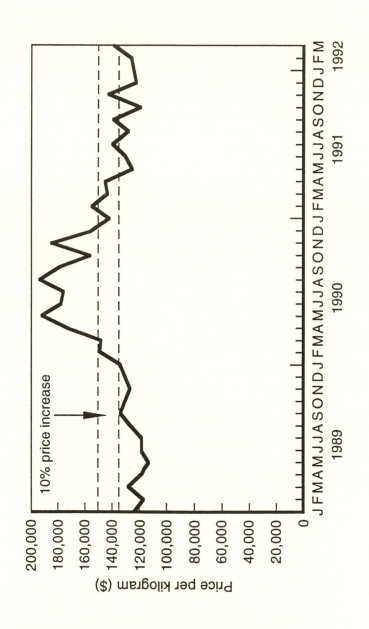

FIGURE 5.2
Drug Industry Murders and Cocaine Prices

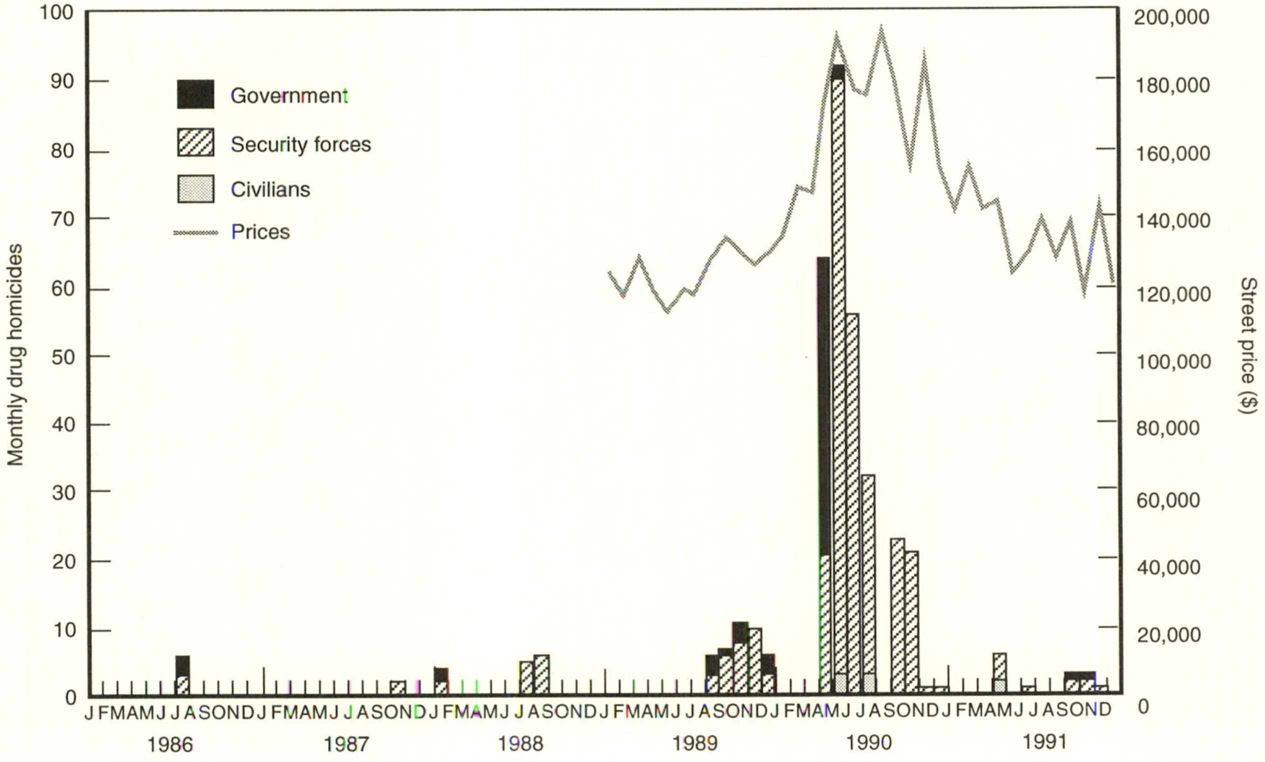

violence further eroded the public's confidence in the state's ability to protect its citizens. Indeed, opinion surveys revealed that a majority of the public favored granting the traffickers leniency, and that a large fraction would not oppose including some traffickers as cabinet members. Implementation of the crackdown itself was expensive. The United States, under the Andean Initiative, provided Colombia with hundreds of millions of dollars of assistance in the form of military equipment, credits, and training.[36] Operational costs are not known, but undoubtedly added millions more to the total.

Colombian security forces killed Jose Gonzalo Rodriguez Gacha in December, 1989, and in January, 1990 the traffickers declared a unilateral truce. In response to the declaration the Colombian government suspended extradition proceedings, but rejected the other terms of the traffickers' offer, including their pleas for amnesty and lenient treatment. The cease fire held until March, 1990, when leftist Presidential candidate Bernardo Jaramillo Ossa was assassinated. As a result, extraditions resumed. In September, 1990, the new Gaviria government offered lenient surrender terms to the traffickers, including a guarantee against extradition in exchange for confession to all crimes. This process ultimately led to the surrender of several leading traffickers, and to a tapering off in the level of drug-related violence.

Lessons Learned

Throughout these efforts, Colombian cocaine exports have continued virtually unabated, the primary exception being a significant disruption of production in late 1989, which persisted into 1990. The 1989-90 crackdown stands out as the one period where source country counternarcotics efforts substantially crippled cocaine exports for a short period. The success of these efforts, which will be discussed in detail throughout this chapter, can be traced to a number of factors. Perhaps most importantly, the scale of the anticocaine effort during 1989 and 1990 substantially exceeded the scale of operations during any other period. In latter 1989 and early 1990 Colombian authorities seized perhaps 10 percent of the cocaine produced in Colombia, and destroyed hundreds of laboratories throughout the country. Additional law enforcement operations in the Transit Zone and at the U.S. border raised losses to between 30 and 40 percent, even before losses in retail markets were considered. Operations during the crackdown also differed in terms of their intensity. That is, the government placed enormous pressure on the leading drug traffickers by seizing their assets, organizing nationwide manhunts, and offering rewards for their capture. At no other time in Colombian history had the state made, and sustained, such an effort against the drug industry. Finally operations against the traffickers occurred across multiple dimensions. The government fully availed itself to legal, law enforcement, and other tools in an effort to curb the drug trade.[37] No aspect of drug trafficking, from production to profits, was spared.

At the same time, the ultimate failure of these efforts to control the Colombian cocaine business can be traced to a small number of factors. Perhaps the most important factor was that all of the Colombian crackdowns, including the 1989–90 crackdown, targeted the Medellin cartel because of the cartel leadership's role in Colombia's assassination wave.[38] The 1989–90 program significantly weakened Medellin but, because it had not been targeted, Cali was able to fill the gap. As a result, trafficking operations, which could have been stifled for many additional months, instead recovered from the crackdown relatively rapidly.

The second major consideration was that the Colombian crackdown was never fully integrated with other counternarcotics measures, both within Colombia and beyond the Colombian borders. This oversight allowed Medellin to recover more rapidly than it otherwise would have. For example, within Colombia, little attention was paid to legal reform that would have strengthened Colombia's ability to prosecute cases that resulted from the crackdown. Similarly, even though the Colombian effort temporarily depressed coca prices, the international community made little effort to capture or extend this result by increasing support to crop substitution and eradication programs in Bolivia and Peru.[39]

Some analysts believe that source country control policies, in their various permutations and combinations, can lead to permanent victory in the war against cocaine.[40] Other analysts, myself included, are not nearly as sanguine about source country control policies' prospects, not only because of the cocaine industry's structure and economics (discussed in chapter 4, and discussed where relevant in this chapter), but because of the potentially high costs associated with implementing source country control policies on a large scale. This statement is not, in any way, meant to deny or denigrate the accomplishments of Colombian and U.S. law enforcement officials. But their acts, however heroic, need to be placed in context: their impact, in practical terms, on the flow of drugs has been, and will continue to be, fleeting at best. And as Colombia's history, particularly the 1989–90 period, indicates, successes in the war on drugs are often accompanied by consequences capable of disrupting Colombian society to its core. Colombia's counternarcotics history, however, offers a unique opportunity to examine the consequences of large scale policy intervention. These consequences will be the focus of this chapter.

The Cartels: Going for Brokerage

For some time now, the term *cartels* has been an inaccurate description of the Colombian drug trafficking organizations. In strict definitional terms, cartels are groups whose members collude to jointly regulate the production, pricing, and marketing of a product. Cocaine cartels, according to the true definition, may have existed briefly in the early 1980s, but they ceased to meet the definition by 1984.[41] The term has stuck, however. Through 1984, Cali and Medellin traffickers met in Colombian hotels, discos, and nightclubs where they mutually planned operations to stabilize prices, insured shipments against loss, and invited small traffickers to consign their loads using the cartels' smuggling routes.[42] At that point, cocaine was an incredibly valuable commodity and such collusion allowed the traffickers to keep prices, and thus revenue and profits, high and under control. The market was sufficiently small and the trafficking network sufficiently cohesive, that the industry could be controlled from a vertically integrated structure.

The collusion may also have been motivated by a security risk the traffickers perceived. Cartel traffickers, as well as other wealthy and influential Colombians, were at risk of being kidnapped by guerrilla organizations in the late 1970s and early 1980s. M-19, founded against the backdrop of allegedly fraudulent 1970 presidential elections and known for its urban attacks and a spectacular raid on the Colombian Palace of justice, frequently kidnapped wealthy citizens as a way of raising funds for guerrilla operations.[43] Among the drug trafficking families, one of the guerrillas' most prominent victims was Marta Nieves Ochoa, sister of the Medellin cartel's Ochoa brothers. M-19 kidnapped her in 1981. The Ochoas refused to pay the ransom and instead convened a meeting of the country's leading traffickers in the Cali territory that was also M-19's home.[44] Shortly after the meeting, the traffickers informed the public and potential kidnappers that they would no longer tolerate the threat, and instead would use a group called MAS (Death to the Kidnappers or *Muerte a Secuestradores*) to crush the problem. Leading traffickers reportedly contributed to a fund that paid for rewards, executions, and equipment, and offered the services of trafficking personnel for MAS operations. Within days of the announcement, MAS itself kidnapped and tortured several M-19 guerrillas. Three months after kidnapping her, M-19 released Marta Nieves Ochoa unharmed. In any event, the kidnapping crisis may also have demonstrated the benefits of working together and the results that could be attained through disciplined unity.

By late 1983 and early 1984, however, several factors had conspired to jeopardize the cartels' hold over production and prices. First, demand and production both expanded precipitously making it much more difficult for Medellin and Cali to control international cocaine markets. As Medellin and Cali built the trafficking infrastructure, bribed the policemen, airport officials, and customs officers, and as they established buying connections in Bolivia and Peru, they also made it easier for competitors to enter the market. Word spread of the easy access to the United States, and of the vast fortunes that could be earned from trafficking. At the retail level the spread of crack, a potent derivative of powdered cocaine, powered a surge in demand.[45] Production escalated rapidly to sate the market's need.

The task of reining in the market was made more difficult by the unprecedented law enforcement pressure put on the leading traffickers in 1984 after the Medellin cartel's murder of Justice Minister Rodrigo Lara Bonilla. The Orejuela brothers' time in jail gave smaller trafficking organizations an opportunity to seize a larger share of cocaine production. No longer able to control the cocaine business, Cali and Medellin began to recoup through higher volume what they lost from declining prices.

By 1987 and 1988 almost any semblance of cooperation between Cali and Medellin had evaporated as the cocaine industry erupted into open conflict. The rancor developed over a number of issues, including Rodriguez Gacha's attempts to acquire a share of the lucrative New York City cocaine market controlled by Cali, and Jorge Ochoa's arrest at a roadblock outside Cali in 1986.[46] Ochoa's arrest, suspicious because it occurred at the hands of a municipal police officer while Ochoa was under heavy guard, placed him in some jeopardy as a consequence of fleeing bail a few months earlier on charges stemming from his in exile in Spain. Medellin's grab sparked a violent conflict in both the United States and Colombia, which pitted the two leading organizations against each other. The combat reached the highest levels in the cartels. A bomb exploded outside one of Pablo Escobar's apartment buildings in the wealthy *El Poblado* section of Medellin in early 1988. Escobar, who was not at home during the explosion, blamed Cali for the detonation. Medellin, in response, initiated a campaign of bombing the chain of pharmacies owned by the Cali cartel's Orejuela family. The government's intense efforts in 1988 to capture Escobar and leading Medellin cartel members intensified the enmity between the groups when Escobar grew suspicious that Cali was providing the government with information it used in its manhunt.[47] Remnants of the hatred between Cali and Medellin were clearly visible through 1993, when the Cali cartel provided Colombian police and military officials with assistance in pursuing Pablo Escobar. Cali went as far as to fund a death squad committed to harassing Pablo Escobar and his family. This group, called PEPES (for People Persecuted by Pablo Escobar), provided intelligence to the government and contributed millions of dollars to the effort that ultimately ended in Escobar's death.[48]

Power Brokers

Despite the evolution in cartel relations over the years, and despite the loss of Medellin's and Cali's chokehold over prices and production, the major drug trafficking organizations still perform the same functions that they did in the late 1970s and early 1980s. The trafficking syndicates' primary role in drug trafficking is to provide brokerage services. Thousands of farmers are required to produce cocaine at the beginning of the production pipeline. At the other end of the pipeline sits the vast distribution and retail network. Somehow, these two parts of the pipeline must connect in order for drug smuggling to work. From a practical standpoint, it would be very risky if the farmers and retailers attempted to deal with each other directly. The number of drug transactions, drug flights, and drug shipments would increase substantially and each farmer-retailer pair would have to supply its own transportation, routes, and protection. With more people conducting a larger number of transactions, the industry's visibility would increase substantially, and so would the risks of trafficking. The cartel leaders saw the need for a small, tightly controlled brokerage service to link these two huge market segments. All that was required for their operations to succeed was a substantial investment in transportation, communications, and security.

The expense and complexity of developing cocaine brokerage capabilities should not be underestimated. Drug trafficking is a risky business. Shippers need short supply lines that provide predictability in, and a large measure of control over, deliveries. Long supply lines, infrequent and unpredictable shipping, and other such perturbations raise the risks for traffickers by increasing the number of individuals involved, or by exposing the operation to greater visibility.[49] Trafficking networks involve extensive spy, intelligence, and bribe arrangements that allow drug shipments to pass through choke points unimpeded, or that provide traffickers with advance warning of law enforcement operations. Many of these functions are international, if not global, in scope, and thus require substantial assets and resources to maintain. For example, the vast majority, if not all, of Colombian aircraft control towers have drug industry informants in them, as do many of the airfields and law enforcement organizations in the countries between Colombia and the United States. As another example of the intricacy and expense, one estimate indicates that over 40 percent of Antioquia Department legislators have accepted money from the traffickers. The traffickers have also invested heavily to establish secure communication networks and develop the ability to eavesdrop on law enforcement organizations' transmissions. Equally importantly, the traffickers need a steady pool of trained pilots and reliable aircraft. Pilots alone may earn $400,000 to $1,000,000 for one flight, with the aircraft costing an additional $1.5 million to $2 million to purchase.[50]

One other component vital to linking producer and retail markets is insurance. That is, the traffickers, in their brokerage capacity, insure suppliers against interdiction losses.[51] This service can be extremely important, considering that individual cocaine shipments can be worth tens of millions of dollars, and considering the potential consequences of failing to complete a cocaine deal. Insurance not only provides shippers with an incentive to use cartel services, but also provides the cartels with a better understanding of how much cocaine is flowing toward retail markets.

Beyond the brokerage function individual traffickers may have varying responsibilities and specializations that pertain to the smooth functioning of the cocaine business. These activities may bear directly on the cartels' brokerage functions, or they may be independent of the brokerage services. For example, Gustavo de Jesus Gaviria Rivero, Escobar's cousin, was thought to be the Medellin cartel's financial planner. It was his job to make sure that Medellin's brokerage services were funded, and to properly launder and dispose of the profits. In contrast, Juan David Ochoa owned and operated a series of cocaine labs. He transported his cocaine using the larger Medellin cartel's trafficking infrastructure, but the cocaine refining was separate from the brokerage function. In other cases, the leading traffickers may provide capital and financing to producers and smugglers in order to ensure that a steady supply of cocaine reaches retail markets. Alternatively, they may sponsor research and investment in areas that will help the cocaine business. For example, the traffickers may pay chemists to investigate new refining techniques and new storage mediums.[52]

A Family Affair

Colombians' involvement in cocaine trafficking can be traced back to Castro's revolution in Cuba. The Cuban revolution not only helped break up the Italian-American organized crime families that dominated the drug trade in Cuba, but scattered Cuban drug traffickers to other havens in South America. It was from the Cubans that the Colombians also learned the manufacturing process for cocaine.[53] The Colombians themselves, however, brought extensive experience to the smuggling profession. Smuggling developed as a national art in Colombia as a mechanism for evading export duties on primary exports and import taxes on most consumer goods. Colombian smugglers have built illicit markets in many goods, but cattle, emeralds, and precious metals are particularly important to the clandestine trade. Many elite families are involved in smuggling, a factor that has helped ease the stigma associated with smuggling. Smuggling organizations are aided by the fact that the Colombian coast is open, with a number of large and small port cities, and by the fact that Colombian businesses are active in international commodity markets, including coffee, flowers, and petroleum products.

Colombians first married drugs and smuggling on a large scale in the 1970s when Mexican authorities successfully (though temporarily) smashed Mexican marijuana production and Colombian exporters stepped in to fill the gap. Logistically, exporting marijuana to the huge American market was simple since Colombia sits atop routes that provide easy access to the United States. Gradually, marijuana smugglers acquired the personnel, skills, money laundering facilities, distribution networks, transportation routes, and other infrastructure that ultimately proved useful to cocaine trafficking. When Mexico reestablished its marijuana industry, Colombia's ability to compete in U.S. marijuana markets quickly waned. Among other factors, Mexico's proximity to the United States provided it a tremendous cost advantage in satisfying the U.S. market so that Colombia was rapidly priced out of the U.S. marijuana market. But as subsequent events soon proved, the eclipse of Colombian marijuana exports was almost immaterial, given the potential for Colombian cocaine exports.

Colombia's latent ability to supply illicit drug markets and the burgeoning demand for cocaine in the United States merged in the late 1970s as cocaine demand started to creep up, and then shoot up. Prior to mass smuggling, cocaine had been a relatively expensive and exotic drug, factors that tended to confine its use to relatively discrete and elite segments of U.S. society, including the Hollywood movie industry. But intense U.S. federal pressure on other drugs, including LSD, simultaneously made them more scarce and raised the risks of consuming these them. Gradually, cocaine emerged as a less risky alternative, if only because it evaded authorities' detection at first. Carlos Lehder recognized these trends and, after a term in a U.S. prison on marijuana possession charges, returned to Colombia and revolutionized the cocaine business. Lehder's insight was that marijuana was, because of its relative weight and bulk, not nearly as lucrative as cocaine. Cocaine's advantage over marijuana is that it can be transported in small packages that are less visible, but still more valuable, than bulky marijuana bales. The risks of shipping large marijuana loads from Colombia became clear as authorities began to clamp down on Caribbean maritime drug smuggling. But the crackdown on boat trafficking did not particularly effect cocaine. Lehder had realized that sufficient amounts of cocaine could be sent by plane to make the effort worthwhile, particularly since authorities were ill-equipped to block air routes at the time.

The traffickers maintain their corporate cartel headquarters and most processing within Colombia, and attempt to repatriate drug dollars to Colombia as well. Confining operations to Colombia minimizes the need for high-level traffickers to travel outside Colombia and maximizes the cartels' influence over local and national governments. The leading trafficking organizations, Colombian and otherwise, are largely built on family, community, and ethnic relations. That is, the cartels rely on kinship, geographic, and generational ties to generate loyalty. Family members, community members and ethnic compatriots can be trusted in a way outsiders cannot. The community structure also instills discipline: a trafficker knows that family members are subject to retribution if cartel ethics are violated. Medellin emerged as one center of the Colombian cocaine trade when its textile industry collapsed and thousands of Colombians headed to New York City in search of employment in the garment industry. This expatriate population provided the core of a retailing market and provided cohesion and fraternity that made it difficult for outsiders to penetrate. Outsiders are easily recognized and their motives challenged. Thus, despite the fact that the United States is the leading consumer of cocaine, relatively few Americans are thought to be high-ranking cartel members. Many pilots and ship captains are non-Colombians, but they are also typically kept insulated from the highest levels of the cartel. In two cases where Americans, Barry Seal and Max Mermelstein, did hold relatively important positions in the cartels, they later defected and provided damaging information to the DEA.[54] Seal's knowledge so threatened cartel operations that the traffickers ordered him assassinated on U.S. soil, despite the fact that the act placed the killers at risk of prosecution in U.S. courts.

The traffickers used their wealth and influence to create a role in Colombian society that, temporarily, gave them influence within the existing social structure. At heart, the traffickers are Colombians and wanted to develop a stake in their country. Social class, in which the family's children are educated, the family is politically active, and entire industries are dominated by extended families, have remained important components of Colombian society. Economic influence is a traditional path to power and respect in Colombia. The importance of wealth and power can be seen in the relatively few families that dominate Colombian institutions. For example, the Colombian political system has traditionally been run by two major parties, one liberal and one conservative, each with a rich history of control by family dynasties. Many of the same families in turn control most of Colombia's major media outlets. Liberal party families own the major daily newspapers, *El Tiempo* and *El Espectador*; the family of former president Mariano Ospina Perez owns the conservative daily *La Republica*; and the children of former presidents run most major national news shows. In a sense, the traffickers tried to build comparable dynasties in the drug business.

The traffickers opened their assault on the Colombian social structure along a number of fronts in the early 1980s. The drug barons began to invest large amounts of cash generated from the drug trade in Colombia. In particular, they bought huge tracts of land in regions of the country where government authority was weak. Terrorist organizations dominated portions of the Colombian countryside. FARC, for example, controlled the Middle Magdalena valley region, and the ranchers and farmers in such areas were at the mercy of the guerrillas. One response was for the ranchers, financially and otherwise supported by the drug lords, to attack the guerrillas. Gradually, the drug lords and their death squads moved in and began to secure the area. The drug lords' purchases, combined with the forceful ejection of the guerrillas, helped shore up property prices and earned the traffickers the allegiance of the region's ranchers and property owners.[55]

Politically, the drug lords were active through campaign contributions and through political organizations that they founded and supported. Pablo Escobar parlayed his political contributions into election as an alternate to the House of Representatives. Carlos Lehder founded a party with bizarre fascist and nationalist beliefs called *Movimiento Latino Nacional*, but also gave generously to the Liberal party.[56] Philanthropy was another mechanism the traffickers used to build public support. Pablo Escobar used his wealth to build public housing, and then reported his largesse in *Medellin Civico,* a newspaper which he owned. Gilberto and Miguel Rodriguez Orejuela bought *Grupo Radial Colombiano,* a prominent Colombian radio network, and owned a popular Colombian soccer team. Drug earnings were also laundered through, and invested in, a number of other legitimate businesses. The Ochoas were prominent horse breeders before the 1984 murder of Lara Bonilla and owned *Pilotos Ejecutivos,* a charter airline service. The Orejuela family still owns a prominent pharmacy chain in Colombia.

The Medellin Cartel

On 3 December 1993, Colombian authorities shot and killed Pablo Escobar in a shootout in Medellin. More than 1500 members of a joint military-police task force searched for Escobar. In addition to official forces, a death squad funded by the Cali cartel PEPES provided Colombian authorities information about Escobar's whereabouts, harassed Escobar's family, destroyed Escobar's assets, attacked Escobar's ranches, and gunned down Escobar's lieutenants and their families for months prior to Escobar's death. Escobar's death brought to a close one of the most tortuous and sordid chapters in the history of Colombian counternarcotics operations. Escobar escaped Envigado prison on 22 July 1992 and continued to evade authorities for over sixteen months. Even while he was confined, however, Pablo "The Godfather" Escobar Gaviria managed to continue his drug operations. Escobar surrendered to Colombian authorities in July, 1991 as part of a settlement negotiated after the Colombian government's crackdown on the Medellin cartel in 1989 and 1990. Escobar, however, dictated many key terms of the settlement, including the provisions that allowed him to design, construct, and staff the Envigado prison from which he escaped.[57]

By the time of Escobar's death, most of the other Medellin cartel leadership was dead or imprisoned. Carlos Lehder Rivas was among the first to go. Lehder's wild, unpredictable behavior and cocaine use had alienated others in the cartel, and thus there is speculation that the Medellin leadership aided the police in capturing him. In any event, Lehder was arrested in Colombia in February, 1987 after an informant told police where to find him. Authorities quickly extradited him to the United States, where he was convicted on a variety of charges in May, 1988. Colombian security forces killed Jose "The Mexican" Gonzalo Rodriguez Gacha in December, 1989 after an intense, nationwide manhunt that ended in the town of Cavenas, along the Colombian coast. Authorities wanted Gacha in connection with the assassination of Luis Carlos Galan, the Liberal party's probable presidential candidate, several months earlier. More than 1000 troops were deployed against Gacha the day he was killed. Jorge Luis "The Fat One" Ochoa Vasquez fled to

Spain shortly after the 1984 assassination of Lara Bonilla. Spanish authorities arrested him on drug related charges in late 1984. Ochoa spent two years in a Spanish prison before he was released to Colombian authorities to be tried on similar charges in his native land. A Colombian magistrate freed him on bond, and Ochoa quickly disappeared. In 1987 he was pulled over for a traffic violation and briefly rearrested again. He remained free until he and his brothers, Fabio and Juan David, surrendered to Colombian authorities in 1991.

These events, culminating in Escobar's death, are widely thought to signal the demise of the Medellin cartel. Of course, many Medellin operants remain free, and have allied themselves with other trafficking organizations, or formed trafficking syndicates of their own. In breaking up the Medellin cartel, however, authorities have eliminated some of the most dangerous and violent criminal personalities in Colombia. These traffickers' deaths and imprisonment have not, of course, eliminated drug trafficking in Colombia, but they have probably contributed to making Colombia safer. Whether Medellin's dismantlement proves to be only the beginning of Colombia's efforts against leading traffickers, or whether it proves to be the pinnacle of Colombian counternarcotics achievements, remains to be seen. Medellin's violence made it a very visible target, and helped motivate Colombian institutions and the Colombian public to confront the drug trade directly. In the absence of Medellin's direct threats to Colombian security, counternarcotics efforts may weaken.

The Cali Cartel

With the collapse of the Medellin cartel, Cali stood as the inheritor to Medellin's lost power and prominence. Through 1995 Cali controlled perhaps 75 percent of Colombia's cocaine exports. While authorities concentrated on the Medellin leadership, much of the original Cali leadership remained free. The Cali leadership cultivated extensive contacts and protection in Colombian political and security institutions, and worked to mask their drug operations under the cover of legitimate businesses. One measure of Cali's influence in the early 1990s can be found in the fact that arrest warrants were not issued for its leaders until September, 1993, or more than a year after the nationwide manhunt for the Medellin cartel's Pablo Escobar began. Figures for 1989 placed Cali's size at between 2500 and 6000 personnel, a number that may have grown since Medellin's collapse, and should be regarded as an approximation given the loose cohesion of cartel affiliations.[58]

Cali's unassailable position was breached in 1995, however, with the arrest of most of Cali's leadership. As this book goes to press, the story of the Cali cartel's unraveling is still being written. Some aspects of the saga are clear, while other aspects of it will undoubtedly be dissected in the coming months and years. The main impetus for the rapid progress against Cali appears to be the allegations that Colombian President Ernesto Samper accepted campaign contributions from the Cali cartel. These allegations placed enormous pressure on the Samper administration to make progress against Cali or risk a severe break in relations with the United States. Samper directed an intensified effort against Cali, which resulted in Gilberto Orejuela Rodriguez's capture in June, 1995. Shortly afterward, Henry Loiaza, who reportedly directed the organization's military operations, turned himself in to authorities. In July, 1995, Colombian authorities captured Jose Santacruz Londono while he dined in a Cali restaurant. Given the ease with which Santacruz avoided capture in the past, it is speculated that he may have cut a deal with the Samper administration. Several days after Santacruz's capture, Phanor Arizabaleta Arzayuz, another Cali leader—and one implicated in many violent crimes—surrendered.

Despite these high-profile arrests, the pressure on Samper continued to mount. Santiago Medina, Samper's 1994 campaign treasurer, implicated Samper's Minister of Defense and former campaign manager Fernando Botero in a scheme to accept campaign contributions from Cali. In exchange for the contributions, the Cali members were allegedly to receive lenient plea-bargain arrangements. Botero resigned in early August, announcing the move as part of an effort to clear his name. In the meantime, Miguel Rodriguez Orejuela was captured. Recent reports indicate that retail markets where Cali's influence was strong have been disrupted by arrests. In New York City, for example, where Cali officials held important roles in retail distribution, press accounts indicate that spot shortages were appearing and retail prices were rising in September, 1995.

Gilberto Rodriguez Orejuela, his brother Miguel Rodriguez Orejuela, and Jose Santacruz Londono were thought to be Cali's three main leaders. Gilberto Rodriguez Orejuela oversaw the logistics of cocaine smuggling and money laundering. Miguel Rodriguez Orejuela temporarily took over Cali operations when Gilberto was imprisoned in Spain and he ostensibly ran the Cali cartel's legitimate businesses, including banks, real estate, and construction companies. At one time he served as Vice-President of First Interamericas Bank of Panama, a country that is one of Cali's primary money-laundering sites.[59] Jose Santacruz Londono is from Cali, and he controlled retail operations that function in a number of U.S. cities, including New York, Chicago, Miami, Los Angeles, and San Francisco. Santacruz is also credited with pioneering sophisticated concealment strategies that exploited weaknesses in cargo inspection procedures. Prior to their arrests, the Orejuela brothers objected, strenuously and publicly, to the government's characterization of them as leading drug traffickers.[60] They contended that they have never been convicted of drug-related crimes, and that media reports linking their names to Colombian drug operations are violating their constitutional rights.

The Cali cartel's stronghold was Valle del Cauca, the department that surrounds Cali. Press reports and other sources indicate that Cali invested heavily in securing the cooperation of local officials in this region. Local police, for example, were reportedly virtually all under Cali's control, as are local politicians. Cali also moved to protect its territory and resources by supporting PEPES. PEPES stood opposed to Escobar's violence, and contributed to information used when Colombian security forces killed him in a December, 1993 shootout. Cali provided intelligence to the government, and contributed millions of dollars to the Escobar manhunt.[61] PEPES also attacked the *La Cristalina,* a farm owned by Escobar's mother, and attacked the *El Poblado* neighborhood in Medellin where several Escobar relatives lived while Escobar was on the run. At this point, it is unclear how the leadership's arrest will affect these local networks and operations.

The Cali cartel largely escaped blame for the drug-related violence that Colombia has suffered through over the last decade because, relative to the Medellin cartel, Cali eschewed violence. Many of Cali's violent acts were aimed against members of rival cartels as part of an ongoing intradrug trade conflict. However, not too much should be made of this claim of alleged nonviolence. First, in the murky world of drug dealing, it is often difficult, if not impossible, to determine responsibility for acts of violence. Second, even if Cali tended to utilize nonviolent means to further the drug trade, its methods have effects on Colombian society that, while difficult to measure, are undoubtedly highly corrosive. For example, the Colombian Prosecutor General's Office has initiated numerous investigations of Colombian legislators and Samper administration officials. Such corruption severely undermines Colombian political and social institutions. Finally, even though the Medellin cartel has largely been dismantled, many mid- and lower-level Medellin members remain at large. Some have joined forces with Cali, and in the process, may have brought along the methods they used as Medellin members.

Other Cartels

In addition to the remnants of Cali and Medellin, a number of other cocaine syndicates operate in Mexico, Colombia, Bolivia, and Peru. Mexico in particular is likely to assume even more importance as a drug center in the coming years. Two factors are primarily responsible for Mexico's increasing importance to cocaine trafficking.[62] First, the U.S. radar barrier in Caribbean Basin succeeded in reducing the number of flights through the Transit Zone and into the United States. However, as Caribbean air routes have become more risky, an increasingly large fraction of cocaine has been sent to Mexico, where it is then smuggled over the land border with the United States. It is estimated that as much as 70 percent of the cocaine entering the United States now moves through Mexico. Mexico was a prime candidate for this displaced traffic not only because it shares a long porous border with the United States, but because it contains many developed port and air transit facilities and has a significant history of corruption and smuggling. The second factor contributing to Mexico's elevation in the trafficking hierarchy is the disarray the Colombian cartels' experiences between 1989 and 1992 and the current pressure on the Cali cartel. Law enforcement efforts imposed financial constraints on the Colombian traffickers in the early 1990s. In response, the Colombian traffickers began to pay their Mexican middlemen in cocaine, rather than cash. One result was that Mexican traffickers developed a significant stake in lucrative U.S. wholesale and retail markets, and rapidly solidified that stake by creating trafficking syndicates and networks of their own. In short, the realignment of cocaine trafficking routes has forced Colombian traffickers to cooperate with Mexican trafficking organizations. However, Mexican traffickers still lack control over vast refining networks in Colombia, which, until recently, guaranteed a continuation of the Colombian syndicates' role. Mexico's role in these aspects of the trade, discussed in more detail in chapter 6, may grow unless replacements to Cali and Medellin emerge in Colombia.

Not much is known, at least from public sources, about these other cocaine smuggling syndicates. Colombia hosts two smaller trafficking organizations. Bogota, Colombia's capital, is home to a prominent cocaine smuggling outfit. The Bogota syndicate began operations smuggling consumer goods, but gradually shifted to primarily cocaine trafficking as it expanded its contacts with U.S. organized crime and retail market elements. The Bogota group has also reputedly worked assiduously to cultivate political connections, and thus protection, in Colombia. The North Atlantic Coast cartel, named for the coastal regions in which operations are concentrated, is among the smaller smuggling organizations. It has established footholds in some large U.S. cities such as Miami and Los Angeles, and has also penetrated cities less well-known as drug centers, including Jacksonsville, Gainsville, and San Diego.[63] Until the demise of the Medellin syndicate, the North Atlantic Coast's major role was to provide smuggling and money laundering services to other cartels. The North Atlantic Coast group's share in international cocaine smuggling remains to be redefined in the aftermath of Medellin's collapse and Cali's uncertain future.

Beyond Colombia's borders, several other prominent cocaine smuggling organizations continue to operate. Most of the other drug groups, while smaller than Cali (and Medellin at its peak), are probably larger and more important than the Bogota and North Atlantic Coast cartels. Peru's largest cartel moves perhaps 50 metric tons of cocaine to the United States every year. The cartel, headed by Demetrio Limonier Chavez-Penaherrera, nicknamed *Vaticano* because he controls Peruvian "churches," or firms, has been under intense pressure from Peruvian. Colombian officials arrested *Vaticano* in 1994 and returned him to Peru for trial.

Historically, Bolivia has been the smallest net cocaine exporter of the three Andean nations. Nevertheless, drug trafficking cocaine syndicates have thrived in the landlocked nation, in part because of government complicity in drug trafficking throughout much of the 1970s and 1980s.[64] The legendary Roberto Suarez Gomez, the so-called king of Cocaine and perhaps Bolivia's most notorious and prolific trafficker, now resides in a Bolivian prison. Convicted in absentia in a 1988 trial, Suarez was caught later in the year during a police raid on a rural ranch. In any event, Suarez's influence as a cocaine trafficker probably peaked in 1984 when Colombian traffickers objected to the prices Suarez demanded for his intermediate products.[65] The dispute, and Suarez's subsequent arrest, did much to diminish Bolivia's direct participation in international cocaine markets. The country remains, however, one of the most important sources of coca leaf, paste, and base.

Laboratories

Cocaine refining constitutes Colombia's second major contribution to the cocaine business. Cocaine refining is done in an extensive set of laboratories dispersed throughout out the plains and jungle regions of the nation. The traffickers use the laboratories to convert cocaine base to cocaine hydrochloride, or powder cocaine. Cocaine base and powder cocaine are essentially the same product, they just get dissolved into the bloodstream in different manners. Powder cocaine is water soluble, and thus will dissolve directly in the bloodstream; cocaine base must be heated to release vapors, which are then absorbed in the bloodstream.

In any event, a number of formulae for converting base to cocaine exist. One factor common to these various formulae, or recipes, is that they each require a variety of chemicals. In many cases, the chemicals required are common and can be easily found throughout Colombia. Kerosene, for example, is widely used as a fuel source in Colombia, and is produced locally as well. The Colombian chemical industry also produces many of the acids used in the cocaine refining process. In other cases, however, key chemicals are not manufactured in Colombia, and must therefore imported into the country. Colombia meets its needs for potassium permanganate, ether, and ether substitutes (acetone, toluene, and methyl ethyl ketone), through imports. Colombia's consumption of these chemicals clearly exceeds the demand for legitimate uses in Colombian industries where they are commonly needed, including pulp, paper, plastics, munitions, rubber, pharmaceuticals, chemicals, and petrochemicals. Colombia's consumption of these chemicals precipitated efforts to make both exporters and importers more accountable for their use of these products. U.S. exporters of chemicals used in drug processing are now required, under the 1988 Chemical Diversion and Trafficking Act of 1988, to report their foreign suppliers and customers to DEA, which in turn verifies the customers' chemical needs.

Whatever recipe is used, the basic procedure for converting base to cocaine is straightforward.[66] Cocaine base is dissolved in a solvent such as acetone or ether. Next, a precipitant such as hydrochloric acid is added, which causes the cocaine to crystallize and fall out of solution. The remaining liquid is decanted off, and the precipitant (cocaine hydrochloride) is dried under heat lamps, in microwaves, or with the aid of fans. The labs in which these operations take place range from the simple to the very sophisticated. Simplicity arises from the need for mobility and the ever-present threat that the laboratory will be destroyed by law enforcement authorities.[67] Sophistication emerges from the volume of cocaine produced and the corresponding scale and number of the laboratories required. The simplest labs may consist of nothing more than a small kitchen supplied with the requisite chemicals, drying equipment, and materials. Often small, crude labs are found in urban areas like Medellin and Cali. Frequently, kitchen labs can be detected by the distinct aroma associated with the processing chemicals. Because the chemicals used to crystallize the cocaine are highly combustible, kitchens without adequate ventilation are subject to explosions. The smell, the explosions, and more generally, the location in urban areas, raise the risks of detection by law enforcement officials. The higher risks, however, are probably offset by the relative ease with which the labs can be assembled and dismantled. Literally any apartment can serve as a small processing laboratory.

In contrast, the most sophisticated laboratories may resemble small towns or villages in size, and indeed may offer more amenities than rural Colombian settlements are capable of providing. These labs are typically designed to process large amounts of cocaine—on the order of hundreds of kilograms per week—and thus typically located in remote regions of Colombia where large volumes of cocaine can be processed with little threat of interference. Labs of this size may employ dozens of individuals, ranging from chemists (or cooks), to security, entertainment, accountants, dock and warehouse workers, and so forth. Few services and supplies are available in these isolated corners of the country, so nearly every need must be satisfied through elaborate supply networks. Processing chemicals, for example, must be brought in by plane or boat (there are not many roads serving rural Colombia), as must food supplies, fuel, and other materials. Large labs often have generators to power drying equipment even though surrounding villages usually do not have electricity. The remoteness of the operations necessitates providing the staff with comforts, including, occasionally, dormitory space for spouses and children, videocassette libraries, and other recreation facilities. Transportation also becomes a seminal issue, as the traffickers must have methods for moving the finished cocaine from the labs to rendezvous points for shipment to the United States. Many of the larger labs are thus located near navigable rivers and airstrips. By virtue of their size and complexity, the larger laboratories are not as mobile as the smaller, kitchen-style labs. However, reports indicate that the traffickers may maintain more processing laboratories than they need to ensure that refining operations can be shifted to other locations if a lab is destroyed. Other reports indicate that, at least in the 1980s, leading traffickers would periodically allow laboratories to be raided and destroyed in order to satisfy law enforcement authorities.[68]

Colombian authorities destroyed 560 cocaine laboratories in 1994, the highest number since they destroyed 452 labs in the 1989 crackdown.[69] In the years between 1989 and 1993, authorities typically destroyed between 200 and 300 cocaine laboratories. Concomitant with the lab destructions, Colombian forces seized more than 32 mt of cocaine and base in 1994, one of the lowest recorded totals in recent years, and substantially less than the 86 mt seized in 1991. One of the most infamous laboratory raids occurred in 1984, when Colombian forces destroyed a lab in rural Colombia called *Tranquilandia*. The counternarcotics forces located the lab by concealing a transponding beacon, or bug, in the bottom of an ether barrel. The lab's remoteness placed some difficult demands on Colombian forces, which were not equipped for operations that had to cover such distances. Although the authorities did not know it at first, the laboratory, reputedly owned by the Medellin cartel, was massive. It contained dormitory space for more than 100 workers, and came complete with a fleet of generators for supplying power. A confiscated logbook revealed that *Tranquilandia* was capable of putting out more than 300 kilograms of cocaine per week, or 15 metric tons of cocaine per year. The traffickers had a fleet of aircraft available at *Tranquilandia* for transporting the finished cocaine.

The success of the raid on *Tranquilandia* probably did much to convince authorities that laboratory raids were a useful tool in the war on drugs. Because it was the first lab of such magnitude to be raided, it was assumed that the facility represented a large portion of the drug industry's capacity. Given its size and output potential, it was simply inconceivable to think that the lab could be destroyed without substantially disrupting cocaine supplies. And indeed, some reports indicate that the raid caused temporary scarcities.[70] But 1984 was also a time of tremendous growth in cocaine production; any shortages induced by the raid on *Tranquilandia* were quickly overcome.

Updating the War Plan

Upon taking office, the Clinton administration subjected international drug control strategy to a review and determined that an interdiction based approach to combatting cocaine was not cost effective, failed to attack the traffic's key vulnerable points, and did not adequately address important host-country repercussions of international drug trafficking.[71] Concerns about the cost effectiveness of international counterdrug operations arose from the tremendous expense associated with detection and monitoring of drug flights in the Transit Zone and the lack of any suitable measure of effectiveness.[72] Certainly, international interdiction has increased over the years, in large part due to improved detection and monitoring, but there is little evidence that these efforts have materially reduced the supply of cocaine reaching the United States.[73] Relatedly, the Clinton review established that these detection and monitoring resources might be better used if they were brought to bear within the source countries, rather than in the Transit Zone. Finally, the review also determined that a greater portion of international drug control resources needs to be devoted to combatting the secondary effects of drug trafficking, including corruption, intimidation, and violence. Accordingly, the Clinton source country strategy has placed increased emphasis on bolstering Colombian judicial and security institutions against these factors. The core of the Clinton administration's strategy is to make more effective use of international drug policy resources by applying them in areas where they will be most beneficial.[74] The shift in strategic emphasis has a number of important implications for the allocation and disposition of drug policy resources.

Air Supremacy

Within Colombia, the vast majority of cocaine is shipped by air. Source country air shipment is seen as a vital link in the cocaine trafficking chain, one that, if successfully broken, might severely weaken the cartels' ability to move cocaine. This assessment, combined with the weaknesses and expense of Transit Zone interdiction, has led to an increased emphasis on controlling air corridors in the source countries. One important objective is to shut down primary trafficking routes within Colombia, before the shipments reach the expanse of the Caribbean basin. By concentrating radar and other resources in Colombia, authorities hope to force the traffickers to find alternative (and riskier) air routes, or to force them into using land routes. A second objective of the strategy is to force up the prices pilots charge. Pilots are a valuable commodity in the trafficking business, and their skills are highly sought after. Recall from earlier in the chapter that they might earn between $400,000 and $1,000,000 for a flight. This compensation represents between 10 and 25 percent of wholesale cocaine prices, and is one of the largest components of the wholesale price. A substantial increase in the law enforcement pressure pilots perceive could substantially force up their asking price, perhaps attracting pilots more willing to take the flight risk, but less skilled at evading detection.[75]

In addition to determining that attacking traffickers at the source makes more strategic sense, the administration has sought to make use of more sophisticated radar systems and detection technologies that will reduce detection and monitoring costs. Transit Zone interdiction, which relies on airborne platforms such as AWACS and E-2 aircraft, is very expensive to maintain. The expenses arise not only because the planes require extensive crews (both in the air and on the ground), but because of the associated fuel, maintenance, and other costs. Operating costs are sufficiently high enough to assure that providing continual detection and monitoring coverage of the entire Caribbean basin is prohibitively expensive. Analysts have repeatedly questioned using such costly tools to search for cocaine in transit.[76] Technology, however, has provided a way to conduct virtually the same operations, but perhaps more cost effectively.

Conventional radar systems are housed in AWACS and other aircraft because microwave radar systems require a direct line of sight to detect targets. Placing conventional radar systems in airplanes improves the angle of vision, and gives the radar a direct line of sight over a larger surface area. The U.S Air Force and the U.S. Navy, however, have recently deployed Over-the-Horizon (OTH) radar systems that provide superior radar detection abilities from the ground more than 2000 miles away. Without the cost of flight and maintenance crews, OTH radar may prove significantly more cost effective than conventional radar.[77]

Developed near the end of cold-war hostilities with the former Soviet Union, OTH technology was originally intended to detect incoming missiles and other such strategic threats to U.S. territory. Since the collapse of the Soviet threat, however, there has been a growing interest in extending the use of OTH radar. OTH radar works similarly to conventional microwave radar. That is, OTH radar works by bouncing a signal off of a moving subject, and then using information about the returned signal to tell a story about the target. For example, the longer the delay in the signal's return, the further away the target is, and the greater the returned signal's frequency shift, the faster the target is moving. The difference between conventional and OTH radar lies in the latter's improved "vision." Conventional radar operates in a line-of-sight-only fashion, meaning that the radar signal travels in a straight line. If obstructions stand between the target and the radar, the target will go undetected. To some extent, this limitation can be compensated for by locating the radar on high ground, in a tower, or on airborne platforms. Stationing the radar on airborne platforms dramatically increases the radar's vision, but at the expense of large increases in operating costs. Stationary radar platforms located along trafficking routes are less expensive, but easier to fly around and vulnerable to attack. In contrast, OTH radar works by bouncing the radar signal off the ionosphere, an electrically conducting layer of the atmosphere that extends from about thirty miles, to more than 250 miles, above the earth's surface. Each bounce off the ionosphere provides a view of a small patch on the ground. By rapidly bouncing the signal off a slightly different spot of the atmospheric layer, OTH radar views adjacent patches and creates a picture of the entire region. OTH can provide a total field of regard of about 2.3 million square miles on virtually a continuous basis.[78] In other words, OTH can view an area the size of the Caribbean Basin around the clock.

Despite the intended cold-war applications, OTH technology was initially deployed in the southwestern United States to assist in counternarcotics detection operations.[79] The main OTH radar in counternarcotics use now is the Navy's R-OTHR (Relocatable Over-the-Horizon Radar), located in Virginia near the North Carolina border. The Air Force has an OTH-B (Over-the-Horizon Backscatter) system located in Bangor, Maine, but the system's ability to see into the Caribbean and Latin America is limited by the need to double bounce the signal off the ionosphere. Once OTH radar installations are completed in Texas (1996) and Puerto Rico (1997), radar coverage of the entire Caribbean region and all of Latin America can be obtained at a fraction of the cost that it would take to provide radar coverage for the entire region using conventional airborne radar. However, unless OTH capability can be projected in all directions—including north into Canada and east into Brazil—OTH ground platforms may ultimately prove more expensive if they have to be relocated in response to changing trafficking patterns or if additional installations need to be built.[80]

According to some sources, OTH technology, if fully deployed, will allow authorities to detect virtually all air traffic moving through the Caribbean basin and the Andean region. Although there is some concern that OTH, which can detect targets from almost 2,000 miles away, may not be as efficient as airborne systems at picking out small targets such as drug smuggling commuter planes, this limitation can generally be compensated for by viewing smaller surface slices. Even with its superior abilities, OTH is not infallible. Atmospheric disruptions, for example, can limit OTH's effectiveness. Moreover, OTH cannot distinguish an aircraft's elevation, an important factor in profiling suspected drug flights. Finally, OTH does not have IFF (Identify Friend/Foe) query capability for interrogating planes in flight. Until this communication element is integrated into OTH, conventional methods will remain important.[81]

Already, OTH is being credited with significantly improving detection and monitoring capabilities in the portions of Latin America now covered. Ironically, however, the United States elected to suspend sharing detection and monitoring information from radar systems, including OTH, with Colombian authorities precisely at a time when detection capability was improving. The suspension, which became effective in May, 1994 and lasted several weeks, arose because Colombia gave its counternarcotics forces shootdown authority in specified restricted air corridors. That is, Colombian forces, which largely rely on U.S. tracking and detection information to identify drug flights, now have the authority under some circumstances to use force against suspected drug flights. Peru maintains an aggressive program, and Peruvian officials have shot down at least twenty-five flights since March, 1995.[82] Colombian officials, to date, have used force to destroy aircraft only after the plane has been forced down and abandoned. Increased surveillance and the use of force have clearly affected trafficking operations, as evidenced by changes in trafficking patterns. Traffickers in Peru are now resorting to land and water routes; to flying east through Brazil, where radar and surveillance coverage is lacking; and to breaking up flights into a series of shorter hops that allow pilots to take off and land before interdiction forces can be launched to intercept and force down the flight. Out of concern that the Colombian and Peruvian shootdown policy endangers legitimate commercial and private air traffic and opens the United States to liability lawsuits, the United States government suspended detection and monitoring support.[83] The conflict has since been resolved, but highlights one of the interdiction policy's central weaknesses: how to ensure the arrest and apprehension of drug traffickers once their flights have been identified by radar.

Courting the Colombians

The Colombian court system has long been recognized as one of the weakest links in the counternarcotics policy chain. Many of these weaknesses are rooted in the structure, described earlier, which places Colombian judges in the unenviable position of investigating drug cases virtually alone. Colombian magistrates became so concerned about their safety and working conditions that they staged a short strike in 1988. But other problems have long plagued Colombian courts. Only in recent years, for example, has Colombia moved to provide its judges with protection. Even state protection, however, is no guarantee against the cartels' resources. The Colombian judicial system also lacks many critical resources, including computers, that would allow it to more effectively monitor and track the disposition of cases. For all of these reasons, Colombian conviction rates stood at an appallingly low level at the end of the 1980s: of the small fraction—perhaps 20 percent—of the crimes committed in Colombia that get reported, less than 5 percent resulted in convictions.[84]

Despite the abysmal state of the Colombian judicial system, the United States is reliant upon it for cooperation in counternarcotics pro-

grams. Drug traffickers not extradited to the United States, an option
currently not allowed for under Colombian law, must be tried in Colombia. In light of the dependence on the Colombian judicial system,
the United States has provided substantial assistance to the Colombian judiciary in recent years. U.S. assistance has been provided across
many fronts. Beginning in 1988, ICITAP (International Criminal Investigative Training Assistance Program) assisted Colombia with judicial protection. This assistance, including bomb mirrors, weapons
detection technology, and personal safety training, has helped Colombia improve its judicial protection system. ICITAP has also provided
Colombian judges with crime scene investigation training, an important skill, given Colombian judges' role in criminal investigations. In
recent years, ICITAP has broadened the range of assistance it provides. Currently, U.S. assistance to Colombia is being used to set up
forensic laboratories and improve forensic procedures (such as han-
dling evidence). Under the aegis of these programs, more than 1500
judges, prosecutors, investigators, and forensic technicians received
U.S.-sponsored training in 1993 in areas ranging from adjudication to
forensic processes.[85] The use of U.S. resources in Colombia now more
closely approximates the uses in other nations to which ICITAP provides assistance.

According to some sources, the Colombians have made great strides
in improving the quality and surety of drug prosecutions.[86] Despite the
improvement, however, U.S. officials remain concerned about
Colombia's ability to effectively prosecute drug cases. In 1993, for example, Colombia convicted several leading traffickers and imposed sentences ranging from nearly four years to twelve years. While the fact
that they were convicted is certainly an improvement over the past, U.S.
officials consider the sentences lenient and not commensurate with the
gravity of the traffickers' crimes.[87] More generally, Colombia's former
Prosecutor General, Gustavo de Greiff, made policy statements that
troubled U.S.-Colombian relations. As prosecutor general, de Greiff and
his staff held the primary responsibility for prosecuting drug cases in
Colombia. de Greiff, however, harshly criticized U.S. and Colombian
counternarcotics policies and openly advocated legalization of drugs,
claiming that it may be the only way to eliminate the profits of drug
trade. These statements, combined with his office's role in negotiating
the settlements with the traffickers, led the United States to review the

procedures under which intelligence and prosecutorial information is shared with the Prosecutor General's office.

On the War Front

In recent years, a number of irritants have emerged in Colombian-U.S. drug policy relations, including Pablo Escobar's escape, former Colombian Prosecutor General Gustavo de Greiff's support of legalization, and the disagreement over Colombia's authorization to use force against suspected drug flights. The constitutional division of the Colombian Supreme Court added to the turmoil in May, 1994, when it ruled that possession of small amounts of drugs, one gram in the case of cocaine, could no longer be considered illegal. The court's ruling determined that drug possession laws violated constitutionally guaranteed personal liberties and freedoms. The ruling had no bearing on the production, trafficking and sale of drugs, all of which remain illegal. But, according to government sources, the only mechanism for challenging the court's ruling is through a constitutional amendment.

These tensions and disagreements over substantive policy issues highlight the difficulties of attempting to coordinate policies between countries. More importantly, they may portend that the United States can no longer rely on Colombia to unswervingly support U.S. drug control policies and objectives. The prospect of break in Colombian-U.S. cooperation over drug issues remains a real possibility, if for no other reason than U.S. and Colombian drug policy objectives appear to be diverging at this point. This juncture, and the differing outcomes that might result from it, make this an appropriate time to evaluate what U.S.-Colombian cooperation has accomplished, what it has yet to accomplish, and what it can never accomplish.

The list of counternarcotics accomplishments for Colombia and the United States over the past decade is very impressive. The leading and most deadly international cocaine traffickers are dead or in prison. Significant progress has been made with the Colombian judicial system. Authorities now offer judges better protection, and the functioning of the criminal justice system has improved markedly. The United States has almost completed its installation of a radar network that will allow continuous monitoring of the Caribbean basin and the Andean region. And, perhaps most importantly, Colombia appears to have beaten back the scourge of drug industry violence against the Colombian government. Yet it is doubtful that the consensus that led to these achievements, particularly those from 1989 through 1990, could now be sustained. The political, economic, and social costs of these policies have been very high for Colombia. These costs can be measured not only by the lives lost and the blood shed, but by the corruption that the drug industry has inculcated throughout Colombia.

If the pressure of the 1989–90 crackdown could have been sustained, would it have mattered? We will probably never know the answer to this question, but the answer is almost assuredly "no." There are any number of reasons why source country control policies cannot be used to control the cocaine trade. Most of the factors, including the cocaine industry's profitability and price structure, have already been covered in other sections of the book. But two factors, surprise and inventory, and their impact on source country policies' effectiveness, merit further attention.

Surprise, Surprise

In the event that a large source country intervention was attempted there are two reasons why its effectiveness would be limited. The first relates to the element of surprise. Basically, source country control policies are successful in the short run, or temporarily, because they catch the drug industry off guard. The element of surprise allows the government to take advantage of the lag between the policy's implementation, in this case interdiction, and the drug traffickers' ability to react to, and compensate for, the policy. The longer the lag, the greater the disruption in production. Depending on the source country policy used, and the scale with which it is implemented, the cocaine business can fully recover from any policy in approximately two years or less. Two years represents the longest lag in the system; it is the approximate amount of time it takes coca farmers to bring new bushes to market.[88]

Advance warning, however, may give the traffickers time to adjust to a policy before it is implemented, and thereby reduce, or even eliminate, any short-run production disruptions. One simple example of the value of advance warning can be found in the archives of laboratory raids. On many occasions, security forces have arrived at laboratory facilities, only to find them emptied of personnel, drugs, and chemicals. Clearly, in many instances the refiners have received advance warning of the raid, and have relocated operations in response. Authorities have moved to guard against such leaks by withholding raid plans from the team members until the last minute. In any event, such incidents, if isolated, can be shrugged off as minor irritants. Unfortunately, advance warning can also occur on a more global scale that seriously compromises strategy.

Consider two factors relating to advance warning and the current interdiction policy. First, it will take the United States and Colombia a significant amount of time to improve interdiction capacity in Colombia. Construction of the OTH radar facilities alone can take months, and that does not even count the lengthy (often public) debates that precede such policy moves. The Clinton administration's review of source country policies, for example, took seven months.[89] All of these delays give the traffickers time to adjust trafficking methods. Admittedly, not all traffickers adjust. That is, many traffickers are still caught and their shipments interdicted, this despite the knowledge that a new policy is forthcoming. These instances, however, may well reflect the traffickers' assessment that the (increased) risk of capture and interdiction is still less costly than changing trafficking routes and methods. In other words, the interdiction campaign is small enough that a radical change in trafficking methods is not warranted.

But now consider the difficulty in keeping an operation of any significant scale a secret. In other words, imagine a very large and successful interdiction program, continuously implemented, that seized half of the cocaine produced.[90] If the program came as a complete surprise, and if authorities seized half of the cocaine as it was shipped, there would be cocaine shortages in retail markets for about two years.[91] That is approximately how long it would take the traffickers to get the coca farmers to double leaf production. After leaf production doubled, the original amount of cocaine would reach the market, and the shortages would disappear. But if the traffickers got wind of that a massive, sustained interdiction effort was forthcoming, they could prepare for it. Clearly, they were not expecting the crackdown in 1989 and 1990, in part because the Colombian government had never before committed itself to such an assault against the drug trade. But would the traffickers expect, and prepare for, such a crackdown if another confrontation with the government seemed imminent? Very likely, they would, particularly after the 1989–90 experience.

Taking Inventory

The second issue that limits source country policies' effectiveness is inventory. Quite simply, inventory allows businesses to respond to fluctuations in market conditions.[92] When demand fluctuates, inventories serve as a buffer, allowing firms to meet changes in demand without incurring costs such as lost sales, the reputation for being an unreliable supplier, and paying staff overtime for crash production efforts. The need to prepare for such instances has logical extensions to the cocaine industry. Wholesalers rushing to meet a surge in cocaine demand expose themselves to greater law enforcement risks, particularly if they are forced to hire new, inexperienced workers.[93] Conversely, when demand is slack, workers may sit idle or be laid off. Consider the ability of disgruntled, laid-off workers to compromise drug operations. One way of avoiding the layoff complication is to use inventory as a way of smoothing production during slack times.[94] At the same time, carrying inventory may impose substantial costs on manufacturers. Inventory, for example, obligates the business to pay for storage, and increases the threat of loss and spoilage, as well as the possibility that the goods may never get sold because of a change in demand.[95] Drug dealers face additional, and not insignificant, potential costs. More inventory held increases the threat of detection by law enforcement officials, as well as increasing the risk that the cache will be stolen. Holding inventory may also increase the risk that the goods will be self-consumed by weak-willed dealers.

Inventory has profoundly negative implications for source country policies' ability to disrupt cocaine production. At a minimum, the presence of inventory increases the size of the policy effort needed to ensure the desired level of market disruption. That is, more law enforcement officers and more raids will be required to achieve a given reduction in the amounts reaching retail markets. At the extreme, if policymakers are ignorant of inventory accumulation, or if the inventory accumulation is sufficiently large, then source country policies may not be able to generate even short-run disruption of markets.

The sparse evidence available indicates that traffickers may use inventory methods in their business transactions, though it is far from clear to what extent.[96] In recent years agents have found cocaine products stored in *aguarica*, or rich water. This product, which is essentially cocaine base or paste suspended in solvents and stored in drums, prolongs cocaine's shelf life by rendering it immune to spoilage from jungle heat and humidity. Discoveries of caches stored as *aguarica* became more frequent after the imposition of an air cap over the Chapare in 1992 temporarily restricted the traffickers' ability to move intermediate cocaine products out of the Chapare to El Beni for further processing.[97] Storage in this medium probably helped smooth out production of drugs, and may account at least partially for the fact that coca leaf prices did not respond as dramatically to the imposition of the air cap as expected.[98]

More ominously, the Peruvian press is rife with stories that the Colombian traffickers have bragged about accumulating a twenty-year inventory of cocaine.[99] It is not clear that such a massive store exists or is necessary, but it is reportedly being accumulated to allow the traffickers to focus on poppy cultivation and heroin production. Certainly, estimates and intelligence sources indicate that heroin production in Latin America is on the rise, but this does not necessarily confirm that the traffickers have amassed a vast store of cocaine.[100]

There is also some indication that the traffickers resorted, at one time, to using smaller, mobile, and redundant processing facilities.[101] That is, they carried an inventory of cocaine processing laboratories. The Colombian crackdown of 1989–90 made a significant dent in the traffickers' refinery capacity for a short period of time, and this program may have convinced the traffickers that extra capacity at this stage of production was worth the cost. Many of the base laboratories raided in 1991 and 1992 were less sophisticated and had less processing capacity than the larger facilities raided in previous years. Moreover, some appeared to be designed for use on a rotating basis.

The movement of retail cocaine prices during the 1989–90 crackdown provides weak support for the inventory hypothesis. Within Colombia, interdiction and laboratory raids seized perhaps 10 percent of the cocaine produced. In addition, U.S. border authorities recorded a 30 percent increase in cocaine seizures over 1988 to nearly a quarter of the amount thought to have been produced and exported in 1989.[102] Additionally, 1989 also saw the seizure of 20 mt of cocaine from a warehouse in Los Angeles, along with numerous other domestic seizures.[103] In total, authorities may have seized 30 to 40 percent of the world's cocaine output for a brief period. The 58 percent increase in retail prices (see figure 5.1) confirms that cocaine markets experienced turmoil.[104] Given that the Colombian government sustained its crackdown for over a year, prices returned to their precrackdown levels relatively quickly (again, see figure 5.1). The best that can be said is that inventories may have had a role in tempering the effects of the 1989-90 events. Beyond those speculations, however, the issue of inventory remains an open, and important, research question.

Summary

In some sense, the search for source country control policies in Colombia is analogous to the search for the Holy Grail. It is a monumental task, and one that exceeds the capacities of mere mortals. Clearly, the cocaine traffickers have a number of vulnerable spots: pilots, their assets, the cartel leadership, and so forth. Equally clearly, source country policies aimed against these exposed points can produce admirable results. One need only look back at 1989-90 to realize what can be accomplished against the traffickers. Likewise, one need only look at 1989-90 to see what costs, over and above the negative consequences of hosting the drug trade, such temporary victories can bring.

Ultimately, however, none of these points appear to be cripplingly vulnerable. No matter how diligently policy pressure is applied, the cocaine industry has the ability to rebound. Certainly, there are those that would quarrel with this argument, and who believe that the traffickers can be defeated, however broadly or narrowly the term *defeated* is defined.[105] Such logic is almost inescapably bound to the notion that we are not trying hard enough (scale), and have not kept the pressure on long enough (sustainment) to truly damage the cartels and cripple cocaine production. As I hope has been demonstrated, there are serious flaws associated with this thinking.

It is easy to be pessimistic about source country control policies. Pessimism, however, begs the question of what should be done about these policies. If they are not effective, why continue them? Should the current set of source country policies be replaced with some other set of choices? Or does some clearly superior choice that does not involve the source countries exist? I hope to answer the first two, and touch upon the third question, in part III of this book.

Notes

1. *Colombia Besieged: Political Violence and State Responsibility* (1989); *The Killings in Colombia* (1989); *The "Drug War" in Colombia: The Neglected Tragedy of Political Violence* (1990); Rosenberg (1991); *The Colombian National Police, Human Rights and U.S. Drug Policy* (1993); Riley (1993); and Duzan (1994).

2. *Colombia Besieged: Political Violence and State Responsibility* (1989); *The Killings in Colombia* (1989); *The "Drug War" in Colombia: The Neglected Tragedy of Political Violence* (1990); Rosenberg (1991); *The Colombian National Police, Human Rights and U.S. Drug Policy* (1993); Riley (1993); and Duzan (1994).

3. *Colombia Besieged: Political Violence and State Responsibility* (1989) and *The Killings in Colombia* (1989) document numerous instances of death-squad massacres apparently ignored by police and military officials.

4. There are other, unmeasurable, ways in which the drug industry contributes to violence. The drug industry, for example, generates indifference and corruption.

5. Riley (1993) reports in more detail on Colombian homicide rates.

6. Rosenberg (1991), especially pages 23–25, describes more of the *plata o plomo* environment.

7. Gugliotta and Leen (1989) and Eddy et. al (1988) provide numerous examples of this behavior.

8. Clawson (1992) provides an overview of the costs.

9. Ehrenfeld (1992); Riley (1993).

10. These forms of cocaine retain many of the pharmacological properties associated with cocaine, and are referred to as "bazooka" or "basuco." Morales (1989), 113, notes the history of such consumption and MacDonald (1989) discusses the extent of cocaine product consumption in BCP. Basuco and bazooka result from errors in processing. As such, they are often impure and laden with processing chemicals that may make them dangerous to the users. A survey of Medellin residents revealed lifetime prevalence of basuco use of approximately 6 percent [*El Tiempo* (3 October 1993)].

11. Riley (1993).

12. Lee (1991).

13. Gugliotta (1993), 123.

14. Ehrenfeld, 74–75.

15. Rosenberg (1991), 25–76 provides an account of how the Colombian judicial system operates. The judiciary's structure has since been modified to relieve magistrates of some of these duties. See *Foreign Assistance: Promising Approach to Judicial Reform in Colombia* (1992).

16. It is estimated that only about 5 percent of the crimes committed in Colombia, including murders, ever reach the court system.

17. *Colombia Besieged* (1989); *The Killings in Colombia* (1989).

18. Gugliotta and Leen (1989), 287.

19. Riley (1993).

20. Accounts of Viafara's story can be found in *Colombia Besieged* (1989) and Duzan (1994), especially 93–114.

21. The DAS reports, such as "Private Justice," on drug-death squad links are referenced in *Colombia Besieged* (1989) and *The Killings in Colombia* (1989).

22. Riley (1993).

23. *Colombia Besieged* (1989) and *The Killings in Colombia* (1989) provide details on military complicity in death-squad massacres.
24. See *The Colombian National Police, Human Rights and U.S. Drug Policy* (1993) for an explication of Colombian National Police human rights abuses.
25. Ehrenfeld, 74–75.
26. Riley (1993) reports on the effects of the government's crackdown on retail cocaine prices and supplies.
27. Riley (1993) provides a look at the targets and tactics used by the drug lords during this period.
28. *The Colombian National Police, Human Rights and U.S. Drug Policy* (1993).
29. *Drug Enforcement Administration and the 1991 Andean Interdiction Operations* (1991).
30. According to EPIC, authorities seized 145 mt of cocaine in 1989, compared to 112 in 1988.
31. There is no single source that records domestic seizures by municipal police forces and other nonfederal organizations.
32. Lee (1991).
33. Andreas et al. (1991–92) report that "cocaine processing and trafficking dropped 70 percent" in the aftermath of the crackdown.
34. The data for this graph are taken from Riley (1993). The death tolls shown represent approximately 10 percent of the drug-related murders that occurred during this period.
35. Lee (1991).
36. See *Andean Strategy* (1991).
37. Gugliotta (1993) terms this a "frontal assault" against the traffickers.
38. Gugliotta (1993).
39. Gugliotta (1993) provides a critique of the Colombian crackdown.
40. See, for example Lupsha (1993) and Gugliotta (1992).
41. Gugliotta (1993) provides a detailed account of trafficker meetings and behavior during the cartel period.
42. Ibid.
43. For more on M-19, the Palace of Justice attack and possible connections to the drug industry, see Gugliotta and Leen (1989), among others.
44. Eddy et al. (1988) provides an account of the meeting.
45. Crack did not gain much national media attention until 1985 and 1986. However, active local markets developed well before crack became a national phenomenon, so that the spread of it was well under way by 1984. Inciardi (1992), 105–32.
46. *Structure of International Drug Cartels* (1989), 131.
47. Gugliotta and Leen (1989).
48. James Brooke, "Drug Spotlight Falls on Unblinking Cali Cartel," *New York Times* (17 December 1993).
49. Indeed, authorities killed Rodriguez Gacha in large part because he emerged from hiding to personally supervise the movement of a cocaine shipment.
50. Lupsha (1993).
51. *Structure of International Drug Cartels* (1989), 122–36.
52. One such new storage medium, *agua rica* (literally "rich water") began to appear in the late 1980s and early 1990s. It consists of refined cocaine suspended in a liquid. Storage in this matter retards spoilage.
53. *Drug Control: U.S. Supported Efforts in Colombia and Bolivia* (1988), 16.
54. The details of these defections can be found in Mermelstein (1990) and Gugliotta and Leen (1989).

55. *Colombia Besieged* (1989); *The Killings in Colombia* (1989); *Drug Trafficking: A Report to the President of the United States* (1989).

56. *Movimiento Latino Nacional* is not to be confused with *Movimiento Nuevo Liberalism,* an offshoot of Colombia's mainstream Liberal party that has pushed many important counterdrug initiatives.

57. *The Future of the Andean War on Drugs After the Escape of Pablo Escobar* (1992).

58. *Structure of International Drug Cartels* (1989), 125.

59. "Cocaine Crisis," *Manchester Guardian* (5 September 1989).

60. Letter submitted to *Cambio 16* by Gilberto and Miguel Rodriguez Orejuela, as reported in JPRS-TDD-94-020-L, 9 May 1994.

61. James Brooke, "Drug Spotlight Falls on Unblinking Cali Cartel," *New York Times* (17 December 1993).

62. Chapter 6 covers transshipment through Mexico in detail.

63. *Drug Trafficking: A Report to the President of the United States* (1989).

64. Hargreaves (1992).

65. Hargreaves (1992).

66. "Recipe Book: Cocaine Processing Techniques," (undated) provides a variety of cocaine processing recipes. See also Cooper (1989).

67. Authorities usually destroy several hundred cocaine laboratories a year. See later in this section for more.

68. Suspicions about the ease with which some labs were destroyed are discussed in a variety of sources, including *INCSR* (various years), Gugliotta and Leen (1989), and Lee (1989).

69. *INCSR* (1994). Colombian authorities also reported destroying ten heroin and morphine labs in 1993, the highest total since heroin lab destructions were first recorded in 1991. The increase in discovery and destruction of heroin labs is, quite likely, indicative of Colombia's increased participation in heroin production.

70. Gugliotta and Leen (1989), 137.

71. *National Drug Control Strategy: Reclaiming our Communities from Drugs and Violence* (1994), 50–58 summarizes the President's international strategy.

72. For an analysis of transit zone operations, see chapter 6.

73. See *Drug Control: Impact of DOD's Detection and Monitoring on Cocaine Flow* (1991); *Drug Control: Expanded Military Surveillance Not Justified by Measurable Goals or Results* (1993); and *Drug Control: Revised Drug Interdiction Approach is Needed in Mexico* (1993).

74. *National Drug Control Strategy: Reclaiming our Communities from Drugs and Violence* (1994), 54.

75. Cave and Reuter (1988) discuss the importance of skill and experience in smuggling.

76. See *Drug Control: Impact of DOD's Detection and Monitoring on Cocaine Flow* (1991); *Drug Control: Expanded Military Surveillance Not Justified by Measurable Goals or Results* (1993); and *Drug Control: Revised Drug Interdiction Approach is Needed in Mexico* (1993).

77. This assertion is challenged in *Over-the-Horizon Radar: Better Justification Needed for DOD Systems' Expansion* (1991).

78. It takes approximately thirty minutes to assemble the patches into a full picture of the complete field of regard.

79. *Over-the-Horizon Radar: Better Justification Needed for DOD Systems" Expansion* (1991).

80. The Navy's R-OTHR, while "relocatable," would still require several million in moving, site preparation, and construction costs.

81. OTH-B radar was initially intended to be used for detecting both bomber and cruise missile attacks. Subsequent testing, however, revealed that OTH-B had was deficient in its ability to detect cruise missile targets. *Over-the-Horizon Radar: Better Justification Needed for DoD Systems' Expansion* (1991).

82. *Drug Enforcement Report*, "Latin Shoot-Down Policy Disrupts Coca Paste Flights" (8 September 1995.)

83. Peru has also granted its forces shootdown authority. Cooperation with Peruvian authorities has likewise been suspended.

84. DANE, the Colombian statistical authority, reported the 20 percent report rate in *El Mundo* (6 August 1987). Other sources, such as Hanratty and Meditz (1991) report similar reporting rates. 85. *INCSR* (1994), 107.

86. *INCSR* (1994) and *National Drug Control Strategy: Reclaiming our Communities from Drugs and Violence* (1994).

87. *INCSR* (1994), 106.

88. Of the four stages of cocaine production (leaf, paste, base, and cocaine), it takes coca leaf the longest to adjust to policies. From the time that they are planted, coca bushes take about eighteen months to reach full maturity and provide full harvests. Factoring in additional time for preparing land, it takes about two years for coca bushes to yield full profits. In contrast, paste pits and base and cocaine laboratories can be replaced in a matter of weeks, and cocaine can be processed in a matter of days. However, interdicting cocaine can directly affects coca farming, and thus interdiction can benefit from coca's two-year lag, even if the coca itself is not directly interdicted. If interdiction is continuous, so that, say, traffickers lose half of their output in every time period, they will eventually request twice as much leaf from coca farmers. Over two years, coca farming will approximately double, and the traffickers will produce twice as much cocaine, eventually losing half to interdiction. The delay between interdiction and an increase in production so that the preinterdiction amount of cocaine reaches the market can be attributed to the time it takes coca bushes to mature. See Riley (1993) for details.

89. *National Drug Control Strategy: Reclaiming our Communities from Drugs and Violence* (1994), 50–58, describes the review and its results.

90. Must be continuous policy.

91. Again, see Riley (1993) for a formal examination of this thesis.

92. See Blanchard (1983), Blinder (1986) and (1981), West (1986) and Holt, Modigliani, and Muth (1960) for a range of theories on inventory and inventory behavior.

93. Cave and Reuter (1988) and Reuter, Crawford, and Cave (1988) address the issue of experience as it relates to trafficking.

94. See Blinder (1986) in particular for more on this model.

95. For more on the costs of carrying inventory, see Holt et. al (1960), 67–91.

96. Note that inventory can also be relevant at the farm level. Coca leaves, once picked, cannot be stored for more than a few days because they rot in the moist climate. There is little indication that farmers are carrying inventory of coca-producing land. However, there is no technical barrier to accumulating an inventory of surplus land; if the leaves are not harvested, the plant will not die. On the other hand, given the uncertainty about the size of the coca plant stock, there could well be excess capacity at this stage of production.

97. Personal communication, DEA, La Paz, Bolivia.

98. Ibid.
99. See, for example, *Expreso* (3 October 1993): A8–A9 (as translated in JPRS-TDD-93-043-L (25 October 1993).
100. *INCSR* (1994) reports on heroin production in the Andes.
101. *Coca Cultivation and Cocaine Processing: An Overview* (1991); personal communication with DEA, La Paz, Bolivia.
102. According to EPIC, authorities seized 145 mt of cocaine in 1989, compared to 112 in 1988.
103. There is no single source that records domestic seizures by municipal police forces and other nonfederal organizations.
104. It is extremely difficult to determine what portion of the price rise can be attributed policy intervention, and what portion is simply due to normal market fluctuations. Generally, cocaine prices had been declining for several years in 1989, but with many ups and downs. Readers should thus be aware that retail prices often move with considerable volatility.
105. Gugliotta (1992) and Lupsha (1993) are two.

References

Andean Strategy, Hearing before the Select Committee on Narcotics Abuse and Control, House of Representatives (Washington, D.C.: USGPO, 1991).

Andreas, Peter R., Eva C. Bertram, Morris J. Blachman, and Kenneth E. Sharpe, "Dead End Drug Wars," *Foreign Policy* 85 (Winter 1991–1992): 106–28.

Blanchard, Olivier, "The Production and Inventory Behavior of the American Automobile Industry," *Journal of Political Economy* 91 (June 1983): 365–400.

Blinder, Alan S., "Can the Production Smoothing Model of Inventory Behavior be Saved?" *Quarterly Journal of Economics* 101, 3 (1986): 431–53.

———, "Retail Inventory Behavior and Business Fluctuations," *Brookings Papers on Economic Activity* 2 (1981).

Brooke, James, "Drug Spotlight Falls on Unblinking Cali Cartel," *New York Times* (17 December 1993).

Cave, Jonathan, and Peter Reuter, *The Interdictor's Lot: A Dynamic Model of the Market for Drug Smuggling Services*, N-2632-USDP (Santa Monica, Calif.: RAND, 1988).

Chernick, Marc W., "The Drug War," *NACLA Report on the Americas* 23, 6 (April 1990): 30–40.

Clawson, Patrick, "How Profitable for Farmers is Cultivation of Coca Leaves?" in *Conference Report: Economics of the Narcotics Industry* (Washington, D.C.: Bureau of Intelligence and Research, U.S. Department of State and the Central Intelligence Agency, 1994).

Coca Cultivation and Cocaine Processing: An Overview (Washington, D.C.: Drug Enforcement Administration, 1991).

Colombia Besieged: Political Violence and State Responsibility (Washington, D.C.: Washington Office on Latin America, 1989).

"Cocaine Crisis," *Manchester Guardian* (5 September 1989).

Collett, Merrill, "The Myth of the 'Narco-Guerrillas,'" *The Nation* (13–August 1988).

The Colombian National Police, Human Rights and U.S. Drug Policy (Washington, D.C.: Washington Office on Latin America, 1993).

Cooper, Donald A., "Clandestine Production Processes for Cocaine and Heroin," in *Clandestinely Produced Drugs, Analogues and Precursors: Problems and Solutions* (Washington, D.C.: DEA, 1989).

Drug Control: Expanded Military Surveillance Not Justified by Measurable Goals or Results (Washington, D.C.: GAO, 1993).

Drug Control: Impact of DOD's Detection and Monitoring on Cocaine Flow (Washington, D.C.: GAO, 1991).

Drug Control: Revised Drug Interdiction Approach is Needed in Mexico (Washington, D.C.: GAO, 1993).

Drug Control: U.S.-Supported Efforts in Colombia and Bolivia (Washington, D.C.: GAO, November 1988).

Drug Enforcement Administration and the 1991 Andean Interdiction Operations, hearing before the Committee on Government Operations, House of Representatives (Washington, D.C.: USGPO, 1991).

Drug Enforcement Report, "Latin Shoot-Down Policy Disrupts Coca Paste Flights" (8 September 1995).

Drug Trafficking: A Report to the President of the United States (1989).

The "Drug War" in Colombia: The Neglected Tragedy of Political Violence (New York: Americas Watch, 1990).

Duzan, Maria Jimena, *Death Beat: A Colombian Journalist's Life Inside the Cocaine Wars* (New York: HarperCollins, 1994).

Eddy, Paul, with Hugo Sabogal, and Sara Walden, *The Cocaine Wars* (New York: W. W. Norton, 1988).

Ehrenfeld, Rachel, *Narco-Terrrorism: How Governments around the World have Used the Drug Trade to Finance and Further Terrorist Activities* (New York: Basic Books, 1990).

Foreign Assistance: Promising Approach to Judicial Reform in Colombia (Washington, D.C.: GAO, 1992).

The Future of the Andean War on Drugs After the Escape of Pablo Escobar, Joint Hearing before the Subcommittee on Western Affairs and Task Force on International Narcotics Control of the Committee on Foreign Affairs, House of Representatives (Washington, D.C.: USGPO, 1992).

Gugliotta, Guy, "The Colombian Cartels and How to Stop Them," in Peter H. Smith, ed., *Drug Policy in the Americas* (Boulder, Colo.: Westview Press, 1992).

Hargreaves, Clare, *Snowfields: The War on Cocaine in the Andes* (London: Holmes & Meier, 1992).

Holt, Charles, Franco Modigliani, John Muth, and Herbert Simon, *Planning, Production, Inventories and Work Force* (Englewood Cliffs, N.J.: Prentice Hall, 1960).

Inciardi, James A., *The War on Drugs II* (Mountain View, Calif.: Mayfield Publishing Company, 1992).

International Narcotics Strategy Report (INCSR), United States Department of State, Bureau of International Narcotics Matters (Washington, D.C.: USGPO, 1994).

The Killings in Colombia (Washington, D.C.: Americas Watch, 1989).

Lee, Rensselaer W., "Making the Most of Colombia's Drug Negotiations," *Orbis* (Spring 1991).

———, *White Labyrinth* (New Brunswick, N.J.: Transaction Publishers), 1989.

Levine, Michael, *Deep Cover* (New York: Delacorte, 1990).

Lupsha, Peter, "The Political Economy of Drug Trafficking," paper presented at *The Role of the Military in the War on Drugs Conference*, San Antonio, Texas (5 January 1993).

MacDonald, Scott B., *Dancing on a Volcano* (New York: Praeger, 1989).

Mermelstein, Max, *The Man Who Made it Snow* (New York: Simon and Schuster, 1990).

Morales, Edmundo, *White Gold Rush in Peru* (Tucson, Ariz.: The University of Arizona Press, 1989).

National Drug Control Strategy: Reclaiming our Communities from Drugs and Violence (The White House, 1994.)

Over-the-Horizon Radar: Better Justification Needed for DOD Systems' Expansion (1991).

"Recipe Book: Cocaine Processing Techniques," (Lima, Peru: DEA, Lima Country Office), undated.

Reuter, Peter, Gordon Crawford, and Jonathan Cave, *Sealing the Borders: The Effects of Increased Military Participation in Drug Interdiction*, R-3594-USDP (Santa Monica, Calif.: RAND, 1988).

Riley, Kevin Jack, *Snow Job? The Efficacy of Source Country Cocaine Control Policies*, RGSD-102 [Santa Monica, Calif.: RAND, 1993(a)].

_____, *The Implications of Colombian Drug Industry and Death Squad Political Violence for U.S. Counternarcotics Policy*, N-3605-U.S.DP [Santa Monica, Calif.: RAND, 1993(b)].

Rosenberg, Tina, *Children of Cain: Violence and the Violent in Latin America* (New York: William Morrow and Company, 1991).

Structure of International Drug Cartels, U.S. Senate, Permanent Subcommittee on Investigations Hearings (Washington, D.C.: USGPO, 1989).

Thoumi, Francisco E., "The Size of the Illegal Drugs Industry in Colombia," *The North-South Agenda Papers*, no. 3 (July 1993).

West, Kenneth, "A Variance Bounds Test for the Linear Quadratic Inventory Model," *Journal of Political Economy* 43 (1986): 374–401.

6

The Border's the Limit

War historians will recall the Maginot Line, a series of fortifications the French emplaced prior World War II to defend against a probable German attack. This much-maligned defensement, conceived in the despair and devastation wrought by World War I, offers a number of instructive lessons for the modern-day Maginot Line that has been erected between Colombia and the United States. In both its length and depth, the real Maginot Line was a marvel. Together with its extension, the Maginot Line stretched from the French border with Germany and Switzerland in the south more than three hundred miles north and west to the French borders with Belgium and Luxembourg. Among the emplacements were antitank barriers to prevent German ground crossings, retractable gun turrets concealed in embankments to defend the line, and antiaircraft cannon to prevent German air incursions.

The Line's main purpose was to stall the German advance at the border long enough for the French military to mobilize in protection of the vital industries and minerals of Alsace-St. Lorraine. Unfortunately for the French, the attacking German forces did not respect the Low Countries' neutrality, and simply outflanked the Line by running around the end point through Belgium. Also, air travel had advanced so much in the decades between the wall's conception and construction, that the antiaircraft emplacements along the Maginot Line were a futile protest against German air power. The Line did prevent a German ground attack over the French-German border for many days after the start of German offensive. This accomplishment is little remembered today, however, in light of the more catastrophic defensive failures that occurred because of the Germans' adaptive behavior.

The analogy between the Maginot Line and interdiction can easily be overdone, but some interesting points do emerge from the comparison.

It is clear that, just as German forces outflanked the Maginot Line, drug traffickers have surmounted the interdiction barrier. Many decry interdiction as a colossal, expensive failure.[1] In a world where every dollar spent on interdiction means one less dollar for other antidrug programs, the critics argue that interdiction is a hollow approach to drug control. In the end, the Maginot Line proved to be a destructive strategy not only because it helped lull French politicians into a false sense of security, but because it forced changes in German behavior that the victims did not anticipate. With the benefit of hindsight, for example, the French probably would have been much better served by building a rapid response force than by committing resource and troops to a fixed location. Would a similar reconsideration benefit U.S. drug control strategy?

In 1994 authorities seized more than 220 metric tons (mt) of cocaine in transit to the United States or at the U.S. border. Not only does this represent about 20 percent of the estimated annual world cocaine production and more than 60 percent of annual U.S. consumption, it is also more cocaine than was produced worldwide and consumed in the United States in the 1970s and early 1980s.[2] Authorities have also confiscated millions of dollars in cash, real estate, cars, boats, trucks, planes, and other assets, all of which can be liquidated to provide law enforcement organizations with more resources to fight drug trafficking. These seizures are impressive figures. Not only do they represent the end result of billions of dollars of public expenditures, but they also attest to the risks and sacrifices undertaken by law enforcement and military personnel.

A search for meaning in the interdiction figures, however, will ultimately prove frustrating. Taken by themselves, the seizures can be construed as a monument to government action and proof positive that lives have been saved through government intervention. But taking the seizure figures at face value is to take them out of context, for what the seizure data fail to convey is how much cocaine gets into the United States. Of course, there is a paucity of data about how much cocaine reaches the United States. The best estimates indicate, however, that as much, and perhaps more, reached U.S. shores in 1994 than in preceding years.[3] The ready availability of cocaine is confirmed by a variety of factors already discussed, including declining retail prices and increasing consumption among some demographic groups.[4] Evidence that interdiction has created long-term shortages and prevented demand from being met is as scarce as cocaine is plentiful.

As a consequence, it is almost universally agreed that seizures are an inappropriate instrument for measuring interdiction's success. This conclusion, however, begs the question of what contribution interdiction makes to the international drug control effort. Indeed, the virtues of international interdiction are difficult to quantify. This chapter explores interdiction and what some of its limitations are.

The Departure Zone

Much of the cocaine that enters the United States is shipped from Colombia, although small amounts are shipped directly to the United States from other countries such as Bolivia and Peru. Within Colombia, drug exporting activity is concentrated in a 600-mile-long strip that stretches from the tip of the Guajira peninsula in the northeast to the Buenaventura-Cali region in the southwest. Little drug production actually takes place along the Departure Zone. Cocaine refining is concentrated in the vast, desolate plains, called *llanos*, of Colombia. The plains, which are isolated from Colombia's population centers by dense jungle and a web of rivers, provide cover for Colombia's cocaine refining. The traffickers have constructed some of Colombia's most notorious refining laboratories, including Tranquilandia, in these isolated regions.[5] Refined cocaine is moved to the Departure Zone through a series of navigable rivers, including the Magdelena, the Cauca and the Atrato, that connect the refining and smuggling regions, over main roadways that run from one end of Colombia to the other, and, of course, by air corridors that connect the two portions of the country. Figure 6.1 provides an overview of the Departure Zone and its proximity to Colombian cocaine refining centers.

Although authorities can never be certain, at one point an estimated 90 percent of the cocaine left Colombia on aircraft. In recent years a greater share of the traffic has moved to ships and the 90 percent estimate has become outdated. As far as air traffic, both commercial and private planes are used. Although a disproportionate share leaves on small commuter planes that depart from clandestine airstrips, the recent years have brought changes here as well. There are now several documented instances of large passenger planes, such as 727 jets, being used to smuggle muliton cocaine shipments from Colombia to intermediate destinations. The story of Colombian cocaine smuggling, and efforts to control it, thus begins with a look at air smuggling operations.

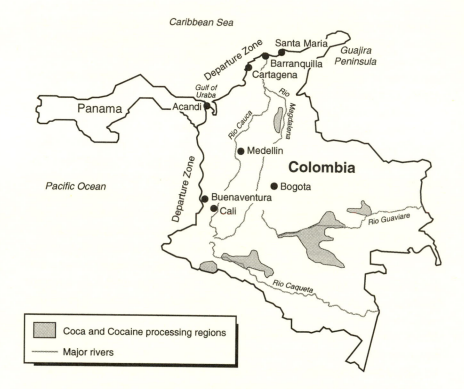

Figure 6.1—Map of Departure Zone

Air Superiority

Several times a week a small commuter airplane, such as a Cessna 210, departs from somewhere inside the Colombian coast for a rendezvous with drug smugglers who will forward the cargo to the U.S border. Laden with perhaps 200 to 300 kilograms of cocaine, though occasionally substantially more, the flights last up to ten hours and cover more than 1,000 miles one way. Many of the smaller planes do not have the fuel capacity for the round-trip between Colombia and the drop-off, and thus have extra fuel tanks added to stretch their ability to fly without refueling. Although the drug pilots are guided by sophisticated electronics and navigation equipment, they must surmount a daunting array of obstacles in order to safely deliver their cargo. Flights out of Colombia are treacherous. Violent thunderstorms periodically strike virtually without warning, causing crashes or forcing the smugglers to return to their landing strips with their drugs undelivered. The flights are also unforgiving of mechanical failures, for there are few safe landing spots along the way and few drug pilots can risk calling for rescue help during an emergency.

Although a portion of the air smuggling activity occurs on commercial airliners, and originates at commercial airports, the majority of the drug smuggling takes place on small commuter craft that leave from private airstrips. Of course the traffickers can bribe personnel to ensure that their shipments are not inspected at the airport, but it is also perhaps safer to conduct operations at private airstrips where the risk from law enforcement intervention is lower. The refueling stations and airstrips range from crude to relatively sophisticated. Some traffickers are reluctant to invest much in their landing facilities because they are frequently uncovered and destroyed by law enforcement authorities. Thus, some airfields consist of little more than a relatively level strip of land, barrels of fuel, and a store of spare parts. There is a price to pay for the crudity, however. Maintenance on the planes is difficult in the remote regions, and a number of pilots have lost their lives because of dirty fuel, broken parts, and bad landing strips.[6] Traffickers have thus been known to build more elaborate landing sites, and to use the region's few paved roads as airstrips.[7]

Traffickers attempt to conduct their operations undetected by law enforcement authorities. Their desire for secrecy not only leads them to depart from remote locations, but to do so under the cover of darkness. Daylight makes trafficking planes vulnerable to visual identification and interception, and so the traffickers tend to avoid flying during the daylight hours. At night there is still the risk of radar detection, but at least the traffickers can complicate the task of interception and trailing by turning out their craft's lights and flying low to the ground.

Another method of avoiding law enforcement is to make the flight look legitimate. Reportedly, the traffickers have expanded their efforts to conceal drug shipments in commercial traffic. In particular, the traffickers have used large passenger jets, such as 727s, to send multiton cocaine shipments to Mexican transshipment centers. Typically, the traffickers control both the source and destination airports. San Andres Island, located off the coast of Nicaragua, but owned by Colombia, is one such location. The traffickers reportedly have corrupted the air traffic controllers, customs inspectors, and other officials at the island's main airport. The airport is large enough to accommodate large aircraft. As a result, passenger jets carrying two or more metric tons of cocaine can depart for transhipment points either under cover of an official flight plan, or surreptitiously to avoid law enforcement. By flying with a plan, at an altitude used by commercial traffic, during daylight hours, these flights are difficult to distinguish from commercial aviation traffic, and less likely to attract law enforcement scrutiny. Conversely, the jet craft are also fast enough to outrun most transit nations' interdiction craft. The jets therefore reduce the risk of making deliveries to transit locations.

Cocaine flights typically originate in one of two major regions: The Guajira Peninsula, which occupies the extreme northeastern portion of Colombia, and the Pacific Lowlands, which stretch from the Gulf of Uraba near the Colombian border with Panama, south to the coastal city of Buenaventura (refer to figure 6.1 for a map of the region). The Guajira peninsula is favored as the launching point for south Florida and southeastern United States destinations. Flights from the Guajira are less than 1500 miles from U.S. territory, but direct flights are increasingly uncommon because of improved radar detection and monitoring of U.S. coastal areas. Instead, many of the small islands between Colombia and the United States have become important stopover points. Some islands, such as the Bahamas, are close enough to the United States that the shipments can be transferred to small boats, which then ferry the drugs into the United States. Puerto Rico is also an increasingly important transit point because of Puerto Rico's commonwealth relationship to the United States. Once drugs have entered Puerto Rico, they can be shipped by commercial means with only limited clearance and inspection procedures. In other cases, the drugs can be given to couriers that will take commercial flights to the United States. The open waters of the Caribbean basin increase the traffickers' vulnerability to radar detection, but they also provide cover in the form of countless tourist, business, and pleasure flights that frequent the region.

The Guajira peninsula of Colombia provides ideal conditions for exporting cocaine by air. Sandwiched between the Gulf of Venezuela and the Caribbean Sea, the peninsula is sparsely populated. The Sierra Nevada de Santa Marta mountain range, with peaks reaching nearly 20,000 feet, separates the Guajira from the rest of Colombia and helps preserve the region's isolation. As is typical throughout most of rural Colombia, the federal government maintains only a nominal presence. Colombia maintains an ongoing dispute with Venezuela over the Gulf's boundaries, and this has, at times precipitated a substantial amount of military traffic in the region, both on and off shore. In general, however, the demographic, geographic, and political situations afford the traffickers ample opportunities to carry out their business virtually unobserved.

The Guajira became an important center of the marijuana trade in the early 1970s when the Mexican government succeeded in dismantling much of its domestic trade in cannabis. The climate of the Guajira, which is semiarid, proved very hospitable to the production of marijuana, and the eastern slopes of the Sierra Nevada de Santa Marta mountains and the flat portions of the Guajira soon became covered with marijuana farms. As the prospects for Colombia's marijuana trade waned and the potential for cocaine consumption in the United States became clear, leading marijuana traffickers adapted their routes, equipment, and personnel to cocaine smuggling.[8] Pioneers in cocaine smuggling, including Carlos Lehder, eventually saw the promise of air smuggling, and the Guajira eventually became home to numerous landing strips.[9]

The peninsula's geography aids the traffickers in their endeavors. Broad flat plains, perfect for constructing temporary airstrips and more elaborate landing fields, are prevalent on the Guajira. These staging grounds provide direct routes to the Mona Passage between Puerto Rico and the Dominican Republic and the Windward Passage between Haiti and Cuba, which in turn provide access to small transit islands such as the Caicos and Turks along the way. In an occupation where every minute spent in transportation adds to the risk of detection and apprehension, flights from the Guajira to the Bahamas and the Straits of Florida are roughly half the distance of the journey from central Colombia through Central America to the Southwest Mexican-U.S. border.

In contrast, shipments destined for California, Texas, and the southwestern United States usually follow a route that leads through Central America or Mexico. These flights are usually launched from the Pacific Lowlands, not only because they are closer to the stopover destinations, but because the risk of radar detection may be lower. The rugged terrain between Colombia and Mexico makes it more difficult for radar to detect drug flights. In addition, many of the Central American nations do not have planes capable of intercepting drug flights, let alone radar systems. U.S. surveillance teams can, of course, use their radar systems to

detect these flights, but must secure permission from the host government to make an interception over foreign territory. In some cases, by
the time permission is received, the flights have already landed.

The Pacific Lowlands, which begin near the Gulf of Uraba and continue south and west to Buenaventura and the Cordillera Occidental range
of the Andes Mountains, are also very sparsely populated. This region
is home to less than 4 percent of Colombia's 30 million residents. It also
receives vast amounts of rain, so much so that portions of the area are
permanently flooded swampland. Despite the wet climate, airstrips located in the lowlands of Colombia offer a number of advantages. Flights
originating on the Caribbean side of the Lowlands enjoy direct overwater
access to the Windward and Mona passages and the transit islands that
lay just the other side of the large Caribbean islands, much like flights
operating out of the Guajira. But, law enforcement authorities have intensified interdiction efforts on the northern and southern rims of the
Caribbean basin, forcing the traffickers to diversify and disperse their
departure and drop-off zones. On the U.S. side, installation of radar coverage along the southern coast severely reduced the traffickers' ability
to fly directly into the United States and drop their shipments on U.S.
soil, while improvements in monitoring and patrolling capabilities off
the eastern Florida peninsula and the Gulf of Mexico helped reduce the
traffickers' ability to make speed boat runs from deep ocean water to
the U.S. shore.[10] The traffickers thus began to ship cocaine up through
Central America and Mexico, and then over the long U.S.-Mexican border using a variety of tactics. Pacific coast airstrips in Colombia made
sense not only because the route from the Panamanian-Colombian border to Mexico was shorter than the route from the Guajira, but because
the increase in shipping activity from the Pacific side helped stretch out
already thin Colombian naval and coast patrolling capacities.[11]

Oceans of Trouble

South and west of the Guajira peninsula and north and east of the
Lowlands, along the jagged coastline, lay the port cities of Barranquilla,
Santa Marta, and Cartagena. These cities, along with the major Pacific
ports of Buenaventura and Tumaco, form the backbone of Colombia's
maritime smuggling. The bulk of Colombian international commerce,
both legal and illegal, that departs Colombia by ship leaves through

these ports. While Buenaventura is perhaps the most important to trade and commerce, Barranquilla handles all of Colombia's oil exports, and thus is of growing importance for Colombia's role in international petroleum markets. To the cocaine trade, these ports, along with dozens of smaller ports found in fishing and coastal villages, have become increasingly important as the risks and costs of air smuggling have increased over the past decade.

Maritime smuggling techniques will vary depending on the perceived law enforcement threat, the availability of crew, size of the ship, and similar considerations. Generally, there are two options for smuggling cocaine out of Colombia by water. One method is to load a large- to medium-sized vessel with large amounts, several tons or more, of cocaine. Ships of this size are capable of delivering the cargo directly to the United States, perhaps with ports of call at various intermediate destinations to provide an air of legitimacy to the operation. Another option is to offload the drug cargo to the uncounted thousands of pleasure craft that ply the waters between the Colombian coast and the United States' shoreline. On the journey toward the United States, the large vessel (called a mother ship) will rendezvous with a series of smaller vessels, each of which take a portion of the drug cargo and delivers it to U.S. territory. The smaller launches are incapable of making the full run from Colombia to the United States, but they are well-suited to making a pick-up in deep water and delivering it to a clandestine U.S. location. Similar arrangements can be made whereby planes, rather than mother ships, drop the cocaine at a predetermined location for retrieval by a small launch. The traffickers have even made use of small (two person) submarinelike craft capable of travelling below the water surface for several hundred miles.

On an average day there are more than 5,000 large ships under way in the Pacific Ocean, and an additional thousand or more in the Caribbean. All of these vessels, which range in size from small fishing trawlers to large cargo container ships, are potential drug carriers since all are suited for transporting cocaine great distances between major ports. Travel time for a ship from Colombia to the United States may be two to three weeks, depending on the size of the ship, the number of stops that it makes, and its final destination. Ocean voyages can be every bit as perilous as the airborne smuggling runs. May to November is hurricane season in the region, but even under normal circumstances, eight- and ten-foot swells are not uncommon in some portions of the Caribbean Basin and the Pacific Ocean. Navy and Coast Guard officials report that many of the ships boarded and seized have been barely seaworthy, particularly smaller vessels that appear to be part of small "mom and pop" smuggling organizations.[12]

Interdiction in the Departure Zone

What happens to a suspicious vessel or aircraft depends largely on where it is identified and intercepted. Inside Colombian territorial limits, the authority for counternarcotics operations is primarily divided between the Colombian National Police (CNP) and the Colombian military.[13] The CNP, who number over 40,000, operate at the national level under the purview of the Minister of National Defense. The CNP, through its operations, air wing, intelligence and investigation units, bears the primary burden for Colombia's counternarcotics operations, including eradication and interdiction. The national police account for more than three quarters of the seizures and raids that occur in Colombia.[14]

The Colombian military numbers perhaps 50 percent larger than the CNP, a level of staffing that nevertheless leaves the force stretched thin.[15] The Colombian military's primary task is to confront and control the guerrilla forces and insurgencies scattered throughout Colombia. While there are perhaps fewer than 5,000 active guerrillas in Colombia, the country's territory is massive, and is substantially larger than the present military force can comfortably control. The military has had substantial counternarcotics duties since 1978, when President Turbay sent Colombian forces to the Guajira peninsula to disrupt the marijuana trade. The military leadership, however, has greeted this responsibility with varying degrees of equanimity. At times, counternarcotics responsibilities have been viewed as a distraction from the primary responsibility of defending against the guerrilla insurgencies, while at other times involvement in counternarcotics operations has been viewed as a mechanism for obtaining increased funding and better equipment. Some observers have noted the military's involvement in counternarcotics operations with alarm, not only because military leaders have colluded with drug traffickers in human rights abuses, particularly against suspected left-wing sympathizers, but because of the potential national security implications of military corruption.[16]

The Colombian military is underequipped for the task of ensuring the integrity of Colombian territorial limits against encroachment by drug smugglers. All told, the Colombian Navy consists of fewer than twenty large craft capable of patrolling the length of the Colombian coast.[17] Four of these ships, the *Almirante Padilla* class frigates, are the pride of the Navy, but have a maximum speed of 27 knots that makes them too slow to catch many drug trafficking vessels. Colombia has five fast-attack craft capable of speeds up to 40 knots, but only the two *Quito Sueno* class ships are appropriate for ocean interdiction. The other three fast-attack craft are confined to river patrol duties.

The situation is similar for Colombia's Air Force. The problems of patrolling Colombia's territory with its small force aside, Colombia lacks trained pilots.[18] The Colombian Air Force consists of less than 350 aircraft, many of which are old and barely serviceable. The age of the procured fleet, combined with the fact that many craft in service were confiscated from traffickers, has hampered the ability to develop an integrated, cohesive force, and complicated the tasks of maintenance and spare parts provisioning. Consequently, the force's ability to provide surveillance and close air support services to interdiction operations is limited.

Between 1989 and 1991 each branch of the Colombian military, as well as law enforcement organizations, received equipment from the United States as part of the Andean Strategy.[19] President Bush announced the transfer and sale of much of this equipment in response to the unprecedented levels of drug industry violence against the Colombian states that erupted in 1989.[20] The United States donated, loaned, or sold a number of aircraft to Colombia for use in counternarcotics operations, including two C-130 Hercules transports, eight A-37 Dragonfly attack craft, five UH-1 Huey helicopters, and eighteen OV-10 craft. Washington delivered additional supplies to the Colombian Air Force ranging from ammunition and grenade launchers to fuel trucks and radios. The Colombian Air Force utilizes UH-60 Black Hawk helicopters to transport troops.

Since U.S. concerns about Colombia's announced policy of forcing down suspected drug trafficking flights have been resolved, the United States has resumed providing operational assistance to the Colombians as well. For example, the United States conducts surveillance over Colombian territory with OTH radar and with flights launched from Panamanian and other bases. This intelligence information is then relayed to the appropriate Colombian counterdrug organizations. Because Colombia controls its airspace, these flights require the permission of the Colombian government. These flights supplement Colombian air operations and the information from Colombian ground radar installations. Indeed, the United States installed the radar facilities Colombia uses in counternarcotics operations and trained the Colombian civilian and military forces that now operate the installations.

The Transit Zone

In the international waters and airspace beyond Colombian territorial limits, the United States assumes the responsibility for direct action against drug smugglers. U.S. forces, both military and civilian, operate on a principle known as defense in depth, by which they attempt to identify and intercept drug shipments as early as possible, but by which they also provide supplementary options in the event that interdiction near the source fails. Near the Departure Zone, this entails conducting sustained patrols close to source countries, both to identify ships as they leave Colombian waters, and to identify aircraft as they head into international airspace. But, failing to identify and intercept a drug shipment as it leaves Colombia, the defense in depth strategy ensures that there are other opportunities for detection and interdiction along the way. Defense in depth consists of echelons of forces arrayed at strategic locations between Colombia and the United States. These forces include land-based radars positioned along the northern Caribbean basin rim, surveillance and interceptor aircraft patrols stationed at key transshipment locations, sea-based aerostats, and ocean patrols located at choke points such as the Yucatan, Windward, Mona, and other passages.

If Transit Zone interdiction operations appear to be a massive endeavor, it is because the Transit Zone itself is enormous. The Transit Zone includes the international waters and airspace spanning from the Colombian-Venezuelan border on the east, Mexico on the west, the Colombian coast line on the south and U.S. territorial limits on the north. The Transit Zone encompasses more than 1.5 million square miles, an area larger than India and nearly half the size of the United States. Given that smuggling planes can fly at altitudes over 10,000 feet, the area under consideration is more than 15 billion cubic miles (see figure 6.2 for

Figure 6.2—The Transit Zone

more detail). Virtually all of the cocaine that ends up in the United States, whether it is shipped by land, air or sea, passes through the Transit Zone.

Within the confines of the Transit Zone, U.S. interdiction forces operate under a number of constraints. U.S. military forces, which have little training in police policies and procedures, evidence gathering and preservation, and matters pertaining to suspects' criminal and civil rights, are proscribed by U.S. law from arresting and apprehending suspected drug smugglers, even in international waters and airspace. Whether they are on air or sea duty, U.S. military forces must limit their operations to detecting and trailing suspected drug smugglers. A strong distinction is made between participation in detection and monitoring activities, and participation in law enforcement activities such as interdiction, arrest, and apprehension.[21] Statutes governing the military's relation to law enforcement organizations were revised in the early 1980s in order to permit the military greater latitude in providing training, equipment, and information to civilian organizations.[22] The 1989 and 1990 Defense Authorization Acts further broadened the military's counternarcotics role by designating the military as the lead agency in the detection and monitoring of aerial and maritime drug smuggling routes, and by requiring the military to provide civilian agencies with greater assistance at, and near, U.S. borders.[23] These proscriptions against military participation in law enforcement operations have been eased to allow indirect military participation in civilian law enforcement operations. Naval vessels that carry civilian law enforcement detachments (LEDETS) may temporarily cede command to the civilian forces so that the military vessel can be used in an arrest and apprehension procedure.

In contrast, U.S. agencies with law enforcement powers, including the Coast Guard, Customs Service, and the Drug Enforcement Administration, are empowered to arrest and apprehend drug smugglers, and to seize contraband and suspicious vessels. There are strict rules of engagement associated with arrest and apprehension, and they vary by mode of transport. What this means is that U.S. law enforcement organizations cannot shoot down suspected drug-smuggling planes, but they are allowed, after following established procedures and securing permission through the chain of command, to use force to disable suspected drug-smuggling ships.[24] Planes must be tracked to a land destination, where the arrests can then be executed by the appropriate LEA.

Transit Zone interdiction operations not only require cooperation between departments and agencies of the U.S. government, but necessitate collaboration across international borders. Tracking a flight from Colombia to the United States, for example, might begin with a radar contact made just off the Colombian coast. Once the suspected plane has been identified it will be continuously tracked and monitored. If the craft's flight profile triggers suspicions, an intercept flight might be launched. The intercept team will attempt to read the craft's registration number, which can then be checked against databases of plane registrations, such as the one maintained at the El Paso Intelligence Center (EPIC). If the plane's flight path takes it over land and overflight of foreign territory will be required to maintain contact, permission from the foreign country in question will be required. Since military personnel have no arrest and law enforcement authority, as the plane draws near its destination the surveillance team must coordinate the tracking with a civilian law enforcement agency such as the DEA, Coast Guard, or appropriate foreign civilian law enforcement agency. U.S. law enforcement agencies have very limited powers in foreign countries, and will in turn have to coordinate arrest procedures with a foreign law enforcement organization if the plane lands in a country other than the United States. If the traffickers' plane does not land, but makes a dropoff instead, and U.S. authorities desire the arrest of the flight crew, the craft must be continuously tracked back to the source country and arrest procedures coordinated with the source country's law enforcement organizations.

Efforts at cooperation can be defeated by matters as mundane as incompatible communications equipment. Prior to DOD's designation as the lead agency for interdiction support, the agencies with interdiction responsibilities had limited abilities to communicate. Not only did interdiction agencies communicate using a variety of different modes, including telephones, radios, satellites, and computers, but even communications using the same mode were difficult. For example, agencies' radios often operated on different frequencies or used different encryption mechanisms to protect transmissions from eavesdropping. The lack of flexible, rapid communications links hampered interdiction operations by preventing coordination between detection and monitoring forces and apprehension and seizure teams. Acting on a communications master plan drawn up in 1988 by the National Drug Policy Board, DOD began to provide limited technical and financial communications assistance to law enforcement organizations, and to develop ADNET (Anti-Drug Network), a data communications system. Although communication procedures have improved substantially since the late 1980s, there are still some limits to interoperability and transmission security.

The Plane Facts

Once drug flights have entered the transit zone, most detection and monitoring is accomplished by air surveillance crews flying in E-2 Hawkeyes, E-3 AWACS, and P-3 Orions.[25] Sea-Based Aerostats (SBAs) and the Small Aerostat Surveillance System (SASS), which consist of small blimps equipped with radar units that are tethered to a surface ship, have, at various times, supplemented airborne surveillance programs.[26] Increasingly, ground-based Over-The-Horizon (OTH) radar systems contribute to detection and monitoring, and are expected to bear the majority of the detection burden in the latter 1990s.

The different radar platforms offer a mixture of strengths and weaknesses. The aircraft use sophisticated radar to patrol the Carribbean basin for air and sea activity and, in certain circumstances, are capable of detecting aircraft at ranges of up to 350 nautical miles. At a distance of 200 miles from base, the Hawkeye can stay on patrol for a time ranging from four and a half hours to over six hours, depending on the fuel configuration with which the plane is equipped. It cannot be refueled in the air, however. The Hawkeye can control forty intercepts and track thousands of targets simultaneously using the most advanced radar configuration. The E-3 AWACS has a more diverse range of radars. While on patrol, AWACS radar can function in modes that allow for optimal scanning of targets flying over a variety of terrains at various elevations and ranges. Yet, between fuel, crew, and maintenance costs, flying surveillance and detection missions is very expensive in comparison to the operation of static radar platforms. When military priorities dictate, airborne platforms may be called to other duties including frigates and cruisers. During the Persian Gulf War, for example, surveillance teams deployed on drug duties were pulled from the Caribbean and deployed to the Middle East. Over-the-Horizon systems can detect targets from almost 2,000 miles away. OTH also provides a much larger field of vision than individual surveillance planes. Although OTH's strengths are impressive, the system has its weaknesses, including susceptibility to atmospheric disturbances, an inability to provide altitude information, and a lack of IFF capabilities, as discussed earlier.[27] Stationary ground platforms may ultimately prove more expensive if they have to be relocated in response to changing trafficking patterns.[28]

Regardless, radar conveys vital information about drug trafficking aircraft and ships, and has been an invaluable tool in drug interdiction. Radar works by detecting both the delay between, and the distortion of, the transmission and return of the radar's signal. The time it takes the radar signal to return indicates the target's range or distance. The target's elevation and heading can be computed by positioning the radar antenna in the direction that yields maximum signal strength. Similarly, the degree of the returned signal's distortion, also known as frequency shift or Doppler effect, represents the craft's velocity. Sophisticated radar systems can also use the frequency shift to construct an image of the aircraft. Images, in conjunction with other flight char-acteristics, can then be compared to smuggler profiles to decide if the target is likely to be engaged in drug trafficking.[29] For example, a very low-flying aircraft moving at a slow speed might be indicative of drug running, while an aircraft following a confirmed flight plan in regular air traffic corridors might not arouse suspicions. Because drug flights typically take place under the cover of darkness, radar, which works in darkness as well as daylight, is an invaluable tool in the detection and monitoring of drug flights.

Radar is not an infallible tool, however. Radar works best when the signal-to-noise ratio is high. In simple terms, the strength of the signal is determined by the aircraft's size. The amount of noise is determined, basically, by everything else. The smoother the path between the radar source and the target, the better the radar signal propagates, or travels, and the better the signal quality. Surfaces such as the sea and the desert are good forward propagating surfaces, and provide good signals. Rough terrain, however, provides irregular surfaces that limit the radar signal's ability to travel forward. Such surfaces not only increase the noise, but limit the signal's forward propagation, which in turn degrades the radar's ability to detect targets at distances. The higher above the target the radar platform is, the better it can see directly down over a target, and thus the fewer problems there are with propagation and clutter. OTH radar, even though it is ground based, functions as if it is stationed di-rectly over its targets because it bounces its radar signals off atmospheric layers located many miles above the earth's surface. Even without OTH, interdiction authorities report with confidence that they detect a high percentage of the aircraft attempting to surreptitiously cross the Carib-bean basin.[30] With OTH, authorities can detect the vast majority of flights that move through the area.

Drug pilots are, of course, aware that the military uses radar to track their flights and they take steps to evade detection. Perhaps the first line of defense for the traffickers is to monitor the communications of the surveillance teams. These communication links, some of which are still not secure, provide the traffickers with information about where sur-veillance activities will be concentrated and, thus, which regions should be avoided. Even when drug planes are flying directly through moni-tored areas, radar detection is by no means certain. Because detection abilities tend to degrade over rugged terrain, the traffickers take advantage of this weakness by flying small planes and following land routes up from Colombia. Similarly, the traffickers will fly low over the ocean in an attempt to fly under radar coverage. Again, OTH radar should work to mitigate the traffickers' countermeasures by providing twenty-four-hour-a-day radar coverage, and by limiting the drug pilots' ability to hide their aircraft in background clutter.

In any event, positive radar contact alone is not conclusive proof that an airplane is on an illicit drug mission. The Caribbean is a popular aviation area. Thousands of commercial and pleasure flights crisscross the region on a daily basis. Thus, after a successful radar detection has been made authorities must determine whether the flight in question is legitimate. One primary indication, of course, is the flight profile, including elevation and bearing. But there are other indicators that will trip the surveillance team's interest. For example, legitimate flights communicate, or "squawk" on known frequencies, so monitoring crews will scan communication frequencies for a target's communication activity. Also, legitimate flights usually file a flight plan with authorities, and then follow it. Monitoring teams thus attempt to verify a target's flight path with the flight plans on file.

If no legitimate flight plan is on record and if the pilot is not broadcasting on regular channels, the surveillance team's suspicions are further aroused. The next step would be to obtain further information about the flight by intercepting it. A variety of planes are used as interceptors. Which interceptor is launched will depend on a number of factors, including where in the Transit Zone the target is detected, how far from its destination it is, and under whose jurisdiction the contact was made. The U.S. Southern Command (USSOUTHCOM) maintains the primary responsibility for military detection and surveillance over the South and Central American land masses. USACOM, based in Norfolk, Virginia, has primary responsibility for operations in the territorial and international waters around South and Central America. SOUTHROC (Southern Regional Operations Center), which SOUTHCOM operates out of Howard Air Force Base in Panama, is the primary command and control center for operations in South and Central America. SOUTHROC collects radar and contact information from both the Caribbean Basin Radar Network (CBRN) and ground-based radar stations in the source countries. USACOM's command and control facility at the Naval Air Station (NAS) in Key West Florida is called CARIBROC. CARIBROC similarly collects intelligence information from CBRN and ground installations in the Caribbean. Under a typical contact and interception scenario, SOUTHROC and CARIBROC would work together to identify potentially suspicious flights. In cases where flights are deemed worthy of a closer look, SOUTHROC and CARIBROC coordinate their information with JTF-4 (Joint Task Force 4) operations. JTF-4, also located at NAS Key West Florida, in turn can seek additional radar monitoring with AWACS and other airborne platforms, and can coordinate interception of suspicious flights so that visual confirmation of aircraft markings and other indicators can be made.

In some cases an F-15 or F-16 interceptor might be launched. These are fast jets, and are capable of catching slow-moving drug targets very quickly. U.S. civilian law enforcement organizations do not have the capability and jurisdiction to conduct intercept operations near the Departure Zone, and thus confine their operations to the northern Caribbean basin. If radar contact is initiated further north in the Caribbean basin, the Customs Service might launch a Cessna II, Customs High-Endurance Tracker (CHET), or a Piper Cheyenne III.[31] These craft are not nearly as fast as military aircraft, but they are also not as expensive to operate and are better suited to the task of trailing slow-moving drug planes.

Interceptors typically approach a suspected drug flight from the rear. This approach allows the interceptor to avoid being detected by the traffickers who, if they thought they were being followed, would probably jettison their cargo and return to Colombia. From this vantage point the interceptor attempts to gather information on the flight. One clue about its intentions will be whether it is flying with its lights on. Lack of lighting is often an indication that the flight is ferrying drugs, although it can also be a sign that the craft is in distress. The interceptor crew can also use infrared and other night-vision equipment to read the craft's tail and body markings, or to observe action in the craft's cabin. Craft identification numbers can then be compared to lists of planes known to be involved in drug trafficking at data centers such as EPIC.

Interceptors also serve another critical purpose by serving as an intermediate link in the tracking chain. If Colombian, Mexican, or other authorities are to make a legal case against a suspected drug-smuggling plane, it is important to have the craft under continuous observation. Fast interceptors, such as the F-16s based at Howard AFB in Panama, can make visual contact with a drug-smuggling plane just after it has entered the transit zone, but before the radar signal is lost to background noise. But, like many other sophisticated pieces of equipment, F-16s are expensive to operate and, because of fuel limitations, cannot remain on station indefinitely. Thus, while fast-moving jet craft are usually responsible for making the initial visual identification and securing the chain of observation, they typically do so in preparation for handing the tailing responsibilities off as the smugglers penetrate deeper into the transit zone and near the arrival zone.

High-Seas Seizures

But not all the cocaine smuggled to the United States heads out on planes. A significant, and some analysts contend, a growing, fraction, moves out of the source countries on ships. Smuggling by ship has grown in popularity, particularly as the radar networks have closed off direct air routes into the continental United States. Ships and maritime craft may also now face increased risks of interdiction, but they offer two advantages over planes. First, large ships provide room in which to hide the contraband. In small planes, drugs may take up virtually all of the cargo space, but in most ships, particularly vessels with larger containers, a load of even a 1000 kilos can easily be concealed in the cargo. The second advantage is that most ships can carry more cargo than commuter planes. In a situation where a plane and a ship face equal odds of apprehension and seizure, the ship will prove to be the more cost-effective method of smuggling, assuming it carries larger loads. Ship cargoes of several thousand kilos are not uncommon, and one naval officer recalled a bust of more than 8000 kilos.

Interdiction forces are on the lookout for suspicious ships and vessels. Surface interdiction teams cannot rely on the bearing, elevation, and speed data that air interdiction teams have at their disposal. Nevertheless, any number of factors might trigger authorities' suspicions about a vessel. Suspicious vessels include fishing boats with equipment in obvious disrepair, boats and ships that take evasive maneuvers, and vessels with superstructures that indicate they are carrying excess fuel capacity. In some cases the smugglers will delete equipment in an effort to save weight, but the actions will trigger suspicion because the vessel no longer matches its profile and obviously is not capable of performing its alleged mission.

For example, a fishing vessel missing reels, lines, buoys, traps, seines, nets, and other equipment relevant to fishing would be marked for attention. There is seasonality to certain types of fishing and trawling, so that some vessels might be suspicious by being out in months, or during times of the day, when their catch is not usually caught. For example, crab is usually not caught from March through October. Other species, such as yellow-fin tuna, are caught year-round, so that vessel profiles are not a perfect guide. Extraneous equipment, such as sophisticated navigation, communications, and surveillance equipment, may also arouse authorities' suspicions. Among smaller craft (which typically operate closer to U.S. territory), interdiction teams look for boats operating without lights, and tend to be suspicious of night operations in general.

The Navy and the Coast Guard use a variety of vessels for their interdiction activities. Generally, Naval vessels and Naval LEDET vessels operate deep in the Caribbean. Naval cruisers, such as the USS *Ticonderoga*, tend to have an important role in detection operations because they have sophisticated radar systems that can simultaneously sort multiple targets. In the latter 1980s, a typical force makeup stationed in the Caribbean included a Coontz (DDG-40) destroyer or Spruance (DD-963) destroyer as the flagship, a Belknap (CG-26) cruiser, a high- or medium-endurance cutter (WHEC/WMEC), and an oiler. Tagos ships equipped with both sonar and radar, and which are largely civilian manned, have assumed a greater share of deep Caribbean operations in recent years. These force configurations operate with a variety of helicopters, including LAMPS I SH-2F and LAMPS III SH-60B. The United States has conducted combined operations the navies and coast guards of Colombia, Venezuela, Honduras, and Jamaica.

The Coast Guard has nearly fifty vessels over sixty-five feet long, called cutters, that it can use in interdiction operations. The cutters, in conjunction with Patrol Combatants Missile (PHM) ships, can operate out of bases such as those in Key West, Florida, Guantanamo Bay, Cuba, and Puerto Rico. The large vessels, capable of being used to stop suspected trafficking vessels, are supplemented by a variety of shore, river, and shallow-water craft. Mark III and Mark IV craft, for example, are used in river operations. A Special Boat Unit with Mark IVs is maintained in Panama, while several Mark IIIs have been delivered to Colombia.

If air interdiction's weakness is that aircraft cannot be forced down, maritime interdiction's weakness is that seizures are difficult in the absence of intelligence. Ships may be boarded and searched with probable cause, but it is often extremely difficult to find the drugs unless the search party has information about where the contraband is hidden. Small cocaine shipments are difficult to locate because much of the cocaine shipped by sea is moved using large-containerized ships that are full of other, legitimate cargoes. Without intelligence about where the drugs are concealed, authorities might never find the illicit cargo. For example, naval vessels and LEDETs do not carry dogs to aid in searching. Only a small fraction of maritime boardings of large ships result in "cold hits," wherein authorities find a drug cargo hidden among a larger cargo without benefit of intelligence.[32] Intelligence experts can use clues from seized and interdicted vessels, including maps, documents, and navigation equipment, to piece together smuggling routes, as well as to pinpoint the locations of other illicit cargoes.

Technological advances have increased the efficiency of searches, and further improvements appear likely. For example, based upon successful field tests, the Coast Guard deployed IONSCAN devices in 1995.[33] IONSCAN technology works by collecting trace vapors and particles given off by chemical substances, electrically charging (or ionizing) the sample, and then analyzing the ions' speed in an electrical field. The speed with which the sample moves in the electrical field will depend on the ions' size and structure. Each chemical substance thus has a signature speed that differentiates it from other chemical substances. Samples for IONSCAN analysis can be collected from surface swipes and portable vacuums. The samples can then be transported back to a ship or vehicle-mounted unit, which is capable of searching for multiple substances simultaneously, for immediate analysis. The Coast Guard's testing revealed that IONSCAN could detect illicit drugs in situations where trained drug-sniffing dogs could not.[34] The Coast Guard will often employ IONSCAN analysis in instances where CINDI (Compact Integrated Narcotics Detection Instrument) has aroused suspicion. CINDI is, in effect, a neutron-based x-ray or radar device; beams of neutrons penetrate surfaces and return a hydrogen profile. The profile, in turn, can be read to provide indication of whether drugs are hidden. Although CINDI's beam can only penetrate about five inches, that depth is sufficient both for finding drug cargoes hidden in surface compartments and for justifying more thorough searches with IONSCAN units. CINDI devices cost about $15,000 compared to $50,000 for IONSCAN systems. Other technologies that may aid in cold searches include AcuPRESS Surface Drug tests. The AcuPRESS system is used by pressing a suspect surface on to a test kit surface (or vice versa). Currently, AcuPRESS kits are substance specific, although future versions of the product may be able to test for multiple substances at once.

The procedures for stopping, boarding, and searching ships vary, depending on the institution involved in trailing the ship, the vessel's flag or registration, and whether the ship is located in international, foreign territorial, or U.S. waters. U.S. Naval personnel cannot stop and board ships, but they get around this restriction by carrying civilian law enforcement detachments. In both international and U.S. waters, LEDET and law enforcement personnel can board a U.S. vessel without a warrant to inspect it. If it is found to be the carrying drugs, U.S. authorities can seize the craft and arrest the crew. Similarly, U.S. authorities can confiscate foreign-registered vessels found to be ferrying contraband in U.S. territorial waters.

Boarding a foreign-registered ship in international waters is slightly more complicated. For example, Colombian and Venezuelan flagged ships cannot be boarded in international waters without a SNO, or a statement of no objection. This is a statement from the vessel's government giving permission for a U.S. LEDET to board and inspect the vessel. Typically, it takes hours for such an statement to be obtained. Often, boats can return to port or otherwise escape in the interim. Nevertheless, the SNO is usually forthcoming. Many nations, however, conform to the laws of the sea, under which a suspicious vessel in open waters may be asked to stop and allow a boarding party on board.

Vessels that do not comply with boarding requests can have warning shots fired over the bow, and eventually may be stopped with a shot to the engine room.[35] The procedures for using force are detailed, and they must be followed carefully up the chain of command. And while there is some risk to the crew and passengers when force is used, it is not as risky as force used against aircraft.

The Arrival Zone

In recent years, Mexican traffickers have become central participants in the drug-smuggling business. As much as 70 percent of the cocaine consumed in the United States now passes through the hands of Mexican middlemen, compared to as little as perhaps 20 percent a decade ago. Mexico became the primary route for cocaine as U.S. drug control operations succeeded in making other Caribbean routes riskier. Before 1989, the limited surveillance assets of civilian law enforcement agencies allowed only intermittent and sporadic coverage of key cocaine smuggling zones in the Caribbean and Pacific. In the late 1980s, however, the United States established a credible radar "picket fence" along the Southern U.S. border. Composed of both law enforcement and military elements, and both static and mobile units, this radar presence allowed U.S. authorities to track drug flights to their destinations inside the United States. There, in many cases, arrests could be coordinated with local law enforcement agencies. Generally, the surety and severity of punishment in the United States for drug offenses is higher than elsewhere, and thus the radar rapidly deterred cocaine pilots from directly entering U.S. territory.

Mexican trafficking organizations were able to gather strength, and ultimately become virtually equal partners with the Colombians, as the cocaine trade increasingly shifted westward. Between 1985 and 1990, officials succeeded in weakening Mexico's largest and most important cocaine trafficking syndicate, the Guadalajara cartel.[36] The cartel's leadership was implicated in the murder of U.S. DEA agent Enrique Camerena. Mexican officials pursued key cartel members for their involvement in this crime, although the leader, Miguel Angel Felix Gallardo, evaded arrest until 1989. Felix Gallardo continued to run his organization from prison, much like Pablo Escobar did, until prison officials tightened security around him in 1990. By the time Felix Gallardo was put out of business, Mexican drug markets had changed in fundamental ways, and these changes brought forth multiple, powerful, Mexican trafficking organizations.

Perhaps most importantly, Colombian trafficking organizations were in disarray because of the Colombian government's crackdown. Law enforcement officials were interdicting Colombian traffickers' cocaine and freezing their assets. At the same time, retail prices in the United States were rising, meaning that the profits associated with supplying U.S. wholesale and retail markets were rising. Finally, Mexican-U.S. drug control cooperation was strained, and Mexican drug control programs were weakened, over the murder of Enrique Camerena. Juan Garcia Abrego saw the confusion in as an opportunity to build a Mexican trafficking syndicate, much like Carlos Lehder saw the potential for air transportation to revolutionize cocaine smuggling. In exchange for half the of the cocaine shipments, Garcia Abrego guaranteed his Colombian suppliers that he would deliver the load anywhere in the United States.[37] This move gave Garcia Abrego's Gulf (or Matamoros) cartel a substantial amount of cocaine to dispose of in the lucrative U.S. wholesale and retail markets. Other factors conspired to augment Mexico's role and opportunities for Mexican trafficking syndicates. For example, NAFTA eased trucking regulations, which in turn gave Mexican syndicates, with their proximity to the U.S. border, an advantage over Colombian organizations. Other syndicates benefitted from their ties to Mexico's dominant political party, PRI. Still others were able to expand their marijuana and heroin trafficking efforts to cocaine, and to forge close relations with Colombian trafficking organizations. Currently, five traffickers, including Juan Garcia Abrego (Gulf/Matamoros), Juan Jose Esparragosa (Guadalajara), Amado Carrillo Fuentes (Ciudad Juarez), and Benjamin and Ramon Arellano Felix (Tijuana) dominate the Mexican cocaine trade. Of these individuals, Carillo Fuentes may be the most important. His influence extends from Ciudad Juarez to Cancun, and embraces land, air, and sea routes. By some estimates there are an additional ten or more major Mexican trafficking syndicates.

With the arrest of leading Cali cartel members, and the collapse of the Medellin cartel, Mexican traffickers may be poised to dominate supplying U.S. drug markets into the next century. Currently, Mexican trafficking organizations exert powerful influence over Mexican political, social, and economic institutions. Drug corruption in Mexico is rampant, and numerous police, military, and political officials have been implicated. In one of the most serious incidents, Mexican soldiers apparently killed seven federal drug agents that were attempting to seize a drug shipment. In 1991, the agents had followed a plane to a remote spot in eastern Mexico. A U.S. Customs surveillance plane, also tailing the flight, captured the raid on videotape. The tape convincingly shows that Mexican soldiers on the scene were providing the traffickers with protection.

Mexican traffickers have also made key inroads into ownership of Mexican businesses, including trucking, shipping, and export-oriented operations. Ownership of these operations has facilitated cross-border smuggling into the United States. With the apparent collapse of the Cali cartel, it remains to be seen whether Mexican traffickers will begin to assume the cartel's brokerage, refining, and transportation roles. Several factors, including Mexican's organizations' wealth and influence, the competition among Mexican organizations for positions in U.S. wholesale and retail markets, and the potential rewards associated with cornering the brokerage market, suggest that at least some Mexican organizations may turn their attention southward.

Operations in Transshipment Nations

Except for those cases where civilian authorities make arrests and complete seizures on the high seas, actual interdiction does not occur until the traffickers jettison their cargoes or land at their destination spot. The lack of interdiction activity in the Transit Zone, particularly with respect to planes, is not because of any failure to detect and monitor ships and planes. Rather, the weak link in the interdiction process is the process of apprehending and arresting suspected smugglers and seizing their cargoes.[38] Most planes reach the Arrival Zone, not because detection and monitoring forces lose track of them along the way, but because no U.S. institution, civil or military, has the authority to force drug-smuggling aircraft to land.

Unfortunately, one consequence of this deterrence is that drug flights and boat shipments now typically end up in foreign countries where it is difficult for U.S. detection and monitoring forces to coordinate arrest and apprehension with foreign law enforcement organizations. While some of the transit nations, including Mexico, have made great strides in their ability to apprehend smugglers and their drug shipments, arrest and apprehension remains one of the weakest components of international interdiction. In many cases, the traffickers are simply able to land, or drop their shipment, in a remote area that law enforcement authorities have difficulty reaching. For example, the increased use of jet transportation has decreased interdiction losses, particularly in Mexico. Jet craft are much faster than propeller-driven airplanes and are thus capable of making short-hop deliveries before Mexican officials are able to identify and interdict the flights.[39] Moreover, the people arrested for smuggling are usually very low level, and thus unable, or unwilling, to report on higher-level activities of the smuggling organization. Trafficking heads have been known to threaten the smugglers' families with reprisal if they confess or implicate higher ups. Some are paid by the smuggling organizations to keep quiet.

Foreign nations' abilities to control ship traffic have suffered as well. As noted before, these ships are extremely difficult to search in the absence of intelligence. Although the ion scanning and other technologies discussed earlier may eventually help the transit nations control their ports and facilities, the sheer volume of legitimate commerce in which contraband can be hidden is daunting. In an average year, more than 300 million visitors, 8 million containers, 100 million vehicles, and 300,000 private and commercial flights will enter the United States, much of which comes over the Mexican border. Cargo truck traffic from Mexico rose by half in 1994 alone, many of which are exempted from border inspections after attaining special Customs Service background checks. In recent years Customs officials succeeded in examining approximately 4 percent of all containers entering the United States, and 20 percent entering from the cocaine producing countries.[40] Mexican cocaine seizures fell by more than one-half in 1994, this despite substantial improvements in Mexican interdiction authorities' communications, air interception, and other related drug-suppression abilities.

Concealing drug shipments in legitimate commercial traffic is only part of the transit nations' control problem. Just as jet aircraft have circumvented transit nations' interdiction capabilities, changes in ocean shipping methods have made interdiction and apprehension more difficult. In particular, submarinelike craft, also called semi-submersibles and LPVs (for Low Profile Vessels) have added a new twist to drug trafficking. LPVs can be as simple as a small fishing or speed boat fitted with a watertight cap, or as complicated as a specially-constructed underwater vessel (see figure 6.3). Whatever their construction, the craft are capable of traveling just below the water's surface, with only a small navigation tower and mast showing. Virtually invisible to both radar and visual sightings, the craft can carry small crews and a metric ton or more of cocaine. Although much slower than air shipments, LPVs are also thought to cost only a small fraction of what propeller and jet aircraft cost.

Commercial and fast pleasure craft present another set of problems. Near the U.S. border and territorial limits, responsibility for interdiction typically falls to either the Customs Service or DEA. U.S. Customs Service not only maintains responsibility for interdiction at U.S. borders

Figure 6.3—Semi-submersible Craft Used in Drug Smuggling

and ports of entry, but also has authority out to the twelve-mile territorial limit. The Coast Guard backs up its maritime forces with air capability, such as C-130s and HU-25 Falcons. DEA has similar interdiction
authority out to the three nautical mile limit. As noted earlier, the ability
to thoroughly inspect craft at sea is limited, developing inspection technologies notwithstanding.

In the transit nations, these craft are difficult to catch, in part because they have access to the thousands of ports, private marinas,
and docks, but also because their speed and range often exceeds that
of transit nations' enforcement vessels, and because they are able to
cloak their activities behind legitimate commerce. Honduran territorial waters, for example, serve as an important link in the transshipment chain. These waters, however, are heavily fished and the

traffickers have been able to conceal their activities behind this commerce. Moreover, the Honduran Navy runs only limited interdiction operations because of fuel and funding limitations. In Costa Rica, speedboats are a popular form of smuggling transportation. Guatemala, El Salvador, and Nicaragua are other important maritime transshipment points.

Interdiction

There is no way to accurately estimate how much cocaine is produced in the Andes and shipped to the United States. Satellite reconnaissance of coca fields, along with other implicit estimates, indicate that the region's cocaine production has continued to grow over the last decade and may now approach 1000 metric tons annually.[41] This number is shocking, not because it is so large, but rather, because it is so small. Consider that other agricultural-based goods (since that is what cocaine is) that are consumed in the United States are measured in the millions of metric tons, and 1000 metric tons takes on a different perspective. The United States' annual cocaine habit could be met by one train pulling thirteen freight cars.[42] Yet, there are literally millions of border crossings each year into the United States, of which Customs can only inspect a small fraction thoroughly. More than 300 million people visit the United States each year, arriving at the thousands of points of entry scattered across the country. More than 100 million vehicles entered the United States in 1992. Then, of course, there are an unknown number of illegal crossings into the United States. Considering the immensity of the task, the real wonder of interdiction policy is not that it fails to completely halt the flow of drugs, but that it stops even a small portion.

The inherent difficulty of interdicting cocaine brings up one of its intrinsic limits, namely, the expense of continuing operations. Interdiction becomes very expensive as a consequence of the cocaine industry's resilience. Moreover, the more interdiction that takes place, the more it costs to seize each additional unit of cocaine. In the language of economists, interdiction faces rising marginal costs, and perhaps extremely significant ones at that. These costs in turn limit the prospects for the type of large-scale policy intervention required to substantially disrupt retail markets.

Marginal Costs

If international cocaine markets are ever to be substantially disrupted, policy intervention of an unprecedented scale will be required. But in addition to bringing potentially dramatic political, economic, and social costs, a large-scale intervention would also probably face very high marginal costs of implementation. Marginal costs refers to how difficult it would be, measured in terms of time and resources, to get the last kilogram of cocaine seized. For example, if the goal was to interdict 50 percent of the cocaine produced, it would cost more to seize the 500th kilogram of cocaine (approximately half of the estimated 1994 production) than it would to seize the first. The greater the percentage of drug production that is being seized or destroyed, the more cunning and skilled the opponents that remain and the longer the search time associated with finding it. Phrased another way, in a general crackdown the least-skilled traffickers, pilots, and refiners will be caught first. The most-skilled participants in the drug industry are better able to evade law enforcement and, by extension, will generally not be caught unless a very large-scale effort is mounted. In operational terms, this means that it might take police, say, five days' effort to catch the least skilled traffickers, but ten days' effort to capture the next least-skilled group, and so forth on up the skill ladder.

Border interdiction provides one example. The U.S. Customs Service inspects only about 4 percent of the cargo entering the United States, although it does review about 20 percent of the cargo coming from the cocaine source countries. That Customs does not inspect a larger fraction of shipments testifies not only to the volume of cargo transactions and the expense of inspecting them, but to the inherent tension between Customs' dual duties of controlling and facilitating commerce. The more intense border control efforts become, the greater the delays that will result for the movement of legitimate commerce. President Nixon ordered *Operation Intercept* in 1969. During this operation, seizures increased substantially, albeit from relatively low levels, but the damage to both the flow of commerce and Mexican-U.S. relations was substantial.

The problem is that previous source country control policies provide very little indication of how difficult, and how costly, it would be to disrupt a large fraction of the cocaine trade with interdiction. Previous crackdowns, including the 1989–90 effort, have disrupted only a small fraction of cocaine production. The 1989–90 crackdown disrupted a larger fraction of the trade, but the portion that was disrupted by policies implemented within Colombia probably did not exceed 10 percent. Our ability to extrapolate that limited experience to a 50 percent disruption rate within Colombia is very limited. However, given the social, political, and economic costs associated with the 1989–90 crackdown, it is extremely unlikely that the Colombians could form a consensus to support a more ambitious disruption effort. Similarly, given the potential costs to U.S. commerce and the potential expense of redoubled Transit Zone operations, it is very unlikely that the United States will ever achieve anything approaching a 50 percent interdiction rate.

Summary

This chapter was deliberately brief. It was primarily intended to acquaint the reader with Transit Zone interdiction procedures, both because these operations consume the largest portion of international drug-control resources, and because Transit Zone interdiction is one of the most visible international drug-control policies. However, the chapter's brevity should not be construed to mean that interdiction is somehow a more effective source country control policy. Instead, a detailed discussion of interdiction could be avoided in this chapter precisely because its weaknesses have been discussed at some length in other sections of the book. Interdiction cannot permanently reduce cocaine output because the cocaine industry is endowed with access to low-cost resources (land and labor), extreme mobility, and short recovery times between policy implementation and industry response. The cost structure of the industry dictates that a substantial disruption must occur before retail prices are significantly affected. Interdiction-induced price increases, massive or otherwise, are destined to be of relatively short duration because cocaine market signals work efficiently and because the factors of production, land and labor, are abundant and not easily regulated. All phases of production recuperate from policy implementation relatively quickly because the production process is extremely simple and mobile. In the case of interdiction, this means the traffickers shift to new routes and modes of transport. Combined, the factors conspire to make the cocaine trafficking relatively impervious to source country control programs. As a result, over the long run interdiction in the Transit Zone will work no better to curb cocaine production than any other source country policy. There were other reasons for avoiding a more detailed discussion of Transit Zone interdiction, including the possibility that traditional Transit Zone interdiction may become less relevant as the Clinton administration's policy evolves. In addition, interdiction will be discussed again in chapter 7, when alternatives to the present source country and international control policies are considered.

This chapter did, however, bring up one potential limit to interdiction that had not been explicitly discussed elsewhere in the book. Interdiction faces high, and perhaps rapidly rising, marginal costs of implementation. This factor can only be added to interdiction's list of shortcomings.

Notes

1. Nadelmann (1992) provides a general critique of the punitive and prohibitionist U.S. drug regime.
2. Estimates of annual production range from approximately 900 to 1100 metric tons, of which approximately 350 mt are consumed in the United States. The balance of global cocaine production is consumed in the source countries, exported to countries other than the United States, or seized in domestic (consuming country) law enforcement operations.
3. *INCSR* (various years). See also the estimates in Rydell and Everingham (1994) and Everingham and Rydell (1994).
4. Chapters 1 and 2 provide overviews on these subjects.
5. Eddy et al. (1988) and Gugliotta and Leen (1989) detail the 1984 discovery and destruction of Tranquilandia by Colombian forces.
6. Mermelstein (1990) provides some details.
7. Gugliotta and Leen (1989), Eddy, et al. (1988), Mermelstein (1990), and Levine (1990) supply additional information regarding landing fields and drug flights.
8. In particular, see Gugliotta and Leen (1989) and Eddy, et al. (1988) for more on the shift from marijuana smuggling to cocaine trafficking.
9. Gugliotta and Leen (1989); Eddy, et al. (1988).
10. *Drug Control: Expanded Military Surveillance Not Justified by Measurable Goals or Results* (1993).
11. Klepak (1991).
12. Lahneman (1989).
13. The *Departamento Administrativo Seguridad* (DAS) serves functions similar to the Federal Bureau of Investigation (FBI) in the United States. As such, DAS has responsibilities that overlap with counternarcotics duties, including investigation of financial and fraud crimes, maintenance of internal security, and protection of human rights.
14. *Clear and Present Dangers* (1991). See also *Stopping the Flood of Cocaine with Operation Snowcap: Is it Working?* (1990).
15. Periscope/USNI Reports (1993); Ehrenfeld (1990), 106-10; and *Clear and Present Dangers* (1991) provide details on Colombian military forces.

16. *Colombia Beseiged* (1989) and Americas Watch Report; *Clear and Present Dangers* (1991); Riley (1993).
17. Periscope/USNI Reports (1993).
18. Ehrenfeld (1990).
19. *Drug War: Observations on Counternarcotics Aid to Colombia* (1991).
20. *Clear and Present Dangers* (1991) covers the Andean strategy in detail.
21. Builder (1993) provides a discussion of the U.S. military's involvement in counternarcotic operations.
22. Bagley (1992) discusses legislation regarding the U.S. military's role in detection and monitoring.
23. The respective statutes are Fiscal Year 1989 Defense Authorization Act (Public Law 100-456, 28 September 1988) and Defense Authorization Act (Public Law 101-510, 5 November 1990).
24. Interdiction forces may fire upon drug smuggling aircraft if fired upon first.
25. The Department of Defense is the lead agency in detection and monitoring activities. However, law enforcement organizations such as Customs, DEA, and the Coast Guard have detection and monitoring capabilities.
26. *Drug Control: DoD Operated Aerostat Ship although Conferees Denied Funds* (1993).
27. OTH-B radar was initially intended to be used for detecting both bomber and cruise missile attacks. Subsequent testing, however, revealed that OTH-B had was deficient in its ability to detect cruise missile targets. *Over-the-Horizon Radar: Better Justification Needed for DOD Systems' Expansion* (1991).
28. Some ground radar systems, such as the Navy's R-OTHR, are mobile.
29. Diaz (1990).
30. *Drug Control: Increased Interdiction and Its Contribution to the War on Drugs* (1993).
31. Klepak (1991).
32. Intelligence-aided seizures are called "hot hits." See Diaz (1990) and Lahneman (1989) for a discussion.
33. *National Drug Control Strategy: Budget Summary* (1995).
34. *National Drug Control Strategy: Budget Summary* (1995).
35. For a discussion, see *Airborne Drug Trafficking and Deterrence Act* (1990).
36. Lupsha (1994) traces the development of Mexican trafficking syndicates.
37. Lupsha (1994).
38. *Drug Control: Increased Interdiction and Its Contribution to the War on Drugs* (1993).
39. See *INCSR* (1995) section on Mexico.
40. *National Drug Control Strategy: Budget Summary* (1992), 174.
41. *INCSR* (various years).
42. Falco (1992).

References

Airborne Drug Trafficking and Deterrence Act, hearing before the Subcommittee on Coast Guard and Navigation of the Committee on the Merchant Marine and Fisheries, U.S. House of Representatives (Washington, D.C.: USGPO, 1990).

Bagley, Bruce, "Myths of Militarization: Enlisting Armed Forces in the War on Drugs," in Peter H. Smith, ed., *Drug Policy in the Americas* (Boulder, Colo.: Westview Press, 1992).

Builder, Carl, *Measuring the Leverage: Assessing Military Contributions to Drug Interdiction*, MR-158-A/AF (Santa Monica, Calif.: RAND, 1993).

Clear and Present Dangers: The U.S. Military and the War on Drugs in the Andes, (Washington, D.C.: Washington Office on Latin America, 1991).

Colombia Besieged: Political Violence and State Responsibility (Washington, D.C.: Washington Office on Latin America, 1989).

Diaz, Charley L., "DOD Plays in the Drug War," *Proceedings of the U.S. Naval Institute/Naval Review* (1990).

Drug Control: DOD Operated Aerostat Ship although Conferees Denied Funds (Washington, D.C.: GAO, 1993).

Drug Control: Expanded Military Surveillance Not Justified by Measurable Goals or Results, General Accounting Office, GAO/T-NSIAD-93-14 (Washington, D.C.: GAO, 1993).

Drug Control: Impact of DOD's Detection and Monitoring on Cocaine Flow, General Accounting Office, GAO/T-NSIAD-91-297 (Washington, D.C.: GAO, 1991).

Drug Control: Increased Interdiction and Its Contribution to the War on Drugs, General Accounting Office, GAO/T-NSIAD-93-4 (Washington, D.C.: GAO, 1993).

Drug Control: Revised Drug Interdiction Approach is Needed in Mexico, General Accounting Office, GAO/T-NSIAD-93-152 (Washington, D.C.: GAO, 1993).

Drug War: Observations on Counternarcotics Aid to Colombia (Washington, D.C.: Government Accounting Office, September 1991).

Eddy, Paul, with Hugo Sabogal, and Sara Walden, *The Cocaine Wars* (New York: W. W. Norton, 1988).

Ehrenfeld, Rachel, *Narco-Terrrorism: How Governments around the World have Used the Drug Trade to Finance and Further Terrorist Activities* (New York: Basic Books, 1990).

Everingham, Susan S., and C. Peter Rydell, "Modeling the Demand for Cocaine," DRR-390-ONDCP/A/DPRC (Santa Monica, Calif.: RAND, 1993).

Falco, Mathea, "Foreign Drugs, Foreign Wars," *Daedalus*, 121, 3 (Summer 1992): 1–14.

Fuss, Charles M., "Lies, Damn Lies, Statistics, and the Drug War," *Proceedings of the U.S. Naval Institute* (December 1989), 65–69.

Gugliotta, Guy, and Jeff Leen, *Kings of Cocaine* (New York: Simon and Schuster, 1989).

International Narcotics Strategy Report (INCSR), United States Department of State, Bureau of International Narcotics Matters (Washington, D.C.: USGPO, various years).

Johnson, Maj. Nelson B., "Intelligence Support to the War on Drugs," *Signal* (September 1989), 47–50.

Klepak, Harold, "SOLIC Drug Interdiction: The Latin American Link," *Jane's Defence Weekly* 15, 8 (23 February 1991): 236–65.

Lahneman, William J., "Interdicting Drugs in the Big Pond," *Proceedings of the U.S. Naval Institute* (July 1989), 56–63.

Levine, Michael, *Deep Cover* (New York: Delacorte, 1990).

Lockwood, Captain John Weldon, "Blocking Caribbean Drug Traffic," *Proceedings of the U.S. Naval Institute* (December 1989), 101–06.

Lupsha, Peter, "The Political Economy of Drug Trafficking," paper presented at *The Role of the Military in the War on Drugs Conference*, San Antonio, Texas (5 January 1993).

Mabry, Donald J., "Andean Drug Trafficking and the Military Option," *Military Review* (March 1990), 29–40.

Mermelstein, Max, *The Man Who Made it Snow* (New York: Simon and Schuster, 1990).

Nadelmann, Ethan, "Thinking Seriously about Alternatives to Drug Prohibition," *Daedalus* 121, 3 (Summer 1992).

National Drug Control Strategy: Budget Summary, The White House (January 1992).

Over-the-Horizon Radar: Better Justification Needed for DOD Systems' Expansion (1991).

Stopping the Flood of Cocaine with Operation Snowcap: Is it Working? Committee on Government Operations, House of Representatives (Washington, D.C.: USGPO, 1990).

Part III

The Warpath not Taken

7

Surrendering the Battle, Winning the War

Recently, a provocative essay in the *Atlantic Monthly* enumerated many of the pitfalls of public policy administration. The essay ruminated on public policy as it relates to the difficulty of changing—or perhaps more precisely, reforming—human behavior and, in the process, identified many of the problems facing national drug control policy today.[1] The tract lamented the incorrigibility of human behavior and begged for patience where public policy to reform behavior is concerned. Specifically, the essay suggested that we be tolerant and allow policies time to influence behavior and that we learn to understand that our best estimates—about costs, effects, and so forth—will often be stunningly off the mark. The author also urged that policymakers not be unduly criticized for attacking the easiest problems first, but rather, savor whatever victories over incredibly complex problems that can be salvaged. In return, however, policymakers were urged not expect (or promise) to solve a problem in its entirety; and not to compare results to ideals, but to the more appropriate standard of the conditions that existed prior to policy intervention. Finally, policymakers were warned that while many problems can, and should, be attacked along multiple fronts, that most policy issues are too complex to address along every dimension.

Even if this lenient standard of judging policy administration is applied to the national drug strategy, after ten years, and more than $100 billion in public expenditures, the United States' crusade against drug use, and cocaine use in particular, has reached an uncomfortable stasis. Some victories are evident, including reductions in cocaine initiation rates relative to the peaks of the 1980s. Particularly important, initiation among teenagers, youth, and students has declined.[2] These users, who are thought to be particularly susceptible to the risks and consequences of drug use, form the core of future generations of cocaine users. At the

245

same time, however, the victory over cocaine is far from complete. Evidence indicates that students' attitudes about cocaine and cocaine use are becoming less critical, and changing toward greater acceptance.[3] Such changes in attitudes are worrisome because they may be indicative of future changes in initiation rates. Additionally, while initiation has slowed, the total quantity of cocaine used has continued to increase.[4] This finding indicates that the remaining population of cocaine users is increasing its consumption, resulting in a large cadre of heavy users.[5]

The dilemma, then, is how to simultaneously protect past gains and make progress in both continuing and emerging problem areas. The constantly shifting state of the drug problem has frustrated the policy community and the public as well. According to a recent survey, a sizeable fraction of the public thinks elected officials are relatively insincere about their interest in addressing the nation's drug problem.[6] Elected officials are perceived to be more concerned about other matters. Public concern about drug issues remains strong, but there is growing cynicism and confusion about what approaches will work. Such skepticism is corrosive, for it undermines policymakers' ability to innovate. Yet progress is more critical now than ever as public resources available for drug programs become increasingly scarce, and as drug policy's cousins, criminal justice and health, provide stiff competition for the public's attention. No longer is there the luxury of fighting over shares of a growing budget pie. Instead, budgets are stagnating, and it thus becomes more important to apply drug dollars in areas where they will be effective.

This chapter, then, has several goals. The first is to explore what justifications exist for continuing source country cocaine control policies. Do they contribute to a resolution of the drug problem as it manifests itself now? One method of examining this question will be to examine source country policies' implications for the other two widely smuggled drugs, heroin and marijuana. A large fraction of international drug control resources is currently devoted to cocaine. But marijuana and heroin flow through many of the same choke points that cocaine does. Thus, to a large degree, particularly with respect to interdiction, policies that are applied against cocaine can also be applied against heroin and marijuana.

If source country policies should be continued, should they be enlarged, scaled down, or left the same? This chapter will attempt to sort out how a revised source country strategy would fit into the larger context of national drug control. The lengthy discussion of source country control policies' inherent weaknesses does not provide a positive prescription for drug policy. Presumably, if significant cuts are made in source country control funding, these freed resources will available for alternate uses. In fact, cuts in one component of the national drug budget do not easily translate into increases in another component. This important limitation aside, are there policy options available that are more effective than international and source country control programs?

Future Wars

Cocaine is far from the only drug with which policymakers are concerned. Scares about new drugs periodically emerge. For example, many policy officials predicted that ice, a crystallized form of methamphetamine, would become the nation's next drug scourge with societal consequences that would dwarf those of crack cocaine.[7] Ice had, in fact, been around for years, and use of it ultimately proved not to be spreading rapidly. It has largely disappeared from the public's view. Other drugs have proven to merit more durable concerns. Heroin and marijuana in particular, consume significant shares of national drug control resources. Heroin is a major concern not only because it is physiologically addictive and is reaching the United States in large volumes at unprecedented purities, but because it poses a substantial public health threat through its role in augmenting transmission of the HIV virus. Marijuana remains a concern because it is used far more widely than cocaine and heroin, and because it is, debatably, thought to be a precursor to harder drug use later in life.

About all that cocaine, marijuana, and heroin share in common is that they have some potential for abuse. Cocaine is a stimulant; heroin is a narcotic. Cocaine is associated with a violent culture; marijuana markets are relatively invisible and less violent. Whereas methadone maintenance may be an appropriate intervention for heroin users, no comparable regimen exists for cocaine or marijuana. Cocaine, heroin, and marijuana do share one common characteristic: they are all imported, in great quantities, from foreign sources. Similarly, there is a degree of inseparability to the extent that policies, such as interdiction, aimed at one drug overlap and affect the other drugs as well. Thus, while source country control policies have disappointing and limited prospects for use against cocaine trafficking, this does not necessarily indicate that source country policies cannot be profitably employed against heroin and marijuana. And indeed, if source country policies could be effectively used against heroin and marijuana, it might provide justification for continuing to use them, despite their disappointing prospects against cocaine.

Essentially, the same tools are available for use against heroin and marijuana as are available for use against cocaine. That is, heroin and marijuana can be interdicted, the crops from which they are produced can be destroyed, and the regions where the drugs are produced can be supplied with development assistance. Analytically, evaluating marijuana and heroin source country control policies is the same as it is for cocaine. Factors such as market structure, the markups between stages of production, and the lags in the production process are all relevant considerations.

Marijuana

Marijuana is the most widely used illicit drug in the United States. Annual prevalence estimates indicate that roughly 20 million Americans consumed marijuana at least once in 1991.[8] Moreover, despite the visibility of cocaine, marijuana programs consume a large portion of the nation's drug budget. By one estimate, one out of every four dollars spent on supply control programs is spent against marijuana.[9] Unlike heroin and cocaine, which involve refining and concentrating steps, marijuana production is very straightforward. Mature marijuana leaves are cut down and dried. Stems and other adulterants are removed from the harvest, and the remaining dried seeds, leaves, and buds are then bundled and sold to wholesalers and intermediaries. The production of hash, hash oil, and sinsemilla involve slightly more complicated procedures, but the vast majority of marijuana used in the United States is smoked in the harvested, dry form.[10] Most marijuana plants provide one harvest per year.

Generally, the markup between the farm stage and the retail stage in marijuana is much less drastic than the markup between similar stages in cocaine and heroin trafficking.[11] Evidence from DEA indicates that prices typically increase by a factor of twenty-one for marijuana between the farm and retail stage, but increase by a factor of 1,710 and 385 for heroin and cocaine, respectively.[12] Marijuana's mark up is lower than heroin's and cocaine's because marijuana sellers bear lower risks at the retail level than heroin and cocaine dealers.[13] In many cases, retail heroin dealers must meet their customers virtually every day, as few heroin users are capable of keeping even a short-term supply of the narcotic on hand. The situation for cocaine, particularly crack, is similar. The necessity of frequent of heroin transactions raises the dealers' risks, and thus the size of the risk markup commanded. In contrast, marijuana consumers, even daily users, keep a larger store of the product in inventory, and thus make purchases less frequently.[14] Heroin dealers appear to face higher risks of predatory crime because of the frequency of the transactions, and the locations where the transactions typically occur.[15] A marijuana dealer might have more clients than a heroin dealer, but they generate less aggregate risk because of their buying practices. Additionally, marijuana's markup is lower because marijuana passes through fewer stages of refinement, and thus there are fewer individuals who bear a law enforcement risk and demand a risk premium.

The lower price markup for marijuana means that marijuana markets may be relatively more sensitive to the effects of source country control programs. That is, if a policy like eradication succeeded in drastically raising farm prices, it would also substantially affect retail prices because intermediate marijuana prices are, compared to intermediate cocaine prices, a relatively large fraction of the retail price.[16] The lower markup provides retail marijuana prices less protection against swings in intermediate stage prices. Consequently, a given size source country control program will work more effectively to raise retail marijuana prices than it will to raise retail cocaine prices.

Marijuana may also be more susceptible to the impact of source country programs because of its bulk. Unlike heroin and cocaine, marijuana's drug content and value are both low relative to marijuana's weight. One mechanism for guarding against interdiction is to move drug shipments in small, highly concentrated packages. Heroin, for example, is brought into the United States in small bundles, which often weigh less than 2.5 kg. Although it is more expensive to transport heroin using this method, it is also more difficult for law enforcement officials to detect couriers transporting such small packages. In contrast, marijuana is almost always transported in multi-hundred kilo shipments, and in many instances on vessels dedicated to marijuana trafficking. Traffickers have no way to concentrate marijuana to reduce its bulk, unlike heroin and cocaine traffickers whose street products may be 350 times or more concentrated than the raw materials from which they are produced.[17] Marijuana traffickers could ship the cannabis in smaller consignments, but there is a point beyond which the shipments become too small to be cost effective. Although it is not clear what the smallest feasible size of marijuana shipment is, it is almost certainly several times larger than small heroin shipments.

History is replete with examples of marijuana control policies disrupting marijuana supplies.[18] For example, Mexican authorities embarked on an eradication campaign in the 1970s that severely reduced Mexican marijuana production between 1976 and 1983. While eradication temporarily reduced supply, it also suppressed demand as many consumers feared the health risks of consuming chemically treated Mexican marijuana. When the demand for Mexican marijuana plunged in response to the chemical eradication program, Colombia quickly stepped in as a major supplier. Similarly, the United States implemented a stringent maritime interdiction program in the early 1980s that led to sharply higher Colombian marijuana prices. With sea lanes virtually shut down, Colombian marijuana traffickers, already high cost producers, found that they could not compete with most other producers.

Several factors militate against marijuana programs' long-term effectiveness. Thus, despite the fact that marijuana is relatively more susceptible to source country control programs effects than cocaine, source country marijuana control programs are no more effective in the long run than source country cocaine policies. The marijuana traffic's ability to rebound is linked to a number of, by now familiar, factors, including the diverse geographic regions in which marijuana can be grown (including domestically) and the plant's relatively rapid maturation cycle. In terms of geography, marijuana grows in a variety of climates and ecologies. Marijuana comes to the United States from such diverse regions as Thailand, Colombia, and Jamaica. Mexico is also a large supplier. In most cases, the United States enjoys excellent relations with the marijuana-producing nations' governments. Many of the marijuana source country governments have strongly supported marijuana suppression efforts. Yet, despite the good governmental relations, the dispersed nature of the marijuana trade makes large-scale disruption of the marijuana trade difficult. Massive disruption of marijuana markets would require truly global intervention, and entail simultaneous operations in several countries. The law enforcement capacity required for such an intervention almost certainly exceeds the source country forces' abilities, and indeed would severely tax U.S. intervention capabilities.

Marijuana's rapid growth cycle also makes it difficult to reduce production for long. When grown from seeds, marijuana can provide full harvests in less than one year, or approximately half the time it takes coca bushes to mature. Recall, however, that the time it takes coca bushes to provide full harvests is not only the longest lag in the cocaine production process, but almost entirely responsible for the temporary production disruptions that source country cocaine control policies can generate. Marijuana's short recovery cycle, coupled with the difficulty of global eradication and interdiction, would make it virtually impossible to create a sustained market disruption.

And, indeed, the evidence indicates that marijuana markets have always been able to recover rapidly from source country interventions. The success against Mexican marijuana, for example, forced innovations in the industry. Shortly after the Mexican campaign of the 1970s got underway, Mexican marijuana farmers dispersed their production to smaller, more remote plots in an effort to make eradication more difficult.[19] This dispersal helped mitigate the impact of the Mexican campaign, and spread marijuana cultivation to regions less susceptible to government policies. Moreover, during the height of the Mexican campaign, Colombia quickly stepped in as the leading supplier to the United States. Similarly, when the maritime interdiction program impaired Colombia's ability to export marijuana, Mexico quickly resumed its role as the leading U.S. supplier. Mexico reestablished its prominence as a supplier to the United States in a matter of a few months, in part because its proximity to the huge U.S. market gave it a large cost advantage over Colombian suppliers.[20] The combination of Colombian and Mexican disruptions also appears to have affected U.S. domestic production, for the United States now supplies a sizable portion of its own demand. High-quality marijuana is cultivated in a variety of states, including Hawaii and California. In fact, significant marijuana cultivation takes place in most of the other states. Together, domestic producers provide enough marijuana to satisfy approximately 30 percent of the U.S. market.[21]

Marijuana provides an instructive example of what may happen in one drug market when large, policy induced changes occur in another drug market.[22] Marijuana is regarded as a substitute for alcohol, at least among teenagers and young adults.[23] During the early 1980s, a Presidential commission established to examine drunk driving issued findings that recommended that the drinking age be raised to twenty-one.

Almost half the states had established a drinking age of twenty-one in the early 1980s, and by 1988 the remaining holdouts had raised their limits as well, in large part because Congress threatened to withhold federal highway trust funds from states that did not require drinkers to be twenty-one or older. The effect of raising the drinking age was to make alcohol more expensive for people under the age of twenty-one. Higher drinking age requirements increased the search time necessary for obtaining alcohol, and increased the penalties (for both vendors and consumers) for cases of underage drinking. As a result of this shift in relative prices, alcohol consumption declined, and marijuana use increased, measurably among teenagers and young adults.

Marijuana has, at times, enjoyed more lenient treatment than most other illicit drugs. A similar case of substitution appears to have occurred in the 1970s when marijuana possession was decriminalized in a number of states.[24] During the 1975–78 period, reports of drug-related emergency room admissions declined for a number of other drugs (including heroin and cocaine), but increased for marijuana.[25] Analysis indicates that this change in emergency room admission patterns may be due to changes in consumption habits that were in turn induced by changes in marijuana laws. Under this theory, as decriminalization took hold, marijuana became less expensive relative to other drugs. Consequently, as relative marijuana prices declined (from decriminalization), marijuana use increased and other drug use decreased.

Two points have emerged from this brief look at marijuana. First, marijuana trafficking, like cocaine trafficking, is subject to disruption from source country control policies. However, although a detailed empirical examination of source country policies' effects on marijuana trafficking is lacking, it appears that source country marijuana policies have even more fleeting effects than source country cocaine policies. The marijuana policies' impact is rooted in the fact that marijuana grows very rapidly, and can be planted in a wide range of geographic areas, so that source country policies are quickly overwhelmed.

The second interesting result is that disruption in one drug market may have unintended results for consumption of other drugs. Studies have revealed that certain population segments will substitute marijuana when alcohol prices increase. Similarly, other researchers have observed that when the relative price of marijuana declines, marijuana use increases and other drug use recedes. Quite probably, a similar substitution phenomenon holds true for cocaine. That is, if cocaine became scarce for a two-year period because of a successful eradication program, it is likely that cocaine users would turn toward other drugs as a mechanism for coping with the shortage. Whether this substitution would generate more or less societal harm than the cocaine consumption it replaces cannot be predicted here. However, it is clear that the potential for substitution to other drugs during a cocaine market disruption must be examined, and if such a substitution exists, it must be counted against the benefits of a cocaine market disruption.

Heroin

Heroin is derived from the opium poppy plant, *papaver somniferum*. The opium poppy, a florid, colorful bloom that can be cultivated in a variety of climates, typically provides two harvests per year. In the first stage of the production process opium, from which heroin is produced, is extracted from oil-bearing pods found in the poppy bloom. Opium is a milky white juice, and the producers obtain it by slicing or crushing the poppy's pods. Once the opium extract is dried, it takes on a brown hue and may be consumed directly as a mood-altering substance.

Raw opium is next converted into an alkaloid called morphine base or morphine. The transformation from opium to morphine is accomplished by soaking, heating, and filtering the raw opium. Morphine base, a fine brown powder, is compressed into bricks and readied for the next stage of processing. Morphine dissolves in water, and therefore can be administered intravenously.

Although morphine itself is a potent narcotic, it is not as powerful as heroin. Heroin is produced from morphine by introducing an acetylating agent. The acetylating agent, such as acetic acid or acetic andydride, attaches additional chemical groups to the morphine that ultimately improve heroin's ability to penetrate the brain. Subsequently, the solution is filtered and diluted with water and sodium carbonate, filtered again, and then dried. The resultant product, heroin base (also known as No. 2 heroin), does not dissolve in water, and therefore is not suitable for intravenous use. To be suitable for injection, heroin base must be converted into heroin through other minor refining operations. Heroin exists in a variety of forms, distinguishable mostly by their purity. The purest form is No. 4 heroin, a white, fluffy powder. No. 3 heroin retains a brownish tint that signifies its relative impurity. Mexican black tar heroin is also available and is notable, as the name suggests, for its dark coloring.

The United States consumes less than 10 percent of worldwide heroin production, in contrast to more than 50 percent of worldwide cocaine production.[26] The U.S. heroin supply comes from a variety of sources in South Asia (20 percent), Southeast Asia (60 percent), and Southern and Central America (20 percent), and U.S. consumption can represent a large share of a country's exports. Virtually all of the heroin produced in Colombia and Mexico, for example, ends up in the United States. However, a very small share of Asia's heroin production ends up in the United States.

Heroin has a very large markup between the farm and retail stages.[27] A number of factors explain the magnitude of the markup. Perhaps most importantly, heroin dealers engage in a large number of transactions at the retail level, primarily because their customers tend to buy small batches on a daily basis. The volume of transactions makes heroin dealers more visible to law enforcement agents, and subjects the heroin dealers to greater law enforcement risks, which they incorporate into the prices they command. Additionally, heroin tends to be smuggled into the United States in small packages distributed among numerous personnel. Nigerian traffickers, for example, are noted for using couriers who have swallowed balloons full of heroin as a primary smuggling method. This too, raises the risks by exposing operations to more potential for compromise. Thus, source country heroin control policies have very weak effects on retail prices because of this price structure. At a minimum, a massive intervention would be necessary in order to severely disrupt heroin prices and production.

However, the prospects for destroying a significant fraction of the world's heroin production are extremely remote. Similar to the task of disrupting marijuana markets, heroin disruption would entail a global operation of massive scale. Even assuming the United States could gather and devote the resources to such a campaign, the United States lacks access to, and support of, many key heroin-producing nations. Thus, it is extremely unlikely that the United States could secure the cooperation of heroin-producing states such as Myanmar and Afghanistan. Even in cases where the United States enjoys good relations with the governments of the heroin-producing nations, heroin suppression efforts could prove very destabilizing. For example, the Pakistani government is sensitive to efforts to halt heroin production among the Pathan tribes because it fears disruption efforts could destabilize the Pakistan-Afghanistan border, which the Pathans have settled.

Operational barriers to global operations notwithstanding, there would be very little purpose to a massive global counter-heroin campaign. Like marijuana, opium poppies can grow in a variety of climates and conditions. And, like marijuana, the poppy produces its bounty very rapidly. Poppies flower approximately four weeks after planting, and can be harvested for opium a few months after flowering. In less than a year, then, poppies can go from seed to opium-bearing stalks.

During the last three decades, the United States has supported three poppy control programs. Much of the modern heroin policy can be traced back to U.S. involvement in the Vietnam war.[28] There, U.S. soldiers experimented with heroin in large numbers. While many, if not most, military personnel abandoned their heroin use upon return to the United States, a small number became important conduits in heroin trafficking. Early reports of heroin abuse in, and trafficking from, Indochina touched off a public and political outcry that resulted in many changes to drug policy. On the international front, President Nixon urged a Turkish ban on opium production and prodded the French to shut down heroin laboratories that processed the Turkish products. The second important poppy control program was erected in Mexico, shortly after the Turkish program was fully implemented.

The Turkish ban began in 1971 after the government reached an agreement with the United States for over $35 million in compensation. At the time, poppy and opium markets provided Turkey with important foreign exchange and revenue. Aid from the United States helped Turkey absorb the losses associated with the ban. Restrictions against illicit cultivation were strict, and Turkish output dropped rapidly. The government was able to enforce the strict ban in part because it did not have to respond to constituent demands. With the return to a representative government in October, 1973 however, pressure soon mounted to discontinue the ban and by 1975 poppy cultivation had resumed in Turkey's seven major producing provinces. Limited control efforts remained in effect, including support for legitimate poppy uses and the introduction of nonopium-bearing poppies into the main cultivation centers.[29]

While Turkey's markets were in turmoil, Mexican producers geared up to fill the market gap. Mexico had little in the way of a domestic heroin market, so that the surge in production was clearly designed for export. Mexico rapidly replaced Turkey as the leading supplier of heroin to the United States. The Mexican government embarked on its own ambitious eradication campaigning that reached its peak against poppy fields in 1975 and 1976. The campaign's effectiveness was increased by the use of aircraft to locate and destroy poppy production centers with herbicides. Mexican heroin production declined substantially between 1976 and 1980.

During the same period, Thailand implemented a long-term control program that succeeded in reducing Thai poppy cultivation 60 to 70 percent between 1965 and 1981. Significant reductions were achieved among Thailand's hill tribes, where Thai poppy cultivation was traditionally concentrated. Thailand's national integration campaign, under which the government sought to extend its legitimacy with the Hill tribes and other ethnic subgroups, proved to be a vital component.[30] The integration campaign not only helped check the influence of the growing communist movement, but also helped ensure that the Hill tribes would be able to find markets for the crops that were substituted for poppies.

Measures of heroin consumption, including estimates of heroin-related deaths and emergency room admissions, indicate that heroin was in relatively short supply for this period.[31] Heroin markets appear to have remained unsteady for substantially longer than would be predicted by the poppy plant's recovery cycle. That is, while the poppy itself is capable of providing opium in less than a year, heroin markets remained in flux for the better part of the decade that began with the 1971–72 Turkish ban. Heroin prices remained elevated and purities low for much of the mid to late 1970s. According to available indicators, such as reduced emergency room admissions, the scarcities lowered consumption.[32] The U.S. heroin drought appeared to end in the early 1980s with the completion of a prolonged (two-year) and severe drought that affected many of the Asian suppliers. Quite probably, the shortage of heroin in the United States can be attributed to a fortuitous confluence of factors. Specifically, the ban on Turkish opium temporarily deprived the United States of an important heroin source. Prior to the intervention, Turkey supplied perhaps 80 percent of the United States' heroin; after the intervention, its share dwindled to less than 2 percent.[33] Asian supplies remained unsteady because of the war in Vietnam and the ultimate U.S. withdrawal. Asian trafficking networks to the United States were slow to develop, both because the U.S. conduits went home at the war's end, and because the Asian immigrant population was not well established, and faced a hostile environment, in the United States at that time. The drought that hit Asia from 1979 to 1980 only prolonged its inability to establish itself as a reliable supplier to the United States. Meanwhile, Mexican efforts to fill the gap were hindered by both persistent Mexican eradication efforts and a Mexican drought. Finally, the purity of the heroin reaching the streets declined substantially, causing some users to avail themselves to synthetic substitutes.[34] In some cases, these manufactured substitutes proved to be fatal as the manufacturers had difficulty controlling the purity and quality of the synthetics. Thus, the risk of using heroin and heroin substitutes increased by an unknown amount during this period, to the point where the demand for heroin was affected as well.[35]

During the dry decade, however, the heroin trade underwent a reorganization that will make future market disruptions more difficult. One important development was the emergence of significant new suppliers to the United States. Colombia, for example, now has a large heroin production capacity, and Peru's is reportedly growing rapidly as well.[36] Equally significantly, reliable domestic supply networks have been established in the United States. Asian trafficking organizations are now very well organized in the United States, having capitalized on both sustained immigration and the strong family ties that prevail in immigrant Asian communities. Similarly, Colombian heroin exporters have been able to use their existing cocaine trafficking infrastructure, and the large Colombian emigre population in the United States. Another major innovation was to locate refining labs near the poppy farms as a mechanism for reducing transport costs and ensuring that farmers had a larger stake in the heroin trade. By 1980, labs were being operated adjacent to farms in most of the heroin-producing nations.

In short, the structure of both the marijuana and heroin trades suggests that they, too will be relatively immune to source country drug control policies' effects. It seems very unlikely that interdiction, eradication, and law enforcement-based strategies will be any more effective against heroin and marijuana than against cocaine. Generally, the explanation for the policies' ineffectiveness can be found in the same causes. Heroin and marijuana have large markups between the source country and retail stages, and their primary inputs can be grown in a variety of geographic areas. As a result, heroin and marijuana markets can react relatively rapidly to policies erected against them. Past successes in curtailing heroin and marijuana supplies in the United States appear to have as much to do with a confluence of circumstantial factors, including severe droughts and major reorganizations of the international drug trade, as well as with temporary changes in demand, as they did with international drug control policies.

Fight to the Finish

Up to this point, this book has been concerned with demonstrating source country control policies' limits. The evidence, while based on a paucity of hard data, is very compelling: cocaine producers rapidly adapt to the pressures of source country programs. What is more, there are potentially tremendous costs associated with source country control policies over and above the budgetary costs of implementation. These costs, or externalities, range from violence and dispersal of the trade in the source countries, to the prevalence and distribution of more concentrated, potent forms of drugs in the consuming nations. Some analysis indicates that one dollar spent on source country interdiction provides only about $0.32 in benefits such as reduced crime and health care costs, and that eradication performs even more dismally.[37] In short, one can reasonably ask, why continue to pursue interdiction, eradication, and development assistance as part of a cocaine control strategy?

Maintaining the present strategy is typically justified on several grounds. Perhaps most obviously, supporters argue that eliminating source country control programs would allow more cocaine to pass through to retail markets. This argument is true as far as it goes, although it ignores complicated market dynamics that might lead to increases, declines, or no change in cocaine consumption and the number of users. The increases in cocaine reaching U.S. markets could force prices down, which in turn might attract new users. Through the ratchet (or hysteresis) effect discussed earlier, these new users might maintain their habit even if prices later increased.[38] Conversely, information asymmetry, in which established users are most aware of prices changes and nonusers become aware of the changes only after a lag, might work to prevent an influx of new users.[39] Since U.S. cocaine markets are now dominated by heavy users, the effect of asymmetric information could be substantial. In any event, concerns about eliminating source country policies are grounded in fears about the potential impact on initiation and use.

In addition, maintaining international control programs is often justified at a symbolic and moral level. That is, it is important to demonstrate a commitment to combatting drug trafficking. International programs are part of a balanced, multidimensional drug control program that attacks the problem from all angles. Moreover, the symbolic element is reinforced by international treaties and bilateral agreements, which obligate the United States to pursue an aggressive drug control program. Finally, there is the moral obligation to apprehend and prosecute the individuals who have committed countless grave and brutal crimes.

In fact, there are alternatives to both maintaining the *status quo*, and to completely abandoning source country control policies. The key to devising an appropriate international control strategy lies in determining what contributions international control programs can make to U.S. national drug-control objectives. This determination is a two-part process. In the first step, international control policies' contributions to national drug control objectives must be considered. As will be evident, there is a substantial gap between the goals set forth for international programs and what they actually contribute to fulfilling the national drug control strategy. In turn, this gap suggests that a different set of objectives for international control programs should be established. With a revised set of objectives in hand, it is then possible to move on to the second step: defining a role for source country programs relative to the treatment, prevention, and domestic enforcement components of the national strategy.

Holding the Line

Reduced to its essential elements, the U.S. international cocaine control strategy embraces three main objectives.[40] Broadly, the first goal is to build and strengthen international cooperation against drug production, trafficking, and consumption by implementing programs that enhance judicial reform, promote the development of competent and honest law enforcement, judicial and penal institutions, and seek the control of money laundering and precursor chemicals. The second goal is to assist the source nations in attacking and destroying the narcotics trafficking organizations. The final goal is to reduce the supply of illicit drugs through judicial use of flexible and responsive interdiction programs.

Combined, these three objectives resulted in expenditures of over $1.6 billion on international drug control programs for 1994, and as much as $2.6 billion in 1991 and 1992.[41] Although all components of international control programs are regarded as important contributors to the international strategy, and although the administration has acknowledged that interdiction has been overemphasized, over 77 percent of international drug control resources were devoted to interdiction activities.[42] An additional 16 percent of international resources was spent on investigations and intelligence. The balance, slightly more than 6 percent of the international budget, was spent on judicial, police, economic, and development assistance. In the case of development assistance, aid has, in the past, been conditioned on meeting eradication objectives, and thus might be rightfully counted as law enforcement-related assistance.

From the given distribution of resources, the reader could be forgiven for thinking that interdiction and law enforcement-based strategies were the most effective international control programs, and that these programs make a clear contribution to the national objectives of reducing both cocaine use and the number of cocaine users. In fact, however, it is very difficult to draw these conclusions on the basis of the available evidence. Interdiction and law enforcement-based approaches are intended to reduce the supply of illicit drugs by deterring drug smuggling. Deterrence itself is a function of destroying drug-yielding crops, cutting off traffickers' smuggling routes, seizing drugs and assets, and arresting traffickers. In theory, these factors should raise the traffickers' costs and convince them to abandon the trafficking business, thereby reducing the supply of drugs reaching the United States. Closer inspection, however, reveals two fundamental flaws with this line of reasoning: source country law enforcement strategies cannot be meaningfully linked to deterring drug trafficking behavior, and consequently they cannot be linked to the ultimate goals of reducing cocaine use. The former flaw implies that a conflict exists between current policies and goals at the source country level, while the latter implies that a strategic conflict exists and that source country control resources might be better applied to other policies.

To understand the conflict between policies and goals, consider the issue of measures of effectiveness. Take interdiction as an example, although the lessons apply to other source country policies such as eradication, arrests, and lab destruction: How do you know if the policy is successful? The level of activity and the outcome of any given mission can be measured, but there is no measure of how interdiction deters drug trafficking behavior.[43] At least six measures of effectiveness have been proposed, but each has severe limits as an indicator of success.[44] Interdiction's success can be judged by the volume of cocaine seized; the percentage of operations leading to seizures; the percentage of shipments using a particular route seized; the percentage of *attempted* shipments using a particular route seized; the markup commanded for a particular route; and the percentage of total market volume shipped using a particular route. But each of these measures is insufficient. Perhaps most important is that the measures require information about drug shipments and drug trafficking that is unavailable. For example, many of the measures, to be meaningful, require knowing the total number of cocaine shipments, a number that is inherently unknowable. Also, most of the proposed measures cannot be updated in a timely manner, and thus cannot be used to revise interdiction operations over any meaningful time horizon.

Without these measures, interdiction cannot be linked to goals such as deterrence. There is no way to tell how much interdiction deters drug traffickers because there is no measure of interdiction's effect. There have been successes that can be directly attributed to interdiction, including the virtual cessation of drug flights directly into U.S. territory, and the shift in trafficking patterns through Peru after the installation of the Yurimaguas radar installation.[45] However, the cost has been an increase in cocaine trafficking through channels that are equally, or more, difficult to detect. Consequently, there is no way to link interdiction to higher-order objectives, such as reducing drug use and the number of users. Increases in arrests, for example, may simply reflect changes in the level of drug trafficking, rather than any change in the efficiency of counterdrug operations. In any case, the volume of arrests reveals nothing about the volume of drugs reaching the United States. Similarly, increases in seizures may simply signal that more drugs are moving through the supply pipeline, rather than reflecting any future shortages of drugs in retail markets.

The lack of connections between source country policies and strategic goals makes it very difficult to justify a particular level of source country funding both in absolute terms (Are we funding enough interdiction?) and relative terms (Should we fund more of other programs at the expense of interdiction?). The difficulty in allocating funding between source country policies and other options lies in the fact that no common standard of comparison, such as each policy's impact on drug use, exists. Certainly, there is a political imperative to continue interdiction. Interdiction demonstrates a commitment to attacking drug trafficking, even if it is an impotent threat.[46] Both elected officials and the public strongly support programs aimed at controlling the foreign sources of drug trafficking. Hence, some level of interdiction will have to be maintained, but only to the extent that it does not jeopardize other objectives, and only to the extent that the costs do not clearly exceed the benefits. Some level of interdiction activity can be justified on the grounds that the U.S. military's participation in detection and monitoring augments military readiness. However, drug detection and monitoring may not be all that useful for sharpening military skills.[47] At a minimum, the evidence indicates that the U.S. military's participation in detection and monitoring could be cut back substantially with no loss in military readiness.

In any event, the existing international and source country strategy cannot be linked to either deterrence or higher-order drug policy goals. Determining the "correct" level of source country funding is extremely difficult because of the schism between policies and goals. Thus, the key to determining an appropriate level of source country control programs is to reexamine source country policy goals. If source country control policies are going to be continued, they must be justified on grounds other than their contribution to counternarcotics objectives.

Redefining Source Country Objectives

In his 1994 drug strategy, President Clinton made explicit the goal of implementing an ineffective program less inefficiently. That is, the administration acknowledged the small benefits and high costs associated with interdiction and, consequently, sought to implement interdiction in a less costly manner without a corresponding decline in interdiction abilities. The major change was to scale back detection and monitoring flights in the Transit Zone, in conjunction with working to provide permanent, ground-based radar coverage of the Caribbean basin and Andean region. While this is an important first step in rethinking international drug control strategy, it is far from an optimal approach. Remember that approximately 75 percent of the 1994 international drug control budget was devoted to interdiction, and that this was the imbalance that remained in 1994, after the President announced the changes in strategy.[48] The reality is that interdiction remains a huge portion of the Clinton administration international strategy, just as it was an essential component of the Reagan and Bush strategies. The continued emphasis on interdiction leaves unresolved the tension between goals (deterrence; reduced drug use) and strategies (source country control policies) discussed in the previous section. This section turns the issue around by examining a different set of source country objectives.

Setting aside the issue of drug trafficking for the moment, what are the United States' and the Andean nations' enduring interests in Bolivia, Colombia, and Peru? Although not an easy question to answer, the response is critical to justifying U.S. intervention in the region. Without a clear understanding of why the United States is involved in the region, it is impossible to determine appropriate policies. Certainly, preservation of Bolivian, Colombian, and Peruvian democratic institutions, however fragile their current existence, would rank near the top of the list. Colombia, because of its size and relative wealth, and because of the duration of its political stability, is a particularly important case. Although Colombia's economic performance has lagged in recent years, Colombia is still one of the region's economic success stories. Colombia has become an important supplier of petroleum products, flowers, and other goods to world markets. International commerce is on the rise in the region and many of the Latin American nations are negotiating free trade pacts. Moreover, Colombia, by virtue of its economic, political, and military strength, has an important role in regional political stability. Reversals to democratic control, whether brought about by guerrillas, death squads, or the drug traffickers, would thus have important regional reverberations.

Peru and Bolivia are less important to regional stability than Colombia but, nevertheless, democratic reversals in either country could prove unsettling to the region. Indeed, one need not go back very far in Bolivia's history to find examples of that country being led by a narco-military alliance. Similarly, Peru stood on the brink of a military takeover in the late 1980s and early 1990s, an event apparently prevented only by the military's desire to avoid assuming the responsibility for Peru's wretched state of affairs.[49] When Peruvian President Alberto Fujimori suspended civil rights and imposed a nationwide state of emergency in 1992, his actions were viewed with alarm. Although Fujimori's actions ultimately brought significant successes against the *Shining Path*, the world community harshly criticized him because it did not want Peru's repressive response to domestic unrest to serve as a template for other nations confronting guerrilla insurgencies in the region. Almost without exception, the Latin American nations either currently confront, or have recently resolved, intense domestic turmoil.

The fact that the Andean governments exert weak control over their national territories compounds the multiple crises they are facing. Elite families often dominate the industrial and political structure, resulting in a system in which power, rather than the rule of law, preserves order. Poverty, poor communications and development infrastructure, and the sheer size of the territory under consideration, make it difficult for the governments to forge relations with their citizenry. In many regions, nongovernmental entities, including drug organizations, paramilitary squads, guerrilla groups, and organized labor, exercise *de facto* sovereign power. Such organizations have won over significant portions of the population by providing services that more typically are provided by governments, including housing, regional security, schools, mediation of property disputes, and regional economic development. In contrast, the states are often hard pressed to provide even basic services to remote regions, even if such moves would assist the state in building legitimacy.

The situation is made more complicated by the fact that official institutions, such as the military and national police, have been implicated in human rights abuses. For example, the Bolivian, Peruvian, and Colombian governments have created special military and police units to address drug trafficking. However, members of these military units have been implicated in drug trafficking.[50] In the case of Colombian police and military officers, there are numerous allegations that they have implicitly condoned and assisted death squads' attacks against guerrilla, civilian, and other targets. These violations are not supported or condoned by the governments, nor do they involve even a substantial fraction of police and military personnel. Typically, the crimes can be attributed to a small number of outlaws, including, regrettably, high-ranking officers. These violations have, in some cases, worked to increase the populace's support for the guerrillas. *Shining Path* operatives, for example, were very adept at parlaying Peruvian Army abuses into support for the guerrilla organization. In Colombia, the death squads have earned the allegiance of rural middle- and upper-class ranchers, largely because the government has been unable to protect these segments of society from guerrilla violence. Official complicity in rights abuses not only undermines public support for government institutions, but limits the United States' willingness and ability to contribute aid. There are restrictions on providing aid to countries and institutions that do not satisfy basic human rights requirements.

That drug policy objectives should be secondary to the larger strategic interests in the Andean region should be clear. The United States would lose the ability to pursue most source country counternarcotics objectives if the governments of the cocaine-producing states collapsed. Similarly, the Andean governments will not be able to cooperate with the United States on counternarcotics issues to the extent that larger principles, such as state survival, are at stake. Indeed, the implicit threat of civil unrest is preventing Bolivia from implementing its promised eradication campaign, despite its desperate need for U.S. funding, and despite the threat of funding being curtailed. The Andean states can succeed in combatting drug trafficking, and the United States can achieve its counternarcotics objectives, only if the Andean political structures and institutions are adequate to the range of threats they face. While it would be misleading to portray the Bolivian, Peruvian, and Colombian governments as on the brink of collapse, it would also be wrong to portray them as completely out of danger. They confront a diverse range of potentially viable threats, of which drug trafficking is only one. With a clearer understanding of vital interests in the region are, it is now possible to examine how these interests are threatened.

Clearly, the presence of the narcotics industry imperils regional stability. Broadly, cocaine trafficking manifests itself in two ways that harm Andean and U.S. interests. First, and perhaps most importantly, the cocaine trade engenders violence, and has brought about unprecedented attacks against political, social, and economic institutions in the source countries. The damage has been most evident in Colombia, where numerous leading political leaders' lives have been sacrificed to the drug trade. Peru, too, has suffered from violence. The *Shining Path* has gained from the drug trade's presence, both by protecting peasant interests against the drug lords, and by deriving revenue from drug trafficking activity. In recent years, Bolivia has shown signs of increasing unrest, including coca union leader Evo Morales's warning that violence would result from a policy of forced eradication. Second, the cocaine trade fosters corruption that is inherently difficult to measure and detect, but pernicious and corrosive nevertheless. Well into the 1980s, Bolivia was essentially governed by drug traffickers. The effects of this corruption still linger, as evidenced by the civilian government's reluctance to entrust counternarcotics responsibilities to the Bolivian army. Policies and measures that addressed these aspects of the drug trade's influence would also help the United States and the cocaine-producing nations address strategic objectives of preserving civilian democratic control.

Yet the drug trade is hardly the only, or even necessarily the most important, factor to threaten strategic interests in the Andes. Colombian society is beset by threats from left-wing guerrillas and right-wing death squads, in addition to that of the drug industry. The death squads' crimes have devastated the countryside, and left significant portions of rural Colombian vulnerable to attack. Meanwhile, the guerrillas' campaigns have inflicted severe damage on Colombian businesses, thrown the political system into prolonged confrontation and chaos, and resulted in thousands of deaths. More generally, the level of nonpolitical, nondrug violence in Colombia is extraordinarily high. Similarly, Peru faces an ongoing challenge from the *Shining Path* that, in many respects, is far more troubling to Peru's stability than the illicit drug trade. Although the violence has abated somewhat with the arrest of the *Sendero*'s charismatic leader, the terrorists still pose a formidable threat to the government. Bolivia has largely escaped the types of organized political violence that plague Colombia and Peru, but it still suffers from weak institutions that have been toppled repeatedly throughout Bolivia's history. In addition, to the extent that Colombian and Peruvian counternarcotics programs displace trafficking into Bolivia, the Bolivian government may be forced to confront the consequences of hosting influential, high-level traffickers again.

The unresolved question, then, is how best to address these diverse threats in a way that supports regional objectives? It is not difficult to see how the focus on interdiction and law enforcement source country control policies can be detrimental to achieving strategic objectives. Interdiction, eradication, and other drug-related law enforcement objectives take the Andean officials away from other, pressing duties not only because drug control consumes scarce law enforcement resource, but because much foreign aid is limited to counternarcotics uses. Such limitations bias the recipients toward counternarcotics activities, perhaps at the expense of other programs that would more effectively address strategic concerns. In addition, the focus on drugs, in the absence of systemic reforms, increases opportunities for corruption by bringing law enforcement and military officials into direct contact with the drug industry.[51] The deepening of the source countries' military involvement in counternarcotics operations is of increasing concern, particularly in light of the long history of authoritarian abuses in regions of Latin America.

There are several steps that, if taken, will ease the imbalances present in the U.S. strategy and strengthen pursuit of higher-order regional objectives. Perhaps the most important step is to recognize and acknowledge that counternarcotics objectives are but a subset of a much larger set of regional concerns. This acknowledgement can be demonstrated through a series of practical steps. Drugs now dominate U.S. bilateral relations with the Andean nations, as evidenced by the conditions placed on U.S. assistance and the State Department's certification process. Such conditions ought to be abandoned, not only because the asked-for reductions in drug production exports cannot be sustained and because they present potentially unbearable costs to the source nations, but because they imperil other regional objectives. For example, nations that are not fully cooperating with the United States on drug trafficking issues are subject to decertification. Among other sanctions, decertification would mandate the cessation of most U.S. aid, obligate the United States to vote against providing aid to the decertified nations in world and multinational forums, and open the way for the United States to implement trade sanctions against the decertified nations. Such sanctions would erode governmental abilities, discourage economic growth, and might worsen social, economic, and political conditions that have already spawned widespread labor unrest, guerrilla movements, and right-wing violence. Although neither Bolivia, Colombia, nor Peru has been completely decertified yet, they have all been placed on warning by being certified on the basis of overriding U.S. national security interests. Bolivia is extremely dependent on U.S. and international aid, and Colombia's economy would be harmed by trade sanctions. As a result, both nations must significantly improve their counternarcotics efforts in the coming years, or face the sanctions described above.

In addition to removing the drug control conditionality from U.S. counternarcotics assistance, the aid should be funnelled through nondrug institutions and programs. In other words, recommendations about program levels should be made outside the Office of National Drug Control, and program implementation should occur outside the various departments' drug-control units. This move would serve multiple purposes. First, divorcing aid from a counterdrug context would provide explicit acknowledgment that problems other than drug trafficking are at stake and that the U.S. is willing to commit resources to them. Second, the move would promote more extensive contact with organizations and institutions that are now only peripherally involved in bilateral U.S.-source country relations. A broader program of assistance, for example, would cultivate trade, economic development, health, human rights, and other such organizations to participate in a dialogue about national issues. While the inclusion of such diverse constituencies might be cacophonous, it may also serve to increase their stake in resolving national issues, as well as extend the government's legitimacy with alienated segments of the population. Finally, removing programs from a strict drug-control context would provide the nations with the flexibility to address pressing problems as the recipient and donor nations mutually see fit. The current focus of resources on counternarcotics issues tends to prevent authorities from considering programs and policies in a larger national context.

One of the major impediments facing the Andean governments is that they lack, to varying degrees, the resources to address their most vexing threats. Generically, the answer is to provide aid that will strengthen the governments against the factors threatening the civilian regimes. In more concrete terms, this means that appropriate government institutions must be supported against violence and corruption. Three institutions in particular seem both critical to the functioning of Andean society and in danger of being overwhelmed by external threats: the judiciary, the police, and the military. Judicial, police, and military assistance certainly do not exhaust the aid and development possibilities. Education, health, and economic development are all areas where the Andean governments could use assistance if for no other reason than that these are societal segments that could help inculcate a culture that rejects drug trafficking, violence, and political insurrection. Certainly, these institutions should be targeted as part of any long-term development strategy.[52] The judiciary, police, and military, however, are the most important to regime stability, and have been subjected to the most severe threats from external actors.

Over the past few years, Colombian authorities, with U.S. assistance, have made evident progress reforming the Colombian judicial system.[53] Where once Colombian judges were almost completely vulnerable to the drug lords' influence, the state has implemented important protective measures. In recognition of the magistrates' physical vulnerability, Colombia has improved its judicial protection program by adding security guards, providing bullet-proof vests, and training judges in personal security. Changes to the Colombian constitution have removed some of the investigatory burden from Colombian judges, and assigned them to police and other agencies that are better equipped to investigate criminal acts. Colombia has also opened a series of "Public Order" courts, which allow judges to try sensitive cases anonymously, and which have helped Colombia ease its tremendous court backlog. Improvements in the functioning of the judicial system may also translate into improved economic and business performance, to the extent that judicial reforms embrace contract enforcement and conflict resolution.[54]

For all of the improvements that have been made in the Colombian judicial system, some glaring deficiencies remain. Generally, justice is still elusive in Colombia. A very small fraction of Colombia's huge number of crimes enters the criminal justice system, and the conviction rate for those cases remains abysmally low.[55] The judicial system's effectiveness is particularly suspect in cases where military and police personnel stand accused of drug and human rights crimes.[56] Civilian courts typically do not have jurisdiction over such cases, particularly where military crimes are involved. Yet, Colombian military courts have not compellingly demonstrated that they take charges of drug, human rights, and death squad crimes seriously.[57] Improvements also need to be made in the penal system, particularly with respect to incarceration. Pablo Escobar's ability to run his drug empire from prison is a legendary, but unfortunately not isolated, example of the penal system's weakness. There is little wisdom in sending more people to jail if they will be able to continue their criminal enterprises while under official protection. Similarly, Bolivia's judicial reforms have been oriented toward improving prosecution of drug trafficking offenses. This focus has not only led to charges that the system violates basic notions of due process, particularly for poor Bolivians and low-level traffickers, but has ignored the need to address a larger set of legal issues that pertain to state legitimacy and control, including defining property rights, promoting civil rights, and curtailing police and military abuses.

Police forces in Bolivia, Colombia, and Peru bear much of the burden for domestic security, as well as for counternarcotics operations. By some estimates, however, half or more of the police in Colombia's large cities accept bribes from the drug industry. Additionally, the Colombian National Police annually commit a significant number of other crimes, including murder and torture.[58] The situation is similar in Bolivia and Peru, particularly in rural areas where the police are subject to less supervision. Bolivia's rural police (UMOPAR) have been accused of a large number of crimes that have inflamed the population's passions. One favorite UMOPAR tactic is to wait for large drug deals in a village to be completed, and then sweep into the area and rob the villagers and townspeople of their profits and possessions.[59] Through 1992, this type of corruption was so blatant that the United States would not share mission plans with Bolivia's UMOPAR teams until the raiding parties were airborne and there was less chance for the operation to be compromised.

Low pay, poor working conditions, and the constant threat of death all contribute to low police moral and, ultimately, corruption. The drug lords routinely offer bribes equivalent to a year's salary in exchange for a few minutes of cooperation. In many cases, the traffickers do not need the policemen's active participation, but rather simply need them to briefly look the other way while drug shipments are loaded. From an officer's perspective, the incentives to cooperate with the drug lords are clear: they and their families are vulnerable to retribution, and they have little recourse for protection. Conversely, some police conspire in human rights abuses against civilians because they—the poor, the guerrillas, the students—are viewed as the root causes of social disarray. Frustrated at the lack of judicial response, some policemen have taken matters into their own hands.

Guarding simultaneously against the police forces' vulnerability to retribution, their susceptibility to corruption, and their complicity in crimes and human rights abuses is no simple task. For example, the police are generally poorly armed in comparison to their adversaries.

Supplying them with better weapons might make them more adept at law enforcement operations, but might also contribute to more severe human rights offenses. Some areas where the Andean forces require assistance are relatively benign. For example, forensic training, protection equipment and training, and communications equipment are all areas where the United States can probably contribute without endangering human rights objectives. Additionally, the United States can work with the source countries to counter corruption by implementing such programs as frequent service rotations, last-minute notification of operations, and periodic reinvestigations of police personnel. Other steps, such as providing better weapons, operations training, and intelligence support can be provided to the extent that acceptable end-use monitoring programs can be implemented.[60] In short, the assistance should address the fact that only a small, albeit substantial, fraction of the violent crimes committed in Colombia are drug related, and that Colombian courts currently prosecute a woefully small fraction of both drug and nondrug crimes.

The Andean militaries face many of the same problems confronted by the police. That is, they are outgunned, poorly paid, and subject to corruption. Within the context of counternarcotics operations, the United States has supplied the Andean nations with substantial amounts of military assistance over the past half decade. But, because of concerns about human rights abuses, and concerns about becoming embroiled in Andean domestic affairs, there are substantial restrictions associated with U.S. military aid. Generally, U.S.-supplied equipment can only be used in pursuit of counternarcotics goals. In Colombia, U.S. equipment can be used against the guerrillas only in cases where collusion between drug traffickers and the insurgents can be proven, or where a strategic relationship between drug traffickers and guerrillas is thought to exist.[61] Such collusion tends to happen relatively rarely, and thus for all practical purposes, U.S. military aid is confined to use against drug traffickers. Ironically, U.S. equipment cannot be used against Colombia's right-wing death squads, despite documented collusion between the drug industry and the paramilitaries. To guard against potential violations of these restrictions, and to ensure that military personnel do not commit human rights abuses with U.S. equipment, the United States requires that end-use monitoring policies be implemented.

The Risks and Rewards of Revising Objectives

By pursuing strategic goals based on institution building and regime stability, the United States can ensure that some, but not all, of its counternarcotics objectives are attained in the process. For example, the Colombian government is negotiating with leading traffickers over terms of surrender. Given that such negotiations will occur, the United States has an interest in ensuring that cocaine traffickers receive the harshest criminal sanctions possible; that any negotiated settlement with the traffickers contain provisions for monitoring the assets and operations of those who surrender; and that those who surrender reveal information about the structure and operation of the cartels. These goals can only be accomplished if the Andean governments negotiate from a position of stability and if Andean penal and judicial institutions are capable of enforcing the law. Clearly, however, pursuit of strategic goals does not contribute directly to reducing U.S. cocaine consumption. Unlike the current law enforcement-based strategy, which has deterrence as its objective, and which fails to meet its goal, the strategic approach labors under no such illusions: the strategic approach is not intended to reduce drug trafficking directly, because it cannot. The strategic approach can, however, ensure that leading traffickers are punished, that their assets seized, and that they serve out reasonable prison sentences. Thus, the institution-based strategy also preserves the moral dimension of international drug control. That is, by helping the drug-producing nations develop their institutional structures, the United States demonstrates a commitment to controlling international drug trafficking while simultaneously preserving the integrity of the Andean political structure.

Strategic goals will not be pursued without presenting risks of their own. By necessity, the types of training and assistance described involve working with institutions in the source countries that have tremendous power over citizens' lives. With this influence and the uncertainty of the political environment comes tremendous potential for abuse. Moreover, a strategy based on institution building presents the potential for deeply involving the United States in the internal politics and policies of sovereign nations. Training and assistance provided to Peru's military, for example, might lead to human rights violations that could be traced back to U.S. training and equipment.

Certainly, end-user monitoring programs would have to accompany the new aid, similar to those that are currently in place for police and military assistance. The alternative is to continue pursuing a strategy that ignores the accumulating tensions and provides little in the way of tangible results.

The new strategy would lose much of its luster if it proved to be prohibitively expensive. How much this new strategy will cost is not clear although, uncertainty notwithstanding, the current level of source country control spending probably exceeds the funding that would be required to address strategic objectives. To put the potential obligation in a more realistic perspective, the Bolivian, Colombian, and Peruvian governments combined spend about $94 billion per year, of which about $2 billion is for military expenditures, and an additional $1 billion for the police and the judiciary.[62] Taking the current $1.6 billion spent on international and source country programs as a potential upper limit to assistance, this represents more than half of the Andean governments' combined military, police, and judicial budgets. Surely, the Andean governments could not efficiently absorb that much aid in one year. A reasonable lower bound would be an addition to the current 6 percent (approximately $102 million) of the international drug control budget earmarked for aid. A doubling of this budget segment, presuming it was devoted to the types of institution building previously described, would make a substantial contribution to regional capabilities. Alternatively, institutional aid could be augmented by directing some of the current 16 percent (or $272 million) of the international budget spent on investigations and intelligence toward institutional aid. While a large fraction of the investigations and intelligence resources contribute to arrests, prosecutions, asset seizures, and investigation of money laundering, a large fraction also gets spent on investigations and intelligence for interdiction, laboratory raids, and other law enforcement actions.

A more difficult question is how much interdiction and law enforcement-based activity to support. To those who would argue that the current $1.3 billion expended on interdiction and law enforcement represents the minimal budget necessary for demonstrating a commitment to combatting international drug trafficking, it should be pointed out that as recently as 1989 the U.S. Department of Defense spent only $71.8 million detection and monitoring operations but that by 1993, without any measurable or discernable impact on drug flows and drug use, total expenditures on the same tasks had risen to $293.1 million.[63] With respect to the military's participation in interdiction and law enforcement-related activities, it is generally agreed that current spending exceeds the amount necessary to maintain and improve military preparedness.

It is no easier to justify the remaining $1 billion or so spent by other organizations on international interdiction and law enforcement-related operations. The measurable benefits of these operations are few and far between. Essentially, the question reduces to how much spending is sufficient to demonstrate a commitment to controlling international drug trafficking. But the question could just as easily be reversed: do we really want to reserve 8 percent of our drug policy resources for symbolic acts of interdiction and law enforcement?

Battle Cry

For many readers, the recommendations that source country control policies be pared back and that counternarcotics goals in the Andes be reoriented toward strategic regional objectives are likely to prove unsatisfactory. For one, the recommendations seem to signal a retreat in the face of the traffickers' power and intimidation and would appear to hand the traffickers an important victory over law enforcement in particular. Additionally, the proposed strategy may leave the impression that little, if anything, can be done to address the United States' cocaine problem. Some pessimism is warranted because there are limits to what the current menu of policy options can achieve. That having been said, however, all is not lost.

In the war on drugs, the policies applied against the various aspects of cocaine use are essentially regulations. We have seen, convincingly I hope, how regulating supply at the source is ineffective. But policies' ineffectiveness in the source countries does not necessarily indicate that all counterdrug policies will be fruitless. Indeed, the impotence at the source country level raises the larger issue of where anticocaine dollars are better, and perhaps best, spent. This is another way of saying that the great risk in continuing down our present course, tilted toward supply control policies, is that we may be forgoing more effective policy options. This argument has been put forth by numerous analysts, and deserves serious scrutiny.[64]

Treating the Wounded

A comparison of four policy options (source country policies, interdiction, domestic enforcement, and treatment) suggests that treatment may accomplish a given reduction in cocaine use for the least cost.[65] Cocaine consumption has matured into a pattern dominated by heavy users. Heavy cocaine users, by virtue of their health care needs, their work habits, and their criminal behavior, inflict the preponderance of cocaine-related costs on society. However, heavy users appear to be relatively insensitive to temporary price changes and shortages, precisely the types of policy successes source country policies are best suited to achieve. Treatment captures the large benefits associated with getting heavy users to quit cocaine. Even though an individual heavy cocaine user might have to enroll in treatment programs several times before successfully abandoning cocaine use, the cost of multiple treatments is still relatively low. Additionally, since most users quit at least for the duration of their program, treatment also reduces consumption in cases that are not successful over the long run.

Treatment's great advantage is that it works by altering the users' consumption patterns, ultimately causing a shift in the demand curve for cocaine. In contrast, source country control policies basically work by shifting the supply curve, which causes *movement along the old demand curve*. The distinction between "shift in demand" and "movement along a demand curve" might not sound important since cocaine consumption is determined by the intersection of supply and demand, but it is. A downward shift in the demand curve means that people's tastes and preferences have changed, and that at a given price for cocaine they will consume less of it than they did before the shift. Tastes and preferences change not only because people learn more about the consequences of cocaine use during treatment, but because they are able to overcome its positively and negatively reinforcing aspects of cocaine consumption.[66] Not only will less cocaine be consumed, but the price will fall, reducing dealers' incentives to enter the market. In contrast, a shift in supply produced by supply control programs does not change the underlying tastes and preferences for cocaine. As supply contracts, the market is equilibrated by a price rise that temporarily pushes some users out of the market. However, the higher price signals that there are profits to be made by producing cocaine, and eventually supply shifts back to the original level. Ultimately the same amount of cocaine is consumed, and the dealers and producers have been enriched along the way.

There are, of course, limits to treatment's utility, the most important of which is that not every cocaine user can be, or is willing to be, treated. Treatment's success, to a large degree, depends on the individual's motivation. Certainly, not all heavy cocaine users are motivated to seek treatment, even if it were available without wait to all those who desired it. Similarly, treatment has a dynamic associated with it that may lead to its undoing over the long run. That is, treatment reduces the demand for cocaine, which leads to lower prices. Lower prices in turn, however, may attract new users by reducing barriers to initiation. The limited available evidence suggests that cocaine use will increase after a price decline, though at this point it is unclear how strong this effect might be, or how long after a large increase in treatment it might occur, let alone what appropriate mitigating steps might be.[67]

In any event, it seems clear that treatment is deserving of some additional funding. There are far more heavy users who would benefit from treatment than there are treatment slots available.[68] In fact, the treatment community is estimated to need more than one million additional treatment slots, a pretty fair indication that treatment's potential effectiveness has not been exhausted.

An Ounce of Prevention

Prevention may turn out to be an important companion to expanded treatment. One of treatment's potential outcomes is a drop in cocaine use and, thus, a drop in cocaine prices. To the extent that any drop in prices stimulates a rise in initiation, prevention programs may become more important because of their potential contribution to limiting the inflow of new users. Also, prevention programs are intended to prevent people who have successfully undergone treatment from relapsing into cocaine use. Again, prevention's cost effectiveness in this capacity has not been formally compared to treatment and supply control programs. The limits to prevention, however, are quite clear. Even if prevention programs stopped all new initiation tomorrow, the United States would still confront a large pool of heavy users that would not decline to 50 percent of its present size for fifteen years.[69]

Not much can be said about prevention's utility relative to other supply and demand control policies because studies comparing prevention to treatment, international control, and domestic control are lacking. Studies of individual prevention programs reveal that prevention's effects generally erode over time, particularly if the prevention message is not periodically reinforced.[70] It is entirely possible that when prevention programs are compared to the other major alternatives, that prevention will prove less expensive than supply control programs for a given reduction in cocaine use. One of prevention's chief benefits is that it can reach large audiences for very low marginal costs. Thus, even if the prevention message has a weak impact on use, and even if it has to be repeated many times before behavior is affected, it still may turn out to be relatively inexpensive to use. On the other hand, prevention may not prove as cost-effective as treatment because prevention's message is relatively indirect and weak.

Enforce, of Course?

The same study that found treatment to be the least costly method for reducing cocaine consumption by a given amount also concluded that domestic enforcement was less costly than source country programs and interdiction.[71] Domestic enforcement has a number of advantages over international and source country control policies. Perhaps most importantly, domestic enforcement increases the full use cost of cocaine much more effectively than source country programs by striking closer to retail markets. For traffickers caught in the United States, the penalties are potentially severe, including lengthy prison sentences, heavy fines, and forfeiture of assets. In addition, it costs traffickers more to replace cocaine seized near the end of the production chain than cocaine seized nearer the source. These enforcement measures increase the traffickers' risks and costs more than policies implemented at the source, and therefore have a more direct and substantial impact on retail prices.

Another form of domestic enforcement, users sanctions, was not considered in the cost comparison analysis. User sanctions are enforcement mechanisms employed against cocaine consumers. Possession laws, for example, are one form of user sanction. Such sanctions figure prominently in the battle against cocaine use, although much work remains to be done with respect to determining their contribution to national drug-control objectives.

Still, domestic enforcement and user sanctions may cost more than they yield.[72] Domestic enforcement is expensive relative to treatment, and it may not effectively reduce crime, morbidity, and mortality associated with cocaine and cocaine markets. User sanctions and domestic enforcement may have notable unintended consequences. For example, heroin users share and reuse needles, which fosters the transmission of HIV, because antiparaphernalia laws have limited the availability of needles and raised the penalties for being caught with them. In some cases, domestic enforcement may increase these costs by stimulating competition for market share among drug retailers. In addition, increased incarceration is one logical consequence of increased domestic enforcement. Incarceration is expensive, and this cost must be accounted for in an analysis of domestic enforcement's utility. Another disadvantage of domestic enforcement is that much of it occurs at the local level, a factor that makes it difficult to enact a uniform national domestic enforcement policy. In other words, domestic enforcement and user sanctions are no different from international programs and interdiction in that they need to be carefully crafted in order to avoid unintended consequences overwhelming their beneficial effects. Domestic enforcement's primary advantage over international programs is that it more directly and effectively affects retail markets.

Where Do We Go from Here?

At the beginning of this book I promised to evaluate source country control policies within the context of the existing drug control regime. There were a number of practical reasons for adopting this approach, not the least of which was that few radical changes to drug policy could be expected. Decriminalization of cocaine is not on the horizon, to say nothing of legalization. Despite these constraints, however, some changes in emphasis are occurring. In particular, a consensus appears to have emerged in the analytic and academic communities that the division of federal drug-control resources between supply control programs (65 percent) and demand control programs (35 percent) needs to be redressed.[73] Balancing the distribution of counterdrug resources can be accomplished one of three ways: the overall drug control budget can be increased, with the majority of new revenues earmarked for demand control; the supply control budget can be cut; or supply control resources can be diverted to demand control programs. Whatever approach is adopted, the question is less whether to rectify the imbalance, since political pressure appears to be leading inexorably in that direction, but rather what issues need to be addressed as we move in that direction. Two issues stand out in particular. The first is how changes in resource allocation might affect the various drug problem indicators with which policymakers are concerned, including prevalence, initiation, and emergency room admissions. In other words, where will additional drug policy resources will do the most good? The second relates to the process through which drug control resources are allocated. In particular, is the resource allocation process adequate for a problem as complex and dynamic as drug control?

Marginal Costs, Marginal Benefits, and Marginal Progress[74]

Despite the billions spent on drug control policy, at a very fundamental level it is not clear whether we are spending too much, not enough, or just the right amount on drug control. As Everingham and Rydell summarized this sentiment:

> The results [of our study] suggest that if an additional dollar is going to be spent on drug control, it should be spent on treatment, not on a supply-control program. [The results] do not, however, indicate whether or not that dollar should be spent in the first place. It might be that [source country control, interdiction, domestic enforcement, and treatment] generate greater benefits than they cost, and treatment is just the best of four good programs. Or, at the other extreme, treatment might merely be the least ineffective of four ineffective programs.[75]

It is unlikely that the U.S. government will ever evaluate its drug-control strategy from the first principles suggested by the excerpt above. The basic divisions of national drug-control policy will remain intact, if for no other reason than that a complete reexamination of drug-control policies is likely to call the very nature of the drug-control regime itself into question. This is an appraisal that few elected officials are willing to undertake. The excerpt, however, introduces the issue of marginal costs and benefits, and this is a much more realistic foundation upon which to build drug policy evaluation.

Integrating marginal cost and benefit thinking into drug-policy analysis matters for one very practical reason: progress (or change to use a less value-laden term) in drug policy will occur incrementally. In other words, changes in drug policy will not be wholesale, but rather will occur at the margin in small increments that the political system can more readily digest. The debate about drug policy is too polarized and the political system too sclerotic to allow for much other than gradual changes in policies.

One problem with subtle changes in policy directions is that it is difficult to determine the changes' effects. But when relatively small changes are the best that can be accomplished, it becomes critical to understand not only where resources are most needed, but where they will be most effective. ONDCP is supposed to provide this type of strategic planning and understanding, but it is fair to say that ONDCP has little ability to estimate how resource reallocations will affect progress toward national drug-control objectives.[76] The types of strategies-to-goals conflicts that plague interdiction (see earlier in this chapter) are prevalent throughout the national strategy. Although ONDCP annually establishes quantitative drug-policy goals, these goals are not meaningfully anchored to existing strategies and programs. In other words, it is not clear how additional funding for most programs will affect the national goals of reduced cocaine use. Obviously, then, it is impossible to determine if the additional funding is better spent in one area or another. Again, this book has established that marginal spending increases in source country control policies are unlikely to be beneficial; it remains to be determined where additional resources could be best used.

One consequence has been the promulgation of a policy that attacks from every angle, doing as much of everything as is politically possible.[77] Now, however, the political environment has evolved to one where less is possible, in part because of resource constraints, and in part because of growing dissatisfaction with programmatic results. Certainly, marginal cost decisionmaking will be difficult, primarily because the data on which these decisions must be made is missing, incomplete, or inappropriate.[78] The lack of credible data, however, is not an argument for continuation of present practices; it is compelling justification for improving data collection and formulating better indicators and measures.

Moving Mountains, Moving Resources

It is very likely that some programs, such as treatment, provide net positive social benefits, and thus are worthy of funding increases. The seemingly logical conclusion would be to take the resources freed up by cuts in source country control policies and apply them to the more effective components of the national drug-control strategy. That decision, or recommendation, is best left to analysts better versed in the marginal benefits of national drug-control programs. But proposing cuts in one area of drug control does raise concern about how resources can be moved between drug-control programs. The point to be made here is not whether such transfers should take place, but rather, how difficult such transfers would be.

Each of the basic divisions of the national drug-control strategy (domestic and international supply control; treatment; prevention) is, by and large, housed separately somewhere in the federal bureaucracy. Each has its budget drafted, and its appropriation set, through a separate bill. Congress must pass, and the President must approve, multiple appropriations bills in order to complete the National Drug Control Strategy's funding. But the reality of funding the drug-control strategy is even more complicated, since most of the funding decisions are made at the Congressional subcommittee level.[79] In effect, the national drug-control strategy is cobbled together by the deliberations of dozens of subcommittees, which are then acted upon at different points during the year.

It should be readily apparent how difficult transferring resources from one drug-control strategy element to another can be. In theory, the Office of National Drug Control Policy should be able to facilitate such transfers by advising Congress and the respective agencies and departments about where resources can best be used. ONDCP cannot, however, reallocate these resources itself. Assume for example that a Foreign Affairs subcommittee approved a cut in the State Department's international drug-control programs. The subcommittee would have few incentives or mechanisms to transfer the resources to Health and Human Services for an increase in treatment funding, regardless of whether such an increase was warranted. It is more likely that the committee membership would find other uses for the resources that fell under the Foreign Affairs committee's domain. Even if the membership of both the Foreign Affairs and the committee with HHS oversight could agree to shift the funding to treatment, the transfer would still be delayed for as long as it took the separate appropriations cycles to be completed. Finally, even if one agency agreed to give up resources, it is not axiomatic that another would be motivated to accept additional counterdrug resources. Often drug policies compete with agencies' and departments' primary missions, and thus ONDCP and its policy prescriptions may be viewed with displeasure. As one example, HHS resisted increasing treatment funding during the Bush administration, in part because it place a higher priority on child immunization and Head Start.[80]

It is not obvious what the solution to this dilemma is. For example, despite the arguments in favor of budget centralization, there are compelling arguments for keeping operational authority scattered among the departments and agencies. ONDCP could be vested with operational authority, but this would not obviously constitute an effective use of resources. Institutions such as the FBI and Health and Human Services have considerable experience with functions such as controlling organized crime and treating drug-dependent patients. These institutions' ability to contribute to drug-control policy depends not only on the drug-control resources they are allocated, but on the accumulated expertise the institutions have developed in related, but nondrug, policy areas. Consolidating operational authority within ONDCP would certainly lead to the loss of some of the expertise found in other parts of the government. One avenue that deserves consideration is a separate drug-control appropriation. This approach would imbue ONDCP with greater allocative authority, but leave operational authority distributed as it presently is. Obviously, this move would create tensions between the budgetary authority (ONDCP) and the operational authorities (the agencies and departments). Whether this tension would be better or worse than the present situation is an open question.

A Final Word

This book set out to examine source country control policies and their limitations, and that is where it should end. The last decade has taught us much about source country drug policies and their effects. Cynics will point out that these lessons have been learned many times before, including during Prohibition and Nixon's war on drugs. While such cynicism resonates with some truth, it also glosses over fundamental changes in drug trafficking, and drug policy options, that have made revisiting and reevaluating drug policy periodically a good idea. However, despite dramatic improvements in law enforcement abilities and detection technologies, the basic laws of supply and demand have not changed.[81] Thus, the major lessons about source country control policies seem relatively clear. The existing source country control programs are small relative to the magnitude of the trade, and the source country components of cocaine account for a minuscule portion of retail cocaine prices. Because of this, losses imposed on cocaine trafficking by source country policies are easily absorbed through the businesses' huge markups, production flexibility, and large profit margins.

Source country policies of a much larger scale have, with rare and localized exceptions, not been implemented.[82] Nevertheless, policies such as widespread forced eradication, and high interdiction rates are possible. These policies, however, would come with extremely high budget costs, and would bring about potentially devastating externalities and social consequences without providing a long-term reduction in cocaine trafficking. Budget costs would grow disproportionately with the fraction of the trade disrupted because of the increasing difficulty, or rising marginal costs, of disrupting successively larger portions of cocaine production. Even assuming the United States and the Andean nations were willing to accept the costs of a massive policy intervention, it is quite probable that the cocaine traffickers could resume full production in two years or less. The cocaine trade's mobility, the ready availability of inputs, and the industry's price structure make it very resilient to control efforts. The coca plant, and the length of time it takes to mature, represents the longest potential lag between a source country policy's implementation and the traffickers' ability to recover. Capturing this lag, however, largely depends on the element of surprise, for if the traffickers anticipate the policy's implementation they may be able to adjust to it in advance. Even with the benefit of surprise, source country policies may not work to disrupt cocaine markets even temporarily if the traffickers compensate for the possibility by accumulating inventory.

A better source country strategy appears to be one that recognizes the severe limits facing interdiction, eradication, and other source country policies, and instead focuses on directing source country resources where they will be most useful. This necessitates defining a regional strategy that elevates political stability and institution building, and demotes traditional counternarcotics objectives. Stability and institution building goals can be accomplished with a modest amount of resources, conceivably freeing up $1 billion or more that was previously devoted to traditional source country policies.

These limits to source country control policies have become increasingly obvious in recent years. Cocaine supplies have continued to rise, and cocaine prices have remained low, despite sharp increases in seizures and other efforts to control drug supplies and production and the source. Similarly, it appears that other policy tools, particularly treatment, are better suited for addressing the cocaine problem as it currently manifests itself. A gradual shift in resource allocations from source country control policies to demand control policies seems both likely and justified. The shift's efficacy will be aided by understanding the marginal benefits of various programmatic funding increases, and by removing institutional barriers so that national drug-control authorities can redirect resources rapidly and flexibly in response to changes in the nature of drug problems. Alas, policy implementation, particularly in a realm as complex, far-reaching, and controversial as drug policy, defies consensus, let alone consensus about policies that reject the conventional wisdom.

Notes

1. Etzioni (1994).
2. See *National Household Survey on Drug Abuse: Main Findings 1991* (1993).
3. Bachman, Johnston, and O'Malley (1990); Johnston, O'Malley, and Bachman (1993a); Johnston, O'Malley, and Bachman (1993b).
4. Everingham and Rydell (1994).
5. See Everingham and Rydell (1994) and Rydell and Everingham (1994) for a discussion of cocaine demand and heavy use.
6. Peter D. Hart Research Associates (1994).
7. Lauderback and Waldorf (1993).
8. *National Household Survey on Drug Abuse: Main Findings 1991* (1993).
9. Kleiman (1989) and (1992).
10. Hashish is produced by extracting the THC resins from marijuana plants. Hash oil results from chemical refinement of hash. The resulting resin and oil compounds are used in a variety of ways. Frequently, for example, hash is smoked, but it is also baked into food products.
    Sinsemilla is marijuana grown exclusively from female plants. Growers eliminate male plants early in the season to stimulate the female plants into producing

richer, larger, and THC-laden buds. Because of the extra steps involved in production, and the higher quality of the marijuana, sinsemilla is more expensive than the commercial-grade products.

11. Reuter and Kleiman (1986), 290.
12. *Source to the Street* (1993). Figures derived from Mexican marijuana, Bolivian cocaine, and Southeast Asian heroin. Ratios calculated using pure kilogram equivalents. For example, the kilogram opium gum price was multiplied by the appropriate factor to yield a quantity (and price) of gum sufficient to produce one kilogram of heroin.
13. Reuter and Kleiman (1986), 294.
14. Kleiman (1989), 97.
15. Moore (1976).
16. Kleiman (1989), 97, notes that while retail marijuana prices might rise relatively rapidly in response to a market disruption, consumption would be affected more slowly because of a variety of factors, including the larger inventories marijuana users tend to keep on hand.
17. Hash and hash oil are less bulky, but do not appear to be commercially viable in the United States, at least on a large scale.
18. See chapter 4 for a discussion of some marijuana control programs. See also Reuter and Ronfeldt (1992), Craig (1978), and *Drug Control: U.S.-Mexico Opium Poppy and Marijuana Aerial Eradication Program* (1988) for more on Mexican programs. One distinguishing factor about marijuana is that it enjoys no legal protections in foreign countries, unlike the poppy and coca crops from which heroin and cocaine are derived. There is no talk of crop substitution or development assistance for marijuana, because marijuana has no recognized legal uses. Consequently, marijuana farmers are not deemed worthy of assistance in transitioning out of marijuana production. Marijuana can be used to make legal products, such as rope. However, it is illegal to use hemp in the manufacture of these legal products. Even if some uses were legal, development assistance's impact on illegal marijuana production would be the same.
19. Reuter and Ronfeldt (1992).
20. *INCSR* (1990) reports the sharp drop in Colombian marijuana cultivation and the sharp rise in Mexican cannabis farming activity. Note, however, that *INCSR* attributes much of the Mexican increase to improved estimating procedures.
21. Kleiman (1989), 71–73, reports on the growth in and organization of domestic marijuana production.
22. Some states decriminalized marijuana use and possession of marijuana, meaning they reduced the sanctions for those caught with small amounts of marijuana, though they did not reduce the penalties for trafficking.
23. DiNardo and Lemieux (1992).
24. Model (1993).
25. Model (1993), 746.
26. *INCSR* (1994).
27. *Source to the Street* (1993).
28. Moore (1976).
29. Spain (1975).
30. Lee (1994) discusses the Thai case in detail.
31. *Heroin Situation Assessment* (1992). Reuter (1984) reports on the problems of determining the number of heroin addicts. See also Reuter (1993).
32. Reuter (1985), 90.

33. *Heroin Situation Assessment* (1992).
34. Reuter (1993) recounts this chapter in the history of heroin use.
35. Reuter (1993) demonstrates that a perceptible substitution effect took place during the heroin shortage. That is, when heroin became scarce, a fraction of the using population appears to have increased its use of substitutes such as codeine, methadone, pentazocine, and so forth.
36. *INCSR* (1994).
37. Rydell and Everingham (1994), 40–42. The authors note that little is known about the societal costs of cocaine use, and thus the measures must be interpreted cautiously.
38. Boyum (1992) discusses this possibility.
39. Ibid.
40. *National Drug Control Strategy: Reclaiming our Communities from Drugs and Violence* (1994).
41. *National Drug Control Strategy: Budget Summary* (1994).
42. Ibid. The interdiction total for 1993 was $1511.1. Counting programs that were directly interdiction-based yielded a total request for 1994 of $1,299.9 million, of which $432.5 was for the Department of Defense; $460.1 million for Customs Service; $313.4 million for the Coast Guard; and $75.6 million for the Immigration and Naturalization Service. The total request for international investigations and intelligence was $264.8 million, of which DEA contributed $109.9 million; Customs $72.3 million; DOD $47.5 million; and INS $35.1. million. Assistance spending totaled $111.3 million, the vast majority of which was funneled through the State Department. Murphy (1994) makes the point that budget figures may overstate the extent of counterdrug activities.
43. See Builder (1993) for a discussion of measuring interdiction's effectiveness.
44. Anderberg (1991).
45. Lupsha (1994).
46. Builder (1993).
47. *Drug Control: Heavy Investment in Military Surveillance is not Paying off* (1993), 31–34.
48. *National Drug Control Strategy: Budget Summary* (1994) provides details on the budgets and cutbacks implemented.
49. McCormick (1992).
50. Hargreaves (1992) provides accounts of Bolivian military forces' complicity in drug trafficking. See *The Colombian National Police, Human Rights and U.S. Drug Policy* (1993) for a perspective on Colombian officials' involvement in the drug trade.
51. Smith (1992), 14–15.
52. See Thoumi (1993), 40–46.
53. See for example *Foreign Assistance: Promising Approach to Judicial Reform in Colombia* (1992).
54. Thoumi (1993).
55. *Foreign Assistance: Promising Approach to Judicial Reform in Colombia* (1992). Also, Hanratty and Meditz (1990).
56. *The Colombian National Police, Human Rights and U.S. Drug Policy* (1993). See also *Colombia Beseiged* (1989) and *The Killings in Colombia* (1989) and, to a lesser extent, *The Colombian National Police, Human Rights and U.S. Drug Policy* (1993), report on the strains in military-judicial relations over abuse charges.
57. See also *Colombia Beseiged* (1989) and *The Killings in Colombia* (1989).
58. *The Colombian National Police, Human Rights and U.S. Drug Policy* (1993).

59. Hargreaves (1992), 96.
60. DOD document, from Riley (1993).
61. *Drug War: Observations on Counternarcotics Aid to Colombia* (1991), 19.
62. *The Military Balance* (1994).
63. *Drug Control: Heavy Investment in Military Surveillance is not Paying off* (1993). *Comprehensive Review DOD Counter Drug Program* (1993) provides similar figures.
64. Kleiman (1992a) and (1992b) presents perhaps the most thorough examination of drug policy regimes. Rydell and Everingham (1994) present a detailed empirical analysis of the national cocaine strategy.
65. Ibid. The study excluded prevention because data on these programs were not available.
66. See chapter 2 for a discussion of positive and negative reinforcement.
67. *Price and Purity of Cocaine: The Relationship to Emergency Room Visits and Deaths, and to Drug Use Among Arrestees* (1992) analyzes cocaine demand in the face of price changes.
68. *National Drug Control Strategy: Reclaiming our Communities from Drugs and Violence* (1994), 23–28.
69. Everingham and Rydell (1994).
70. Montagne and Scott (1993); Ellickson, Bell, and McGuigan (1993).
71. Rydell and Everingham (1994).
72. Ibid.
73. This is the approximate distribution of federal resources. If state and local resources were included, the distribution would be much more heavily tilted toward law enforcement programs. Murphy (1994) touches on this.
74. For this section, I am particularly indebted to Zimring and Hawkins (1992) and Rydell and Everingham (1994).
75. Rydell and Everingham (1994), xvi.
76. Reuter and Caulkins (1995).
77. Ibid., 5.
78. Reuter and Caulkins (1995); Ebener, et al. (1994).
79. Murphy (1994).
80. Ibid., 5.
81. Thornton (1991).
82. The Colombian crackdown in 1989 and 1990 is, of course, a primary example. *Operation Blast Furnace,* which Bolivia executed with U.S. assistance in 1986, is a localized example. Hargreaves (1992) and Menzel (1989) examine *Operation Blast Furnace* in detail.

References

Anderberg, Michael, *MOEs for Drug Interdiction: Simple Tests Expose Critical Flaws,* CRM 91-48 (Arlington, Va.: Center for Naval Analyses, 1991).

Bachman, Jerald G., Lloyd D. Johnston, and Patrick M. O'Malley, "Explaining the Recent Decline in Cocaine Use among Young Adults: Further Evidence that Perceived Risks and Disapproval Lead to Reduced Drug Use," *Journal of Health and Social Behavior* 31 (June 1990): 173–84.

Boyum, David Anders, *Reflections on Economic Theory and Drug Enforcement* (dissertation, Harvard University, 1992).

Builder, Carl, *Measuring the Leverage: Assessing Military Contributions to Drug Interdiction*, MR-158-A/AF (Santa Monica, Calif.: RAND, 1993).

Childress, Michael, *A System Description of the Heroin Trade*, MR-234-A/DPRC (Santa Monica, Calif.: RAND, 1994).

_____, *A System Description of the Marijuana Trade*, MR-235-A/DPRC (Santa Monica, Calif.: RAND, 1994).

Clark, Andrew, "Adding up the Pros and Cons of Legalization," *International Journal of Drug Policy* 4, 3 (1993): 116–21.

Colombia Besieged: Political Violence and State Responsibility (Washington, D.C.: Washington Office on Latin America, 1989).

The Colombian National Police, Human Rights and U.S. Drug Policy (Washington, D.C.: Washington Office on Latin America, 1993).

Craig, Richard, "La Campana Permanente: Mexico's Antidrug Campaign," *Journal of Interamerican Studies and World Affairs* 20, 2 (May 1978).

Dennis, R. J., "The Economics of Legalizing Drugs," *The Atlantic Monthly* (November 1990): 126–32.

Dinardo, John, "Law Enforcement, the Price of Cocaine and Cocaine Use," *Mathematical and Computer Modelling* 17, 2 (1993): 53–64.

DiNardo, John, and Thomas Lemieux, *Alcohol, Marijuana and American Youth: The Unintended Effects of Government Regulation*, NBER Working Paper #4212 (November 1992).

Dombey-Moore, Bonnie, Susan Resetar, and Michael Childress, *A System Description of the Cocaine Trade*, MR-236-A/AF/DPRC (Santa Monica, Calif.: RAND, 1994).

Drug Control: Heavy Investment in Military Surveillance is not Paying off (Washington, D.C.: GAO, 1993).

Drug Control: U.S.-Mexico Opium Poppy and Marijuana Aerial Eradication Program (Washington, D.C.: GAO, 1988).

Drug War: Observations on Counternarcotics Aid to Colombia (Washington, D.C.: Government Accounting Office, September 1991).

Ebener, Patricia, Jonathan Caulkins, Sandy Geschwind, Daniel McCaffrey, and Hilary Saner, *Improving Data and Analysis to Support National Substance Abuse Policy* (Santa Monica, Calif.: RAND, 1994).

Etzioni, Amitai, "Incorrigible: Bringing Social Hope and Political Rhetoric into Instructive Contact with What it Means to be Human," *The Atlantic Monthly* 274, 1 (July 1994): 14–16).

Everingham, Susan, and C. Peter Rydell, *Modeling the Demand for Cocaine*, MR-332-ONDCP/A/DPRC (Santa Monica, Calif.: RAND, 1994).

Foreign Assistance: Promising Approach to Judicial Reform in Colombia (Washington, D.C.: GAO, 1992).

Hanratty, Dennis M., and Sandra W. Meditz, eds., *Colombia: A Country Study* (Washington, D.C.: Department of the Army, 1990).

Hargreaves, Clare, *Snowfields: The War on Cocaine in the Andes* (London: Holmes & Meier, 1992).

Peter D. Hart Research Associates, poll on drug problem (2 and 3 February 1994).

Heroin Situation Assessment: A Report Prepared for the Office of National Drug Control Policy (Cambridge, Mass.: BOTEC Analysis Corporation, 1992).

International Narcotics Strategy Report (INCSR), United States Department of State, Bureau of International Narcotics Matters (Washington, D.C.: USGPO, various years).

Jarvik, M. E., "The Drug Dilemma: Manipulating the Demand," *Science* 250 (1990): 387–92.

Johnston, L. D. ,P. M. O'Malley, and J. G. Bachman, *National Survey Results on Drug Use from the Monitoring the Future Study, 1975–1992, Volume I: Secondary School Students*, National Institute of Health Publication 93-3597 (Rockville, Md.: National Institute on Drug Abuse, 1993a).

Johnston, L. D., P. M. O'Malley, and J. G. Bachman, *National Survey Results on Drug Use from the Monitoring the Future Study, 1975-1992, Volume I: College Students and Young Adults*, National Institute of Health Publication 93-3598 (Rockville, Md.: National Institute on Drug Abuse, 1993b).

Kennedy, Michael, Peter Reuter, and Kevin Jack Riley, *A Simple Economic Model of Cocaine Production*, MR-201-USDP (Santa Monica, Calif.: RAND, 1994).

The Killings in Colombia (Washington, D.C.: Americas Watch, 1989).

Kleiman, Mark A. R., *Marijuana: Costs of Abuse, Costs of Control* (New York: Greenwood Press, 1989).

Lauderback, Dave, and Dan Waldorf, "Whatever Happened to Ice? The Latest Drug Scare," *The Journal of Drug Issues* 23, 4 (1993): 597–613.

Lee, Rensselear, "Controlling Production of Opiates: The Case of Thailand," in *Conference Report: Economics of the Narcotics Industry, sponsored by Bureau of Intelligence and Research* (Washington, D.C.: U.S. Department of State and Central Intellegence Agency, 21-22 November 1994).

_____, "Making the Most of Colombia's Drug Negotiations," *Orbis* (Spring 1991).

Lupsha, Peter, "The Political Economy of Drug Trafficking," paper presented at *The Role of the Military in the War on Drugs Conference*, San Antonio, Texas (5 January 1993).

McCormick, Gordon H., *From the Sierra to the Cities: The Urban Campaign of the Shining Path*, R-4150-U.S.DP, (Santa Monica, Calif.: RAND, 1992).

_____, *The Shining Path and the Future of Peru*, R-3781-DOS/OSD (Santa Monica, Calif.: RAND, 1990).

Menzel, Sewall H., "Operation Blast Furnace," *Army* (November 1989): 24–32.

Military Balance, International Institute for Strategic Studies (London: Brassey's, 1995).

Model, Karyn, "The Effect of Marijuana Decriminalization on Hospital Emergency Room Drug Episodes: 1975-1978," *Journal of the American Statistical Association* 88, 423 (September 1993): 737–47.

Montagne, Michael, and David M. Scott, "Prevention of Substance Abuse Problems: Models, Factors, and Processes," *International Journal of the Addictions* 28, 12 (1993): 1177–1208.

Moore, Mark, *Buy and Bust: The Effective Regulation of an Illicit Marke in Heroin* (Lexington, Mass.: Heath, 1976).

Murphy, Patrick, "Keeping Score: The Frailties of the Federal Drug Budget," RAND Drug Policy Research Center Issue Paper (January 1994).

National Drug Control Strategy: Reclaiming our Communities from Drugs and Violence, The White House (1994).

National Drug Control Strategy: Budget Summary, The White House (1994).

National Household Survey on Drug Abuse: Main Findings 1991 [Washington, D.C.: U.S. Department of Health and Human Services, 1991 (1993)].

Ostrowski, J., "The Moral and Practical Case for Drug Legalization," *Hofstra Law Review* 18 (1990): 607–702.

Plotnick, R. D., "Applying Benefit-Cost Analysis to Substance Abuse Prevention Programs," *The International Journal of the Addictions* 29, 3 (1994): 339–59.

Price and Purity of Cocaine: The Relationship to Emergency Room Visits and Deaths, and to Drug Use Among Arrestees (Washington, D.C.: Office of National Drug Control Policy, 1992).

Reuter, Peter, "After the Borders Are Sealed: Can Domestic Sources Substitute for Imported Drugs," in *Drug Policy in the Americas: Vol. 1, Strategies for Supply Reduction*, Peter Smith, ed. (New York: Markus Weiner, 1993).

———, "Eternal Hope: America's Quest for Narcotics Control," *The Public Interest* 79, 2 (1985): 79–95.

Reuter, Peter and Jonathan Caulkins, "Redefining the Goals of National Drug Policy: Recommendations from a Working Group," *American Journal of Public Health* 85 (August 1991): 1059–63.

Reuter, Peter, and David Ronfeldt, *Quest for Integrity: The Mexican-U.S. Drug Issue in the 1980s*, N-3266-USDP (Santa Monica, Calif.: RAND, 1992).

Reuter, Peter, Gordon Crawford, and Jonathan Cave, *Sealing the Borders: The Effects of Increased Military Participation in Drug Interdiction*, R-3594-USDP (Santa Monica, Calif.: RAND, 1988).

Reuter, Peter, and Mark A. R. Kleiman, "Risks and Prices: An Economic Analysis of Drug Enforcement," in Michael Tonry and Norval Morris eds., *Crime and Justice: An Annual Review, Volume 7*, (University of Chicago: Chicago), 1986.

Riley, Kevin Jack, *Snow Job? The Efficacy of Source Country Cocaine Control Policies*, RGSD-102, (RAND: Santa Monica, CA), 1993.

———, *The Implications of Colombian Drug Industry and Death Squad Political Violence for U.S. Counternarcotics Policy*, N-3605-USDP (Santa Monica, Calif.: RAND, 1993).

Rydell, C. Peter, and Susan Everingham, *Controlling Cocaine: Supply Versus Demand Programs*, MR-331-ONDCP/A/DPRC (Santa Monica, Calif.: RAND, 1994).

Smith, Peter H., ed., *Drug Policy in the Americas* (Boulder, Colo.: Westview Press, 1992).

Source to the Street: Drug Intelligence Report (Washington, D.C.: Drug Enforcement Administration, 1993).

Spain, James W., "The United States, Turkey and the Poppy," *The Middle East Journal* 29, 3 (1975): 295–309.

Thornton, Mark, *Alcohol Prohibition was a Failure*, Policy Analysis Series no. 157 (Washington, D.C.: Cato Institute, 1991).

Thoumi, Francisco E., "The Size of the Illegal Drugs Industry in Colombia," *The North-South Agenda Papers*, no. 3 (July 1993).

Warner, Kenneth E., "Legalizing Drugs: Lessons from (and about) Economics," *The Milbank Quarterly* 69, 4 (1991): 641–61.

Westermeyer, Joseph, "Substance Use Disorders: Predictions for the 1990s," *American Journal of Drug and Alcohol Abuse* 18, 1 (1992): 1–11.

Zimring, Franklin E., and Gordon Hawkins, *The Search for Rational Drug Control* (Cambridge University Press, 1992).

Index

NATIONAL UNIVERSITY
LIBRARY   SAN DIEGO